DATE DUE

DE 1 5 '99			

DEMCO 38-296

Evangelism and Apostasy
The Evolution and Impact of Evangelicals in Modern Mexico

Evangelical, conservative Protestantism of a largely Pentecostal cast is growing so rapidly throughout Latin America that a religious revolution may be taking place. Mexican evangelicals have grown from almost 900,000 in 1970 to nearly 4,000,000 in 1990. In *Evangelism and Apostasy*, the first sociological survey of evangelicals in present -day Mexico, Kurt Bowen evaluates the appeal, character, and future growth of the evangelical community.

Highlighting the demographic, social, and political character of the evangelical movement in the 1980s and 1990s, Bowen pays particular attention to their conversion processes, commitment mechanisms, schisms, and distinctive beliefs. He also considers the controversial issues of American missionary influence and religious persecution.

Bowen reveals that evangelicalism's appeal is so pervasive in Mexico that, if evangelical converts all remained faithful, it could become the dominant religion by 2006. This is unlikely to occur, however, because of high drop-out rates. Bowen argues that evangelical apostasy is rooted in the most basic of their beliefs and practices.

KURT BOWEN is associate professor of sociology, Acadia University.

McGill-Queen's Studies in the History of Religion
G.A. Rawlyk, Editor

Volumes in this series have been supported by the
Jackman Foundation of Toronto.

Evangelism and Apostasy

The Evolution and Impact of Evangelicals in Modern Mexico

KURT BOWEN

McGill-Queen's University Press
Montreal & Kingston • London • Buffalo

BR1642.M6 B69 1996
Bowen, Kurt Derek.
Evangelism and apostasy :   p of a
the evolution and impact of Canada,
evangelicals in modern   s and

McGill-Queen's University Press is grateful to the
Canada Council for support of its publishing program.

Canadian Cataloguing in Publication Data

Bowen, Kurt, 1946–
  Evangelism and apostasy: the evolution and impact
  of evangelicals in modern Mexico
  (McGill-Queen's studies in the history of religion; 23)
  Includes bibliographical references and index.
  ISBN 0-7735-1379-5
  1. Evangelicalism – Mexico. 2. Mexico – Church
  history. 3. Protestant churches – Mexico. I. Title.
  II. Series.
  BR1642.M4B69 1996   306.6'804'0972   C96-900021-9

Typeset in Palatino 10/12
by Chris McDonell, Hawkline Graphics.

Contents

Tables

Acknowledgments

After a research project that has stretched over the better part of a decade, I owe thanks to a huge number of people. All the information that follows was obtained by interviews with people who gave of their time and shared their personal knowledge and insights with me. Among those who were particularly influential at the beginning of my inquiries, I would like to mention Juan and Elizabeth Isais, Alfonso de los Reyes, Jean Bastian, and Alfredo Miranda. At a later point David Nellis, Ed Farris, and Sergio Morales gave me great insight into the world of missionaries. Promises of confidentiality prevent me from mentioning the over six hundred *hermanos* across the length and breadth of Mexico who invited me into their homes and spoke so freely of their lives and faith. All that is valuable in this book is the fruit of their insight and shared reflection. The subsequent analysis and interpretation is, of course, solely my responsibility.

My research was made possible by a three-year grant from the Social Sciences and Humanities Research Council of Canada. I also owe noteworthy thanks to Acadia University for providing me with initial funding and for allowing me to devote two sabbaticals and the intervening summers to work in Mexico.

I am especially grateful to Miranda and Jonathan, who spent a major chunk of their childhood in Mexico or travelling to and from in the back seat of our car. In ever-changing circumstances, without the comfort of home and friends, they were always adaptable and outgoing. My affection for them is exceeded only by my envy for their flawless Spanish. I also feel a gratitude more than I can convey to my wife Dale, who contributed so much to the work and abundant pleasures at every stage of our journey together.

Evangelism and Apostasy

1 Introduction

Dramatic, recent, pervasive – these are the qualities frequently attributed to the growth of Protestantism in Latin America today. David Martin subtitles his highly regarded book *Tongues of Fire: The Explosion of Protestantism in Latin America*. David Stoll asks *Is Latin America Turning Protestant?* Although any predictions of Catholicism's demise would still be premature, the growth potential of Protestantism is the theme that underlies the following effort to describe, analyse, and assess the Evangelical or Protestant world in modern-day Mexico.

Before the nineteenth century the Catholic church throughout Latin America held a carefully guarded monopoly, in law and in fact, tolerating only some syncretic residues in its Indigenous and slave populations. In the second half of the last century a measure of formal religious toleration was initiated in some but not all countries. Until the 1930s Protestants everywhere remained tiny, scattered minorities. Subsequently greater vitality became evident here and there, but it was only after 1960 that Protestant growth became a pervasive feature of Latin American society. Even today the findings of church growth experts, surveyed by Martin and Stoll, show substantial variation by country. In Colombia, Ecuador, Uruguay, and Venezuela, 3 per cent or less of the population were Protestant in the mid-1980s.[1] At the other end of the scale, the most recent estimates for 1993 put Protestants at 22 per cent in Brazil and 28 per cent in Chile.[2] In Central America, Protestants grew from 7 per cent of El Salvador's population to as much as 23 per cent between 1978 and 1987.[3] Guatemala, which is typically cited as about 30 per cent Protestant, was the first Latin American country to elect a Protestant president, Jorge Serrano Elias, in 1990.[4] In Mexico, according to the census of 1990, the four million Protestants were a far more modest 5 per cent. Some widely circulated "guesstimates" put Protestants at as much as 17.5 per cent,[5] but even the more trustworthy and prosaic census figures show a remarkable degree of vitality and outreach among Mexican Protestants.

Extrapolated into the future, these figures imply a transformation of Latin America so basic and fundamental that it deserves to be called revolutionary. The close ties between Catholicism and Latin American culture have their roots in the Iberian, post-Columbian conquest and the colonial society it produced. The conquest was justified on the religious grounds that the Indigenous heathen needed to be brought to Christianity. In Mexico, where the Indigenous vastly outnumbered the colonists, their pacification and incorporation into a new colonial society meant their Christianization in Catholic terms. So disparate were the material interests, ethnic origins, and secular cultures of colonists and colonized that their primary common bond was their shared Catholicism, with its attendant symbols, rituals, and beliefs. National identity throughout Latin America became in turn so permeated with a generalized sense of Catholicism that its repudiation inevitably raises questions about national identity and loyalty. When to this are added the links between Protestantism and the United States, the now resented but indisputable superpower of the region, then religious change becomes an even more highly charged issue in Latin America. Conservative Catholics, nationalists, and leftists agree about very little, but they are one in affirming that Protestantism is an alien, divisive, and destructive force, driven by American imperialist interests.

Protestant growth in much of Latin America seems to belie or call into question the inevitability of secularization in the modern world. Sociology's first generation of armchair theorists almost all agreed that religion would and perhaps should decline as traditional society fell in the face of encroaching capitalism, modernization, and rationalization.[6] Some current theorists continue to affirm that secularization is the dominant trend.[7] Others would disagree by pointing to the United States, where church membership rates have grown over the centuries and high church attendance rates have not appreciably changed over the last fifty years.[8] Others argue on the more theoretical grounds that individual religions may decline but the demand for religion in general is constant, because humans will always seek supernatural compensation for thwarted desires, scarcity, and suffering. This "self-limiting" theory of secularization, propounded by Stark and Bainbridge, is buttressed, I think, by less than compelling evidence from the United States,[9] but there remains a suggestive core to their argument. It would be foolhardy to suggest that secularization's limits have been reached in Mexico. Even so, Protestantism's growth throughout Latin America, which is everywhere seen as the product of rapid social change, surely flies in the face of the logic of secularization.

Some have viewed Protestantism as itself part of the secularization process in that it demystifies and disenchants the world by conceiving a distant God, who created the laws of existence but who no longer intervenes in the daily affairs of his faithful.[10] However, Pentecostalism, which is now the faith of the majority of Latin American Protestants, is the antithesis of such historical Protestant conceptions. For Pentecostals, theirs is a personal relationship with a God who is concerned with the lives of each one of his followers and who intervenes constantly in their lives in response to prayer. Ecstatic eruptions have occurred periodically throughout Christian history, but the Pentecostal movement is very much a product of the modern world, first manifesting itself in religious revival in Los Angeles in 1906. By the middle of the 1980s Pentecostals were reckoned to account for 21 per cent of all Christians world-wide.[11] In Canada and the United States, liberal mainstream Protestantism is in decline, while Pentecostalism grows in the secular heartland[12] as well as less secularized regions such as Latin America. It is this pervasive growth that makes Pentecostalism such a fascinating and crucial determinant in the future prospects of Christianity as a whole. Are we seeing here the challenge to secularization's reach, to which Stark and Bainbridge allude, or is Pentecostalism destined to remain a marginal but vibrant sect of religious virtuosos, incapable of becoming a mass movement? This too will be a recurring theme in what follows.

SUBJECT AND METHOD: SOME PRELIMINARY CLARIFICATIONS

The people under scrutiny here call themselves "Evangelicos." This should be literally translated "Gospellers," but they are better called by the more familiar "Evangelical." They are less comfortable with the label "Protestant" because they see it as having negative, critical connotations. They prefer to emphasize the positive aspects of their proclamation of the Gospel, or message of salvation through Jesus Christ. They are conservative Protestants. They regard the liberal

Protestant agenda of religious tolerance, ecumenism, and social action as misguided in its neglect of personal salvation and as heretical in its condoning of Catholicism. For Evangelicals, Catholicism does not preach true Christianity. They are also Evangelical in the broader Christian sense of this word. They place heavy stress on the Bible, which they regard as divinely inspired and as the ultimate source of authority. They also stress the divinity of Jesus and the necessity of having a personal faith in him in order to achieve salvation. Many though not all Evangelical Mexicans might also be labelled fundamentalists, in that they embrace a highly "literal" interpretation of Scripture and a dispensationalist pre-millennialism.[13] The details and consequences of their beliefs will be further explored in chapter 5. By their own definition Pentecostals and members of the "historical" Protestant denominations, such as Presbyterians, Methodists, Baptists, and Congregationalists, are "Evangelicos." No significant rump of liberal Protestants exists in the historical denominations. The few scattered liberals, and they do exist, are everywhere regarded with great suspicion. On the margins are the Adventists, whose doubts over the failure of other Evangelicals to recognize the Jewish Sabbath are counterbalanced by the latter's suspicions that Adventists pay too much heed to the Old Testament. These are the limits of the Evangelical world as Mexican Evangelicals define it.

Outside are all others, including Jehovah's Witnesses, Mormons, and, of course, Roman Catholics. The former two groups share with Evangelicals the common status of being recent religious dissidents. They may also all be regarded as sects, to anticipate a technical term to be discussed immediately below. However, I excluded Mormons and Witnesses from my analysis because of the mutual antipathies between Evangelicals and them, because of the corresponding lack of any real communion or fellowship, and because their inclusion in my fieldwork would have disturbed Evangelicals. I present some very limited information on these two largest of the "other" religions in chapter 3. However, as Evangelicals were 76 per cent of all who had a religion other than Catholicism in the 1990 census, they are the predominant tradition of religious dissent in Mexico.

The study of sects in sociology goes back to the original formulation of Weber. For Weber, sects are voluntary and exclusive religious organizations requiring choice, proof of individual worthiness for admission, and high commitment. Their opposite, the church, is inclusive or monopolistic, incorporating all within a given society or area within its fold, though it makes fewer demands upon its members. Weber's original distinction has been elaborated on by many others, most notably Troeltsch, Niebuhr, and Wilson, who portray sects as new or renewed religious movements that sometimes evolve into churches. Many additional characteristics are attributed to the typical sect, including the sense of being a chosen few or "elect"; an ideal of a priesthood of all believers, whereby special clerical functions are de-emphasized and lay involvement encouraged; informal, spontaneous worship; and indifference or hostility to the state and public realm.[14] Some would argue that the sect would be better identified with a single factor, on the grounds that these traits do not always cohere in a unitary fashion. Thus Johnson and, more recently, Stark and Bainbridge have argued that sects are religious movements of renewal in high tension with their surrounding environment.[15] Single variable definitions may have the virtue of greater simplicity, but the multi-variable sort are surely the more allusive. In the case of Mexican Evangelicals, the latter complex definition illuminates a variety of their most distinctive features.

Some have argued that the term "sect" should be dropped because of its many misleading and unfortunate associations. Providing the present usage is clear in context, I have no qualms about using the word. Two objections, however, touch on issues that deserve mention. First, the term is rejected by some because it is seen to imply a false, divisive, or destructive faith.[16] No such intention exists on my part or in the bulk of the theorizing identified above and below. It may also be worth emphasizing that I will not and feel I cannot comment on the intrinsic merits of the varied denominational practices and doctrines outlined in subsequent chapters. Secondly, others have pointed out that sectarian theorizing is Eurocentric and Cristocentric, in that it assumes the existence of an established church with which the sect shares a common, if disputed heritage.[17] Such assumptions will therefore hinder understanding in situations where no religion is clearly dominant or in non-Christian contexts. As a rule there is much to be said for this second concern, but the notion of sect surely remains useful in analysing the Christian world. This is especially true of Latin America, where Evangelicals are so clearly in opposition to the Roman Catholic church. Thus I retain the notion of sect, shorn of its ideological meanings, because it fosters many illuminating links with other similar cases and with theorizing that enhances our understanding of Mexican Evangelicals.

Comments on methods of collecting information often cause a reader's eyes to glaze. I ask forbearance here because my findings are heavily reliant on surveys, which need some description in order to permit assessments of their representativeness and utility. Questionnaire data are especially crucial here, since I was rarely able to rely on written sources. With the exception of a few recent anthropological studies of Evangelicals in the approximately 8 per cent of Mexico's population that is Indigenous, little hard evidence is elsewhere available on contemporary Mexican Evangelicals. There are a large number of denominational associations and agencies, but there is no substantial body of reports and documents available for a scholar to study. Before the 1930s, when foreign mission boards exerted substantial influence, data of this sort were available, but they have faded away as the influence of missionaries has declined. Over the last twenty years, which is the principal focus of my study, the bureaucratic arts of record-keeping, documentation, and the like have been little valued or practised by Mexican Evangelicals.

The bulk of my data was obtained through interviews and participant observation between 1987 and 1993. During a sabbatical in 1985–86 I studied Spanish, contacted church leaders and denominational offices, and visited the major regions of the country. Systematic data-gathering was then conducted for three months of each of the following five summers. Then, in 1992–93 I spent thirteen months in southern Mexico on another sabbatical, writing a first draft and filling in research gaps. A minimum of one summer was spent in each of the four major regions of the country.

Promises of anonymity to respondents prevent me from naming specific villages, towns, or neighbourhoods, but the general character of each region and site deserves brief mention. The north,[18] not significantly populated till this century, is less deeply rooted in Mexican traditions than elsewhere. I worked in the booming maquilladora or branch-plant city of Matamoros, which has grown from under 20,000 to perhaps as many as 750,000 in the last forty years. Right on the border, it is a crucial test of American influence in all its forms. From here I sallied to three rural congregations. The central region[19] is the colonial and Catholic heartland of Mexico. I was based in and around Morelia, Michoacan, because I happened to do my Spanish-language training there. It is a conservative, very Catholic centre. In Mexico City, with a total population now said to be near twenty million, the vagaries of seeking accommodation led me to the south-east of the city, where Evangelical concentrations are greatest. Four of the seven congregations here are located in Nezahualcoyotl, an instant city of migrants, now with two million or more inhabitants, which scarcely existed twenty-five years ago. In the south[20] I spent a summer in Tabasco, which was the first area to experience a

significant degree of Evangelical growth. I also worked in five congregations in the state of Oaxaca, which had the second-highest concentration of Indigenous peoples (39 per cent in 1990) in the country.
Religious conflict and persecution have been particularly marked
here. As a rule the south has always been geographically, politically,
and socially marginal to the central core of Mexico.

At each base I endeavoured to select a cross-section of congregations typical of the denominational, rural-urban, and class mixture
of local Evangelicals. The willingness of the pastor was also a consideration, though I found relatively few were resistant. In large
measure this was because I had generous letters of introduction
from several denominations and prominent leaders. Advice was
everywhere proffered, but the final decision in selecting between
many small and similar congregations was always mine. Nowhere
was there a complete listing of congregations, which might have enabled random sampling. At the main service I was usually presented by the pastor to the congregation. During the service I
estimated the mix of genders, ages, and classes of those attending. I
then selected a representative sample of between eight to fifteen,
whom I approached after the service, with the aid of my wife, to
arrange an interview in their homes during the coming week. At the
very beginning I followed the advice of a few pastors in selecting respondents, but they were inclined to direct me to a rather narrow
group of dominant males in the congregation. A far more diverse
sample emerged when I selected respondents at the main service.

In theory this is the one level at which random sampling might
have been attempted, but practical experience soon taught me that
pastors very rarely had an up-to-date list of their membership. Only
after pressing several times, at the end of my time in most congregations, was I able to obtain something like a complete listing of the
congregation. From the pastor I then obtained a census of basic
background characteristics of the members. All baptized in the previous year and every second, third, or fifth of all others, depending
on the size of the congregation, were enumerated. This yielded what
I call the congregational sample of 1,410, though it is sometimes broken down into its two components of new and older members.

In all, this multi-stage sampling process produced six samples.
Apart from the congregational sample (N=1410) referred to above,
two more samples come from the 485 laity and 49 pastors I interviewed in the forty-three congregations where I worked. A questionnaire on the history, organization, and activities of each of these
congregational samples yielded a fourth sample. Their regional distribution, compared with the 1990 census figures, are presented in

Table 1.1
Evangelicals by region, 1990 census and samples

	Census %	Lay Sample %	Pastor Sample %	Congregation Sample %
North	20	22	20	23
Mexico	12	15	16	16
Centre	37	37	33	28
South	31	26	31	33
Nation	100% (3,969,858)	100% (485)	100% (49)	100% (43)

Table 1.1. There is a reasonable goodness of fit, though the sample of laity is somewhat underrepresented in the south, as are the pastors and the congregations in the centre. I also gathered information on the current religious affiliation and basic demographics of all the siblings and children of the respondents in the main laity sample who had attended an Evangelical church as children. This fifth sample of 1,198 casts light on patterns of second-generation religious commitment. The 17 missionaries I interviewed make up the sixth and final data base.

Though concern with representativeness pervaded every stage in the selection of my samples, there is no independent means of testing this effort. The religion question in the census cannot help because it is not cross-classified by any other variable, apart from population distribution, to which reference has already been made in Table 1.1. There are, however, four ways in which the samples, particularly that of the laity, might be said to be less than fully representative. First, only 4 per cent of my lay sample and three (7 per cent) of the forty-three congregations are Indigenous, in contrast to the 8 per cent who were so enumerated in all Mexico in 1990. To compensate, I spent approximately six weeks in the highlands of the adjacent southern state of Chiapas familiarizing myself with some of the more Evangelical municipios or counties that had already been studied by anthropologists. The fact remains that Indigenous peoples are underrepresented in the lay sample. Secondly, though the 36 per cent in my sample in rural communities with fewer than 5,000 inhabitants compares favourably with the national census figure of 35 per cent, I suspect my sample has fewer remote rural communities than it might. Thirdly, in an effort to obtain a cross-section of denominations, the 62 per cent in the lay sample who are Pentecostal are probably less than the national average. Received wisdom puts Pentecostals at about 75 per cent of all Evangelicals, though there is no means of proving this. Lastly, it is likely that my sample is biased towards the more active of members, despite my sampling precautions, though the high levels of commitment typically expected put pressure on the lukewarm to reform or to drop out.

This is not and could never be a random sample. Random sampling requires that the entire universe be enumerated before random selection takes place. As we have seen, no universal enumeration of Evangelicals, or even their churches, is available. My inability to meet the requirements of random sampling is, of course, far more widespread in survey research than is commonly recognized. What I have gathered here are "purposive" samples, in which "the investigator relies on his or her expert judgement to select units that are 'representative' or 'typical' of the population."[21] I have therefore not calculated tests of significance in the tables that follow because the prerequisite of random sampling could not be met. Readers must form their own opinions of whether I have succeeded in drawing a representative sample. It is also worth bearing in mind that tests of significance measure the likelihood that the observed difference is or is not due to chance. They do not assess whether the recorded difference is sufficiently large to be regarded as substantively important. The latter qualitative judgment is surely the more important.

SECTARIAN THEORIZING AND LATIN AMERICAN CONCERNS

The signs of rapid Evangelical growth touched on earlier raise the issue of how such growth is possible. Logically, there are two possibilities. The first is for Evangelicals to socialize and then to recruit their own children as the latter mature into adulthood. For Evangelicals to grow faster than others by such a method would imply that they have distinctively high rates of fertility or natural increase. In fact there is no reason to think this is true of Evangelicals, or at least of Mexican Evangelicals. We shall also see that retention of the second generation is far from certain or universal. Evangelical growth – indeed, the emergence and subsequent expansion of most new sects – hinges on the degree to which religious outsiders are prepared or induced to shift allegiance to the new faith. Conversion is the term typically applied to this process. Two different attributes or motifs linked to the idea of conversion deserve mention.

First, conversion is typically confined to situations where there is a radical realignment of attachments, beliefs, attitudes, and identity. The key motif or requirement is that there be a dramatic personal change on the part of converts. When the change in allegiance is less radical, as in the case of shifting membership from a Presbyterian to a Baptist church in Mexico, which are both deemed to be part of the same Evangelical world, commentators are inclined to speak of "switching" or of "alternation."[22] The distinction, it must be admitted, is not always as clear as it might be in certain cases,[23] but a Mexican Catholic's embrace of Evangelicalism is an unambiguous case of conversion. This is so because all Evangelical denominations are in high tension with Catholicism and because they place such high demands on their members. Massive change in attachments, beliefs, and identity are explicitly required of all converts to the Evangelical world. Indeed, the generalization holds for all outsiders attaching themselves to sects.

A second, more ambiguous motif associated with conversion is the degree to which the transferred allegiance may be regarded as voluntary or self-directed, as opposed to being manipulated or caused by others.[24] The extreme charge of coercive brainwashing as a means of obtaining members, commonly alleged against groups like the "Moonies" or the Hare Krishnas in the West, has no real application to Mexican Evangelicals. Capture, forced detention, denial of food and sleep, and the like play no part in Evangelical recruitment methods, though not a few of the converts I interviewed had angry Catholic relatives who thought otherwise. More pervasive is the view that Evangelicals, and American missionaries in particular, seduce or buy converts through offers of food, clothing, and other material benefits. Betrayal of one's patrimony for "bread and dollars," as one priest I interviewed aptly put it, is the standard and perhaps predictable explanation offered by the Catholic church. Similar charges are evident in the phrases "rice bowl" Christianity in China or "souperism" in Ireland. One must look elsewhere to assess the validity of the latter two charges, but I shall argue against them in Mexico's case. It is none the less true that Evangelicals devote a great deal of time, energy, and thought to the development of effective methods of evangelism, recruitment, and persuasion. There is no more truth to the notion of irresistible manipulation in conversion than there is of an extreme voluntarism, unaffected by the efforts of others, by learned predispositions, or by a variety of social needs. How conversion among Mexican Evangelicals fits on this continuum is the subject of chapter 4.

Questions about religious commitment over the long term ought to be separate from the chronologically prior event of conversion. The ability of any sect, or really any religious group, to grow is dependent on its ability to recruit outsiders, but so too is it influenced by its capacity to retain the commitment of its converts and their offspring, the next generation. The success of a sect in recruiting need not necessarily translate into a comparable capacity to retain commitment. Thus studies of the Pentecostal movement in the United States show that its growth and success in evangelism has been curbed by a 36 per cent drop-out rate among their childhood members.[25] In other parts of Latin America and in Mexico there have been intimations that short-term commitment and high drop-out rates may prevail in the Evangelical world,[26] but the possibility has not been explored in any systematic manner. I endeavour to rectify this neglect.

In chapters 5 and 6 I explore the various psychological, material, and social rewards that accrue from membership in Evangelical churches and might be said to strengthen or reinforce commitment. To the degree that potential converts experiment with the sectarian world for a time prior to becoming members, such rewards might also be regarded as causes of their conversion. There is, however, a further line of reasoning, most frequently associated with the work of Rosabeth Kanter and Dean Kelley, which suggests that groups that make high demands on their members are most successful in eliciting high commitment. Kanter concludes from her study of nineteenth-century utopian commitment that the successful were distinguished by their requirements of sacrifice, renunciation, and mortification.[27] Kelley, in trying to explain why conservative American Protestantism grows while its liberal counterpart declines, argues that it is the "seriousness" and "strictness" of the former in their demands on their members that give them their strength and appeal.[28] There is no disputing that high commitment is characteristic of the examples cited, and of sects in general, but there remains the dilemma that such demands and mechanisms would be better described as the fruit or sign of commitment rather than its antecedent cause. At best they reinforce a commitment that is the product of other factors.[29] Might it not also be equally probable that high commitment expectations, rather than fostering growth and allegiance, cause some to defect or drop out?

The questions of why people convert and why sects emerge are analytically separate, but in practice they tend to be fused. The answers given may be grouped into three broad categories, though here too there is, in practice, quite a bit of overlap.

The social disorganization model has its roots in anthropology, in Linton's theory of "nativistic movements," which he describes as "any organized attempt on the part of a society's members to revive or perpetuate selected aspects of its culture."[30] Such movements are portrayed as a common response by Native or Indigenous peoples to the intrusions of the modern world and its attendant pressures. Evangelicalism can hardly be regarded as a conscious attempt to revive Latin American culture, but many explanations of Pentecostalism in America have stressed that it too is a response to social and cultural disorganization. In this case, those suffering from maladjustment and uncertainty have been recent urban migrants who find in Pentecostalism a functional substitute for the lost intimacies, supports, and certainties of their former lives. Similar themes are also evident in Lalive D'Epinay's highly influential study of Evangelical, largely Pentecostal growth in Chile and Argentina after 1930. Neglect by the Catholic church and new guarantees of religious freedom were combined with the essential impetus of worsening economic conditions and runaway urbanization. The result was the destruction of the traditional social order modelled on the hacienda, which was both "oppressive and protective" in its paternalism. This in turn caused a "general spread of social anomie among the working classes, who live in an uprooted state, while still nostalgically regretting the lost father-figure"[31] of the hacienda. Into this vacuum stepped Pentecostalism, offering "an attractive substitute society because it relates back to the known model and at the same time renews it."[32] In the Pentecostal congregation the security of a fictive kin network is recreated and new opportunities for mobility are offered, but the price is a hierarchical, authoritarian, and anti-democratic system, now headed by the pastor rather than the former patron.

In the second broad class of theories I would place the well-known works of Willems and Martin, which share in common an emphasis on modernization as the key force causing Evangelical advance. In this respect they have no obvious parallel with the main traditions of sectarian theorizing elsewhere in the world. Only with diffidence do I put them together in a common category. Willems, writing in the 1960s on Brazil and Chile, stresses how Evangelical growth emerged in those sectors of society undergoing rapid change caused by urbanization and industrialization. In this and in his recognition that Protestantism provides a "meaningful system of primary relations in an atomised society,"[33] Willems anticipates and closely parallels the later analysis of Lalive D'Epinay. Where they part company is in Willems' stress on how Protestantism fosters egalitarianism, local autonomy, ethical values of industry, thrift, and sobriety, and a measure of upward mobility, which has in turn "contributed to loosening up the once tight class structures of Brazil and Chile."[34] Rather than portraying Protestantism as recreating a lost world, as Lalive D'Epinay does, Willems stresses its progressive character as a product of and contributor to a broad process of religious and cultural differentiation.

Much the same general logic pervades Martin's analysis, which reviews research done by others throughout Latin America. He places Evangelical growth in the "long term historical context" of Latin America's "political and economic defeat at the hands of the North American heirs of the British Empire."[35] Democracy, industrialism, and religious pluralism first came out of England, where Protestantism, "a voluntary, participatory, and enthusiastic form of faith," played a major role in "the differentiation of spheres,"[36] or what others might label modernization. Channelled through the United States, where the absence of religious monopoly allowed religion to escape secularization's inroads, Protestantism was then disseminated to Latin America, where it was initially "a minor movement alongside other militantly anti-Catholic movements,"[37] such as Masonry and positivism. Large-scale Protestant growth only occurred when it became Pentecostal and embraced Latin American cultural forms (which the historical denominations could never do) and when social differentiation became more advanced. The "process would have occurred independently"[38] of American influence, but it was accelerated as the later became more pervasive. "As the sacred canopy is rent and the all encompassing system cracks, evangelical Christianity pours in and by its own autonomous native power creates free social space."[39] Advance was most marked where the Catholic church was most weak, among neglected and abused tribal peoples and in the sprawling new cities of recent rural migrants. Here a "new faith is able to implant new disciplines, re-order priorities, counter corruption and destructive machismo, and reverse the indifferent and injurious hierarchies of the outside world."[40] It is this characterization of Evangelicalism as "an advanced form of social differentiation" and the notion that the latter gives rise to the former that puts Martin's interpretation in the modernization school, along with Willems.

Deprivation is by far the most common model accounting for the emergence of sects. From at least the time of Niebuhr it has been recognized that sects are the religions of "the disinherited," who tend to be neglected by the churches and are drawn by the sect's radical condemnation of a world that excludes and oppresses them. Religious dissent is thus fuelled by economic and other material discontents. In one of the most widely cited modern versions of this view, Glock defines deprivation as "any and all of the ways that an individual or group may be, or feel disadvantaged in comparison either to other individuals or groups or to any internalized set of standards."[41] Deprivation is not absolute but relative to others. Glock identifies various types of deprivation, most notably economic and social deprivation. The former implies suffering from "limited access ... to the necessities and luxuries of life." Social deprivation refers to suffering from social exclusion and belittlement because of a disparaged social status, as in the case of the Indigenous peoples in Mexico. (Glock also lists other types of deprivation, but his organismic, psychic, and ethical variants have less direct applicability to Mexico and need not concern us here.) For an organized religious movement or sect to emerge, he further considers it necessary "that the deprivation be shared, that no alternative arrangements for its resolution are perceived, and that a leadership emerge with an innovative idea for building a movement out of the existing deprivation."[42] Even then, Glock avers that the response to the deprivation may be secular rather than religious in form. In cases of economic or social deprivation, "religious resolutions are more likely to occur when the nature of the deprivation is inaccurately perceived or those experiencing the deprivation are not in a position to work directly at eliminating the causes."[43]

It is best left to chapters 3 and 4 to explore how well disorganization and deprivation theories apply to and illuminate Evangelical growth and conversion in Mexico. There are, however, a number of general implications that derive from the above theories that need to be clarified and evaluated. The first is a dismissive, anti-religious tendency, which is most striking in deprivation theory. Glock's analysis surely suggests that people will only embrace religious answers to their problems when pragmatic material responses are not possible in the face of repression, or when ignorance, false consciousness, or stupidity prevent the sect members from seeing the "true" cause of their plight.[44] Christianity explicitly presents itself as compensation for the problems of deprivation, suffering, and evil. The famous passage from Matthew 2: 8 ("Come unto me, all ye that labour and are heavy laden, and I will give you rest") is commonly displayed and frequently cited in Mexican Evangelical churches. Christianity should therefore take no offence at sociology's identification of deprivation as a source of religious commitment.[45] What are gratuitous, unprovable, and therefore unnecessary are the further implications that sectarians are mentally defective and their response to evil inherently inferior to political and economic movements of reform. Personal convictions regarding the efficacy of religious solutions to life's problems should play no part in objective analysis. Such biases only cloud efforts to elucidate the social forces that shape the emergence and growth of religious sects.

There is a further implication to be found in some variants of both disorganization and deprivation theory, and perhaps in all sociological analysis, that might be described as the reductionist fallacy. By this I mean the failure to acknowledge that religious motivations have a force and existence independent of more pragmatic worldly interests. The dominant thrust in the sociology of religion has been to emphasize what have come to be known as the latent functions of religion. The emphasis has usually been on the often unintended ways in which religious commitment has met various psychological, emotional, social, political, and material needs of its adherents. However, in pursuing this traditional sociological analysis, we would do well to pay heed to the advice of Bryan Wilson not to neglect the manifest function of religion.[46] In the case of sects, where religious commitment is high and tensions with the wider society so clearly cast in religious terms, the advice is all the more pointed. This primary and explicit goal of religion, and of Mexican Evangelicals in particular, is the attainment of salvation, by which is meant a solution to the problems of the world, most notably that of evil, by supernatural means. This pursuit is often shaped by political, economic, and status interests, but its essentially non-material objective cannot be reduced to such pragmatic interests. Without reference to their religious beliefs and values, we will never understand the appeal, character, and subsequent evolution of the Mexican Evangelical community.

In accounting for any new religious phenomenon, it is part of a standard checklist to consider the influence of internal and external forces. When applied to Latin American Evangelicals, this issue touches deep cultural nerves because the external source, the United States, is the region's superpower. In the popular press there have long been periodic denunciations of the "sects," with lurid examples of bizarre behaviour by the Children of God, Hare Krishnas, and Moonies, which are presented as typical of all "sects," including the Pentecostals and historical Protestant denominations – despite the fierce protestations of Evangelicals. Accusations of American manipulation, cultural imperialism, and CIA plotting abound.[47] Missionaries working among Indigenous or Native peoples are favourite targets, presumed to be bent on a policy of cultural genocide in the service of American imperialist interests. Even the presumably informed College of Anthropologists and Ethnologists of Mexico called in 1979 for the expulsion of the Summer Institute of Linguistics, a well-known missionary agency, for its promulgation of an individualistic, pro-American, and hence anti-national ideology among Indigenous people.[48] Public paranoia in part arose because of the indisputable fact that American economic interests and political intervention sometimes play a part in regions where foreign missionaries and Latin American Evangelicals are also present. Particularly in Central America during Ronald Reagan's presidency, conservative Protestant organizations from the southern United States were as vocal in their condemnations of communism as they were of Catholicism. Some were also visible in their support for the Contra war in Nicaragua and for the military dictators of Guatemala, of whom the most notable was the Pentecostal general Rios Montt.[49] However, David Stoll, who is the only scholar to have looked into these issues empirically, shows that the missionaries on the ground in Nicaragua, Guatemala, and Ecuador were much more varied in their political opinions than these extreme examples suggest. He also suggests that Evangelical growth in each country was little affected by the actions and rhetoric of the American Evangelical right.[50] I will explore these issues as they apply to Mexico in chapter 7, paying particular heed to the influence of missionaries among Indigenous peoples.

Intimately linked to the above is the question of the political stance and role of Evangelicals. To nationalists and leftists of many stripes it was entirely predictable that the faith of the imperial power would foster passivity and resignation in the face of oppression. The behaviour of Pentecostals in the United States seemed to give credence to such fears. Prior to the 1960s they preached radical disengagement from unions and political parties, "rejecting all secular solutions to their problems."[51] When they did later begin to vote, they supported the most conservative of candidates. Bastian argues that Protestantism throughout Latin America was a key agent in the struggles for greater democracy and political reform as long as the historical denominations were the dominant force, but he too fears that this progressive element has been eroded with the rise of Pentecostalism.[52] Lalive D'Epinay's research in Argentina and Chile and Rolim's work in Brazil confirm these impressions, pointing out that Pentecostals practise a passive conformism by preaching that political issues are not Christian concerns, that trade unions and political parties are places of damnation, and that submission to authority is God's will.[53] If Evangelicals were prepared to accept the leftist regime of Allende, they also embraced Pinochet's military dictatorship for a time,[54] though the continuing economic crisis subsequently caused them to become more politically divided. Their essential passivity has in turn been engendered by crushing oppression and a millennialist belief that offers hope of salvation at the same time it preaches expectant waiting for divine – not human – action.[55]

Lalive D'Epinay's conclusions are not universally shared. Willems, whose differences are more of emphasis than content, stresses that

Protestants of all stripes were formerly wary of political involvement because it might provoke Catholic repression. While acknowledging that Pentecostals differ from the historical denominations, Willems notes that both became a visible and growing presence in electoral politics, though their goals were primarily defensive, centred on defending religious liberty rather than supporting any particular party or program.[56] In Colombia, Pentecostals have sometimes supported populist movements of protest,[57] while survey evidence suggests that Pentecostals were actually more likely than Catholics to support Allende in Chile.[58] In Nicaragua, Evangelical support for the Sandinistas was initially quite strong, though it faded as the economy deteriorated and the government sporadically repressed Evangelicals because some, though by no means all, supported the Contras.[59] Next door, in war-torn El Salvador, where about one-fifth of the population are now Evangelical, Evangelicals were less likely than Catholics to support the guerrilla movement, but they were just as likely to favour negotiating a settlement with the rebels and to make concessions to do so. They were also slightly less likely than Catholics to vote in 1989, but those who did were less likely to vote for the conservative ARENA party.[60] And again, in Colombia, Evangelical growth among the indigenous Quichau has come to be viewed as an ethnic revitalization movement, prompted by leftist and Catholic paternalism as much as Mestizo oppression. In 1984, Evangelical votes "went overwhelmingly for centre and left candidates."[61] Such varied responses in such different contexts give little support to any idea that Evangelicals are always or inherently a movement of political protest, though they effectively undermine models of inevitable political passivity.[62] Where and whether Mexican Evangelicals fit on such a continuum is the subject of chapter 8.

There remains one major theme to which the reader should be sensitized before tackling the main body of analysis. This revolves around the past and future trajectory of Evangelicals since their beginnings in Latin America in the last century. It brings us back to the question raised in the very beginning. Are we seeing a revolution whereby Latin America will become Protestant in the future, or is it all a temporary effervescence, brought on by foreign intervention, deprivation, and disorder? Because Evangelicals are such a new presence, little has been said on the topic by Latin American investigators, but the range of options can be delineated from the general body of sectarian writings. Three possibilities suggest themselves.

The first and least likely, I think, for the foreseeable future, is that the Evangelical movement may die out. Massive Catholic revival or rampant secularization are both possible but not probable projections, as we shall see in subsequent chapters. It is a truism that few religions survive from among the many being constantly born, but the critical stage is typically at the very beginning. Particularly at the death of the founder there arise problems of authority, of doctrinal stability, and of commitment.[63] The first and third of these issues will come up again when the related topic of schism is addressed in chapter 6, but the stark option of extinction or survival does not arise here. In part this is because the Evangelical movement in Mexico has already left behind this precarious first period. It is also because these dilemmas of a founding charismatic leader, on whose succession everything hinges, simply do not apply in Mexico. Because the Evangelical and Pentecostal traditions initially emerged outside of Mexico, they may be better regarded as established branches within Protestantism rather than entirely new faiths. Thus working Pentecostal and/or Evangelical faith systems were either introduced from abroad or set an example for Latin Americans to follow.

The second possibility or option is that of sustained growth for Mexican Evangelicals. In the United States there are a host of examples of originally sect-like Protestant bodies that have since undergone growth and expansion. A classic example would be the Methodists, whom Martin identifies as a significant prototype of later Pentecostal growth.[64] Their growth, however, is also portrayed as often involving a fundamental transformation in their character, now known as the tendency to denominationalize. Niebuhr, who first identified this common trend, suggests that true sectarianism is almost inevitably confined to the first generation. Religious commitment grows less intense as subsequent generations are raised in the faith without the obligation of making a personal faith. Evangelism and numerical expansion often lead to the creation of trained, professional clergy and bureaucracies, which are more typical of churches than of sects. The typical asceticism and puritanism of sectarians sometimes creates upward mobility in later generations, which may lead to the neglect and alienation of the poor, who were the original constituency of the sects. Upward mobility also inclines the membership to embrace a more tolerant, less tension-ridden view of the secular world and other faiths. In short, sects have a tendency to become transformed into church-like denominational bodies over time.[65]

For Niebuhr, the theologian, denominationalization is a betrayal of Christian morality and principle. Subsequent sociologists have steered clear of such an explicitly doctrinal judgment, though they remain fascinated by the breadth of his vision. For rather different reasons Mexican Evangelicals would feel uncomfortable with much of Niebuhr's theology, but they too would shudder if they thought their subsequent growth would entail all the changes identified above.

Equally unpalatable for Evangelicals is the third option proffered by sociology, namely that Mexican Evangelicals may remain an "established sect."[66] This option suggests that Mexican Evangelicals might retain their sectarian vigour but at the price of remaining relatively small and marginal. Such a possibility is a clear challenge to the enticing simplicity of Niebuhr's original model. Now it is recognized that the transition from sect to church is neither universal nor inevitable. Not all sects denominationalize.[67] Some that do also experience very modest rates of growth, though growth and denominationalization often go hand in hand.[68] Those that do denominationalize, to use Wilson's terminology, tend to be conversionist sects, which "stress simple affirmation of intense subjective experience as a criterion of admission, ... which emphasize evangelism, ... and which seek to accommodate groups dislocated by rapid social change."[69] Pentecostals, he rightly says, are a prime example of a conversionist sect, but Mexican Pentecostals show few signs of denominationalization. Why this is so and how it affects their growth potential and future trajectory are two of the most basic questions that underlie what follows.

In a later work Wilson raises the intriguing question of whether a thaumaturgical orientation in Latin American Pentecostalism might not differentiate it from the conversionist format of European and North American Pentecostalism. By thaumaturgy Wilson means the practice of magic, or the manipulations of religious symbols to achieve very specific and limited ends. Conversionists, in contrast, seek a total transformation of self and deny that the supernatural can be manipulated or controlled. The dilemma with such conceptual distinctions, which are rooted in the long-established distinction between magic and religion, is that the boundaries are not always so clear or certain in specific empirical cases. Nevertheless, the presence of a thaumaturgical or magical strain is indisputable among the Toba Indians of Argentina, cited by Wilson, whose Iglesia Evangelica Unida so mixed Pentecostalism with pre-Hispanic practice that other Pentecostal churches and pastors condemned it as pagan.[70]

Apart from such extreme cases, opinions are more mixed. Thus Willems acknowledges that folk Catholicism may have predisposed Brazilians and Argentinians to Pentecostalism, but he insists that the latter makes "no allowance for religious syncretism ... insists on doctrinal purity and, more often than not, aggressively opposes competing faiths." He also stresses how its asceticism puts it in sharp opposition to many elements in traditional culture.[71] Jean Bastian, by contrast, stresses the continuities, in practice if not in theology, of Pentecostalism with folk Catholicism, which has always been centred on the saints and existed apart from the clerically dominated institutional church. Pentecostalism, Bastian suggests, is lay led, magically oriented in its emphasis on faith-healing, and inclined to lengthy ritual and oral tradition. Echoing Lalive D'Epinay, Bastian also suggests that it is now a world dominated by authoritarian, nepotistic pastors whose behaviour in running their churches matches that of the *caudillos* or political bosses of old. He thus questions Martin's and Willems' portrayal of Evangelicals today as a movement of religious reform, carrying the seeds of a more modern culture. It is true, he says, that the historical Protestant denominations, which dominated the Evangelical world before the 1960s, were important incubators of "democratic modernity," but they are now a minority who have been obliged to mimic the newly dominant Pentecostal tradition. Given this metamorphosis, he believes the modern Evangelical movement is best seen as "a patchwork kind of renewal of popular religion" that reproduces but does not challenge traditional structures and methods of control.[72]

Bastian's provocative analysis has a marked theological or ideological cast to it in that it so clearly calls for us to distinguish the progressive from the regressive, or the good from the bad. In this sense it is a secular variant of Niebuhr's theological critique of the established churches, though in Bastian's case the objects of scorn are the sects. A similar tendency can be discerned in Lalive D'Epinay and, to a lesser extent, in Stoll, while the modernization thesis of Martin and Willems naturally inclines them to view Evangelicals as a progressive force. Criticism is not my intent in making this observation. Any really good analysis surely causes us to confront the question of what is and is not desirable in the human condition. But in acknowledging the importance of this and other issues raised here, I also want to keep a sustained focus on whether the Evangelical movement has the capacity to embrace a substantial and growing body of Mexicans. The ability to recruit and maintain commitment is the underlying factor that determines how important a force the Evangelical faith is or will be in Mexico. Is it capable of generating sustained commitment among enough Mexicans to make it an agent of transformation in society as a whole? Or is it destined to a permanent status as a small minority? I begin the detailed description needed to answer this question by exploring, in the next chapter, the historical roots and evolution of Mexican Evangelicals.

2 Historical Background

The entrance and subsequent evolution of the Evangelical tradition in Mexico was most decisively determined by indigenous forces. Protestantism was, of course, first established elsewhere. American missionaries then came to control the organizational structures of the Evangelical movement for many years. Neither can we ignore the pervasive economic, political, and cultural influence of the United States, which has invaded Mexico on three occasions in the last two centuries and so shapes modern Mexican sensibilities and conditions. Nevertheless, it was political and religious conflicts internal to Mexico that led some to seek a religious alternative to Catholicism. It was the struggles of Mexicans, in the build-up to and aftermath of their revolution, that defined the context in which the Evangelical movement operated and in which people accepted or ignored the new faith. This turbulent historical background is the subject of this chapter.

PRE-1910: LIBERAL BEGINNINGS

Discontent with the Catholic church existed long before the arrival of the missionaries. That discontent was centred on the church's colonial structure and legacy. Endowed with great wealth, established as the only legal, true, and acceptable faith, and granted many special privileges or *fueros*, including exemption from all taxation and the authority of state law, it was the most powerful institution in colonial Mexico. The *patronato royale* may have given the state a final say in ecclesiastical appointments, but the two were so intricately intertwined that the church saw itself as the ultimate defender of all that was Spanish, Catholic, and civilized in New Spain. Though some priests were leaders of the independence movement, the higher clergy and the church as a whole were vehemently opposed, excommunicating the insurgents. Only the prospect of liberal reform in Mother Spain caused the church's landed allies to embrace independence in 1821, to protect their privileges.[1] This failure of independent Mexico to address or resolve the tensions of its colonial legacy set the foundations for the struggles that culminated in the revolution of 1910.

Though the new constitution of 1824 was republican and liberal in principle, all the old colonial powers and privileges of the Catholic church were reaffirmed. At first it was the more intellectual of liberals who came to believe that the advance of individual liberties and social progress would only be achieved when the powers of the Catholic church were curbed. Thus Mora, a well-known liberal writer, helped James Thomson of the English Bible Society to distribute Bibles for a few years in the late 1820s, until Thompson was driven out. Though Mora continued to serve as an agent of the Bible Society into the 1840s, he and most of his contemporaries were wary of Protestantism, which they feared might weaken national identity.[2] The major liberal concern at this time was to curb the church's wealth and thereby replenish the state's empty coffers. Anti-clerical sentiments among liberals were strengthened when the Catholic church proved reluctant to help fund the war with the United States in the mid-1840s. Americans occupied Mexico City for a year and annexed Texas and California under the imposed treaty of Guadalupe-Hidalgo of 1848.[3] In 1857 the liberals disestablished the church, obliged it to sell off its huge holdings, and established a measure of religious freedom. The conservative opposition revolted, leading to a bitter and very bloody three-year war, eventually won by liberals under the leadership of Benito Juarez. During the war he promulgated his far more restrictive "laws of reform," which suppressed all male religious orders, nationalized all church property without compensation, gave state governors the right to regulate the number of churches, and granted complete freedom of religious belief and practice. The new, more virulently anti-Catholic sentiments of a growing number of Mexicans were then additionally fuelled when Mexico was invaded by French troops and the Austrian Archduke Maximilian, at the invitation of Mexican conservatives and the Catholic church, which sought to overthrow the reform laws. Again a bitter three-year war was fought, during which Juarez decreed, in 1863, that all who supported or aided the intervention would be regarded as traitors. When the United States pressured the French troops to withdraw, the liberals were again victorious, causing many clergy and two of the three archbishops to flee.[4]

In this climate a small group of renegade priests known as the Constitutionalist Fathers proposed that an independent national church be established. The new institution they envisaged would retain Catholic doctrine and ritual but would acquiesce to liberal reforms and would no longer be subject to the authority of Rome or the former Catholic hierarchy. When Juarez returned to Mexico City, he volunteered his support and gave them a recently confiscated church in the capital. The next year Augustin Palacio, a prominent priest, and Sostenes Juarez, a relative of the president, proposed founding a new church under a lay committee headed by prominent liberals, including the then magistrate of the Supreme Court. In 1864 the dissidents formed themselves into the Church of Jesus. Their numbers grew, but they were plagued by financial problems, by their failure to attract a significant number of Catholic clergy, and by their lack of any bishops to ordain new clergy. They turned to the Episcopal church in the United States for aid, but no formal commitment was made until 1872. Little money was forthcoming, and the only Episcopal missionary on the scene proved to be a poor administrator.[5] At the same time, other small reformed Christian groups emerged in different parts of the country. Some were led by Mexican liberals, and others were linked to American and English Protestants resident in the country. Bastian, whose account of the period is most thorough, estimates that in the early 1870s there were some fifty congregations outside the Catholic church, of which only a small minority had any links to foreigners. None had been founded by missionaries,[6] but all were in need of guidance and aid.

Faced with the failure to create an autonomous Mexican church, the liberal government opened its doors to American Protestant missionary agencies as the only available means of creating a viable alternative to the Catholic church. According to the fulsome rhetoric of Juarez, "the future prosperity and happiness of my nation now depend on the development of Protestantism." A Zapotec Indian by upbringing and ethnic origin, he claimed that "Protestants would become Mexican by conquering the Indians; they need a religion to compel them to read and not to spend their savings on candles for their saints."[7] The assimilationist assumption of such rhetoric may offend some today, but the idea of Indians coming to be part of Mexican society was progressive, radical, and even revolutionary for its time.

Once the American civil war was over and peace under the liberals secure, the large Protestant establishment in a prosperous United

States became ever more attentive to stories they had heard for a number of years of Mexican discontent with Catholicism. In 1871 the Quakers and Northern Baptists made their very first contacts. They were followed by the Northern Presbyterians and Congregationalists in 1872, by the Northern and Southern Methodists in 1873, and by the Southern Presbyterians in 1874.[8] The bulk of the already established dissident churches, as well as their leaders Sostenes Juarez, Augustin Palacio, and Arcadio Morales, joined the new Protestant denominations, while the remaining small rump of the Church of Jesus affiliated to the American Episcopal Church, which has not since shown much vitality.[9] There later arrived the Disciples of Christ, very small numbers of Adventists, and the Nazarenes, who are part of the Holiness movement that was the precursor of Pentecostalism.[10] In 1910, on the eve of the revolution, the initial group of historical Protestant denominations continued to dominate the Evangelical world.[11]

The missionaries were highly educated: most of their leaders were graduates of prestigious eastern institutions like Yale and Princeton. Their religious world-view had been formed by the revivalist era of the Second Great Awakening in New England, which emphasized individual conversion rather than social reform. Ethics and morality, not doctrine or ritual, were their prime concerns. They gave particular emphasis to the founding of schools as a means of propagating their message and gaining converts. The social gospel had no significant impact until the end of this pre-revolution era. Progress, betterment, and the like were central to their thinking, but the locus of reform continued to be the individual, not society as a whole.[12]

By 1882 there were a total of some 85 missionaries stationed in Mexico. By 1910 their number had risen to 300. In the same year there were 600 Mexican preachers, of whom about half were ordained. Many of the Mexican preachers also taught in a Protestant network of 163 schools. Together missionaries and nationals had founded about 1,000 congregations, "of which perhaps two-thirds are organized churches."[13] As this network expanded and the number of Mexican preachers grew, direct missionary responsibility for local congregations diminished. Baldwin estimates that by 1910 62 per cent of the preaching stations were run exclusively by Mexicans; the figure is probably even higher for the smaller mission sites attached to each station.[14] Missionaries were always looking to make their churches as financially self-sufficient as possible, but "the major portion of all salaries"[15] continued to come from abroad. It seems fair to assume that capital expenses for church, school, and mission construction derived even more overwhelmingly from the United States. For 1905 Bastian estimates that about 28 per cent of the costs of Presbyterian day schools came from local sources, though the great majority of the children were not Protestant.[16] By 1911 the head of the Methodist mission could claim that it received "nearly as much from indigenous sources as the parent society,"[17] but the administration of mission funds remained firmly in missionary hands. "Mexican ministers were rarely invited to the annual mission meetings and when they were invited it was usually as nonvoting participants."[18] Though more and more of the pastoral work was done by Mexicans, they remained employees.

Estimates of the total Evangelical population vary according to source and the way in which membership is defined, but the missionary estimates coincided closely with the 1910 census, which put the total Protestant community at 68,839, or 0.5 per cent of Mexico's 15 million inhabitants.[19] Evangelicals and missionaries tended to be disproportionately concentrated in the north and along railways, which eased access for missionaries. Besides the simple matter of northern proximity to foreign influence, it was a relatively recent area of settlement, with many migrants, less deeply rooted customs, and little Catholic institutional presence. Conversely, Evangelicals were largely absent in the distant south, in the many remote Indian communities, and on the larger estates or "haciendas," where landlord and priest retained tight control. Those sectors and regions of Mexico most traditional in character had no noteworthy Evangelical presence. Evangelicals grew where Mexican society was changing, where the old structures were least deeply embedded, and where opposition to the status quo was most evident. Recruitment among the upper class and highly educated was non-existent. Baldwin stresses Evangelical success in the newly emergent middle class of craftsmen and urban workers. Bastian, the other major investigator of this era, stresses Evangelical growth among the poorer strata of miners, small landholders, textile workers, and rural folk pressured by expanding haciendas. Beyond the differing labels Baldwin and Bastian use, they seem to agree that the new faith emerged among strata or factions whose worlds were new or changing. None could remotely be described as privileged.[20] Where they did establish a presence, their small numbers insured that it was rarely more than a toehold.

The impact and relative importance of these varied factors in shaping Evangelical growth emerges more clearly from the two brief case studies that follow. In the tropical coastal state of Tabasco in 1884 there were no bishops and only four priests, who were located in the larger towns. The absence of colonial institutions helped to make Tabasco a liberal stronghold, which defeated the French invaders under the leadership of Gregorio Mendez. When a radical faction of liberals took over the governorship of the state in 1881, Mendez, who was part of this group, a Mason, and a federal senator – but not an Evangelical – invited the Presbyterians to make their presence known in his home state. A Mexican lay preacher, arriving for six months in 1881, found that the Chontalpa region, from which Mendez came, was especially open. The first group of converts came from a local Masonic lodge whose members had all been invited to a service by Mendez's brother. After 1883 there were usually one or two Mexican Presbyterian pastors resident in the state. With land donated by Mendez, the first church was built in 1888 in Comalcalco. Thus a small network of schools and several small congregations were built up. Missionaries paid the salaries of the Mexican pastors: they subsidized the schools, and they dominated the regional meetings of Presbyterians, but they visited briefly only once a year.[21]

A similar though rather more extreme pattern occurred in the Zitacuaro region of western Michoacan. It too was a liberal centre, fighting on the side of Juarez, first against Mexican conservatives between 1858 and 1861 and then later against the French. Travelling Bible distributors and preachers, probably supported by the Presbyterian mission, held the first house services in 1876. A Mexican pastor was not sent to the area until 1879. Some 10 per cent of the population had become Evangelical by 1882, organized into sixteen congregations. A missionary couple later settled in the area, but only after the early period of rapid growth, which was largely promoted through Masonic lodges and liberal networks.[22] In neither of these two cases of Evangelical breakthrough were missionaries responsible for the propagation or spread of the faith. They did provide leadership training and subsequent material aid to the pastors, but the keys to Evangelical success surely lie in the combination of Catholic neglect and/or a radical liberal opposition to the Catholic church and the established social order.

Lerdo de Tejada, Juarez's successor in the early 1870s, pressed the Catholic church even more than Juarez by trying to implement fully all the reform laws and by expelling over four hundred Catholic brothers in 1875. He offered to sell former Catholic churches to Evangelicals. He went out of his way to assure worried Evangelicals that he welcomed their presence and would defend them against

Catholic aggression. In 1876 Lerdo was overthrown by General Porfirio Diaz, who ruled Mexico with an iron fist until the eruption of the revolution in 1910. Evangelicals were initially worried, but Diaz quickly made it clear that he supported the liberal reforms, that he was not opposed to the presence of American missionaries, and that he did not condone persecution of Evangelicals. In fact, Lerdo's anti-Catholic policies had provoked aggressions and demonstrations against Evangelicals that the central government had sometimes been helpless to prevent.[23] These attacks continued and probably grew in the early years under Diaz, though he expressed his deep regret at the murder of twenty-five Evangelicals in 1878 in the town of Atzala, and he promised to defend religious liberty. The most widely cited figure for the period 1873 to 1892 puts the number of Evangelicals killed for their religion at fifty-eight, of whom only one was American. Thereafter overt violence appears to have diminished, but Evangelicals continued to experience social ostracism, sometimes finding it difficult to buy, rent, or gain employment.[24] The pervasive, deeply rooted hostility to Evangelicals suggested by such incidents helps to explain their less than overwhelming rate of growth in these years, despite a weak Catholic church and a sympathetic government.

Like Juarez and unlike Lerdo, Diaz sought to restore social harmony by improving relations with the Catholic church. Though Diaz was not prepared to alter or remove any of the reform era legislation, he did not apply it. The unstated if clear condition was that the church not involve itself in politics, a condition it abided by until nearly the end of the "Porfiriato," the years of Diaz's rule. The number of prelates grew from 4 to 36. The number of priests more than tripled, from 1,600 to 5,000, as did the number of churches. Religious orders were allowed to return and increase in number, from 8 in 1851 to 18 in 1910. Outdoor religious ceremonies and processions were allowed, culminating in the coronation in 1895 of the Virgin of Guadalupe, whose symbolic role as the "Mother of Mexico" is outlined in chapter 5. Diaz did not resume official relations with the Vatican, which had been broken in the 1860s, but he received a visit by a papal delegate in 1896, and another delegate took up residence in Mexico City after 1905.[25] Such reconciliation can only have further hindered Evangelical growth.

Missionaries remained universally supportive of the Diaz regime till 1905, though they never involved themselves directly in political debates. They were grateful for the free access Diaz allowed them to Mexico and for his general promise of religious liberty. Yet they were conscious that the promise often meant little in the particular region where they worked. They were aware of his dictatorial, anti-democratic ways but were inclined to rationalize them on the grounds that he gave Mexico stability and progress. The occasional younger missionary, under the influence of the social gospel, began to be more critical, after 1905, of Porfirian injustice. Most others, especially those older and in positions of higher authority, were disinclined by their individualistic and evangelistic inclinations to pay much heed to political and economic matters unless they directly affected their mission. Though long standing, missionary support for Diaz was far from deep. When his regime fell in 1910, they quickly gave their support to Madero, since he too supported religious tolerance and they could see that the Diaz regime was clearly over.[26]

Far less sanguine were Mexican Evangelicals, who had to endure the growing inequities and pervasive injustices of the Porfiriato. With no significant presence among the privileged, Evangelicals had no material or practical interest in preserving a regime that so obviously favoured the few at the expense of the many. Such sentiments may initially have been slow to emerge. Since the 1870s Evangelicals had been quick to assert their patriotism in order to counter Catholic propaganda emphasizing their "gringo" connections.[27] No general sounding of Evangelical opinion is available for this period, but Evangelicals were a striking and voluble minority in the liberal press and clubs that emerged in the 1890s to condemn Diaz's fraudulent elections and his conciliation with the Catholic church. By 1905 the former emphasis on patriotism had been replaced by a new stress on liberty, civil rights, their centrality in Evangelical life, and the many hindrances to their achievement in secular society. Few Evangelicals, it seemed, were prepared to embrace the demands of the Mexican Liberal Party for immediate insurrection and widespread economic and social change. However, Evangelicals all over the country responded vigorously to Madero's call in 1909 for peaceful electoral change on the principle of no re-election. Moderate as these proposals were, they were a direct challenge to Porfirian rule.[28]

1910–1940: REVOLUTION AND REPRESSION

When Madero looked as if he would be a serious opposition candidate at the 1910 presidential elections, Diaz had him put under house arrest prior to the election, as he had done to other opponents before. This time the state of unrest was such that Madero and his supporters opted for insurrection. In October he fled to the U.S. From there he proclaimed illegitimate the just-completed elections and called for an armed uprising on 20 November. The north, Madero's home and the site of the greatest concentrations of Protestants, was most responsive to his call. One of the first rebel leaders to rise to arms was Pascual Orozco Jr, who had been raised a Methodist in western Chihuahua and who, along with Pancho Villa, provided Madero with his first base in Mexico in his six-month campaign. "Almost all the evangelicos are revolutionists and even the pastor [Grijalva] goes with them" claimed the nearby missionary, who had baptized Orozco and many of his followers.[29] Other prominent Evangelicals in the north were Braulio Hernandez and I.M. Lopez, both pastors, and Moises Saenz. Support for the revolution was far more spotty and localized elsewhere in the country, but wherever the uprising was evident, Bastian's careful research reveals Evangelical leadership and participation. In the Chontalpa, for instance, to which reference has already been made, the anti-Porfirian forces were led by Ignacio Gutierrez, a Presbyterian convert and active member of his church, whose co-religionists followed him in substantial number.[30] Evangelicals never dominated the ranks of the revolutionaries as much as these two examples might seem to imply, but the general level of their involvement was certainly greater than their percentage of the total population.

Madero's triumphal arrival in Mexico City in June 1911 was celebrated by the Evangelical press as the arrival of democracy,[31] while the Catholic church opposed him "as a matter of course."[32] However, his early victory turned out to be the very first phase of a lengthy, bloody struggle that transformed Mexico, though it did not make it democratic. From the beginning Madero's regime was confronted with armed uprisings among various factions on both the left and the right. The first to withdraw support was Zapata, who distrusted Madero's reliance on so many from the old regime and who wanted radical agrarian reform, which had never been part of Madero's vision. Not long after, in early 1912, Pascual Orozco, the Evangelical from Chihuahua, denounced Madero, called for greater reforms, and took control of most of his home state and part of Coahuila before being defeated by Madero's forces, led by Huerta, a former Porfirian soldier.[33] Two other small uprisings from the right also occurred before Huerta, with the support of a newly created Catholic party, used his military force to take power in 1913, executing Madero and his vice-president, Pino Suarez. Evangelical support for Madero had grown increasingly tepid in the face of the continuing chaos, but Evangelicals were vehemently opposed to the Huerta regime because of its savagery, its conservative cast, and its anti-Evangelical tendencies.[34] The Catholic church, seeing Huerta as the last stand against liberalism or worse, condemned all who later rebelled against it and even lent Huerta money to pay his troops. In so doing, it put itself in opposition to all strands of the victorious revolution.[35]

The bloodiest phase of the revolution then took place, as resistance to Huerta coalesced around a northern coalition headed by Carranza. As the war spread, the revolutionary forces everywhere plundered church buildings, extorted money from clergy, and generally intimidated them, causing most of the bishops and many of the clergy to flee.[36] By the summer of 1914 Carranza had defeated Huerta and entered Mexico City, but he was soon obliged to flee in his fight with his former ally, Pancho Villa. By August 1915 Carranza was back in Mexico City, where he established himself as interim head and then president of the new regime. He stayed in power until 1920, fighting Villa in the north and Zapata in the south. Carranza tried to overcome the constitutional prohibition on re-election by nominating as the official candidate for the presidency a virtual unknown whom he, Carranza, would subsequently control. Obregon, his leading general and ally, revolted, took Mexico City, and killed Carranza. Revolutionary continuity but not democracy was maintained.

From the beginning, Evangelical support, among both missionaries and Mexicans, was widespread for Carranza, and hence for the winning faction in the revolutionary struggles. Their shared northern origins may have fostered Evangelical support for Carranza, but behind it was their broad attachment to the rhetoric of democracy, progress, and liberal reform, which he claimed to represent. Villa and Zapata were generally regarded by Evangelicals as unstable extremists, though some Evangelicals in Zapata's home state of Morelos did back him. A goodly number of Evangelicals also served in Carranza's army and later administration. Since no more than 10 per cent of Mexicans were then literate, Evangelical graduates of their school system were sought out as senior staff officers around generals, who sometimes could not read. As early as 1914 the head of the information and propaganda office, Gregorio Velasquez, was a Methodist preacher who filled his department with many other Evangelicals. Three of Carranza's governors were Evangelicals, as were between seven and ten of those elected to his Chamber of Deputies. The total Evangelical presence, given their small numbers, was never large, but it was sufficiently striking for Catholic and other critics of the Carranza regime to complain of it constantly.[37]

The most far-reaching of the actions of the Carranza era was the creation of a new constitution in 1917. Carranza's initial proposals were modelled on the 1857 constitution, but people of far more radical persuasion dominated the constitutional congress. The final documents swept the old liberal principles aside, giving way "to a militant nationalism and to a native, non-Marxian, socialism"[38] in such areas as land reform, labour relations, and education. Rather than full separation of church and state, there were now to be clear state restrictions on religious practice.

The state was denied the right to establish or prohibit any religion (article 130), while freedom of speech was affirmed, except where public order was threatened (article 6). Individuals were also free to profess their religious beliefs and to hold services in their homes or in places of public worship. However, article 24 stipulated that public worship could only take place indoors and under government supervision. The time, place, and number of services were now all in theory under government control. Most notable was the banning of the religious processions and outdoor campaigns so loved by Catholics and Evangelicals respectively. Under article 27 churches could own no property, including their places of worship, which were to be transferred to state ownership. Any future places of worship acquired by churches required government approval and had to be nationalized or given to the state (article 130). All subsequent modification of such properties also required state approval.

Article 5 prohibited religious orders. Article 130 stipulated that only Mexicans by birth could be ministers of religious creeds. The latter article further decreed that the state could set the number of ministers for each religion according to the needs of each locality. Moreover, all ministers had to be registered with the state. The result if not the intent of this stipulation was that the government now possessed a veto over the appointment of all ministers. Politically, ministers were denied the vote and the right to take part in political activities. They were also forbidden to criticize, in public or private, "the fundamental laws of the country, the authorities in particular, or the government in general." Article 3 prohibited all religious education in both state and private schools. It also barred all religious bodies or ministers from founding or owning primary schools, while leaving open the possibility of religious control at higher levels. Lastly, article 130 stipulated that the infraction of these provisions could not be subject to trial by jury, thereby leaving all control in the hands of the federal authorities.[39]

The restrictive potential of the document was breathtaking, ranging from the exclusion of missionaries to the prospect of losing all church property and to seeing the treasured school network shut down. Catholics were predictably vocal in their condemnation, but the Evangelical response was far more muted. In large measure this was because Evangelicals in government were privately assured by the president that the restrictive elements of the constitution were aimed at the Catholic church and would be interpreted so as not to hinder Evangelical work. These assurances were then disseminated to all the major denominations and mission boards.[40] In fact, nothing really changed, since, by Mexican law, each constitutional article requires an implementing law, passed by Congress, that outlines the specific rules and penalties. Without such a law the article could not be enforced. Carranza, the old liberal, who was opposed in principle to the new constitution, made no move to introduce the necessary regulatory laws.[41] The right to do so, of course, remained.

Obregon was of a more radical mind than Carranza, but he too did not apply the religiously restrictive constitutional articles. He had other more pressing economic problems and did not wish to provoke American opinion. The Catholic church, for its part, showed little interest in conciliation. It threatened excommunication to any parents who sent their children to the expanding secular state school system, though Obregon made no move against the Catholic school system, which continued to expand. It also condemned the first steps towards agrarian reform, and told the faithful that it was a mortal sin to join the new secular unions being promoted by government.[42]

Calles, Obregon's successor, was far more vehemently anti-Catholic, having previously, as governor of Sonora in 1916, expelled all clergy because of their presumed opposition to the revolutionary cause. In hindsight there seems a certain inevitability to the ever more intransigent positions taken by both sides in 1925 and into 1926. Already in 1925 the state of Tabasco had passed a law requiring that practising ministers be married and over forty years of age. In early 1926 the archbishop of Mexico stated that his church did not recognize and would fight the constitutional restrictions, which in turn caused Calles to announce that he would enforce the relevant articles. Foreign nuns and priests were expelled; schools run by foreign religious orders were closed, and states everywhere began to impose severe limits on the number of priests allowed. It was also announced that the priests for all churches built since 1917 would have to be registered with local governments. Catholic opposition centred on this last requirement, although the implementary laws for most of the remaining restrictions followed a few months later. The hierarchy responded by saying that it would suspend all church services if the offending legislation was not withdrawn. Calles did not blink. For three years, until 1929, no services were held in Catholic churches throughout Mexico, and the constitutional restrictions were enforced with vigour.[43] The call for a national boycott failed, but in the western and most Catholic regions of the country the Cristero rebellion raged on and off for three years, with considerable loss of life in rural areas. In the end the rebellion ceased and the churches were reopened when the Catholic church agreed to register its clergy. The government, for its part, stated that registration in no way implied interference with church appointments by government, and it agreed to allow religious education of children in church. Otherwise the government made no appreciable concession.[44]

Repression did not stop; for a time it even intensified. In 1931 a large ceremony was held in honour of the Virgin of Guadalupe, which was attended by most bishops, many priests, and large numbers of the faithful. Interpreting the event as a challenge, the government passed further legislation stipulating that only the registered official of a church could officiate in it. The next year a papal encyclical condemning the Mexican government drove the Chamber of Deputies to hold extraordinary sessions in reply. More critically, state governments imposed even tighter restrictions on the number of ministers a religion might have. The states of Vera Cruz, Chiapas, Sonora, and Tabasco prohibited all religious services, though this most repressive phase came to a close after Cardenas became president in 1934. In 1935 the Garrido regime in Tabasco was removed; its ban on church services was lifted, and nation-wide limitations on the circulation of religious literature were removed. The next year Cardenas declared a moratorium on the anti-religion campaign, on the grounds that it hindered the economic progress of the country.[45]

Catholicism's difficulties and Evangelical prominence in the revolution together seemed to offer an unprecedented opportunity for Evangelical advance. In 1921 Obregon invited Evangelical leaders to the official celebrations commemorating one hundred years of independence.[46] Several Evangelicals held important posts in the expanding state educational system, which was given the task of preaching revolutionary ideals and creating a modern, Mestizo identity. The most prominent of this group was Moises Saenz, a Presbyterian from Tamaulipas, who served as sub-secretary of public education under Obregon. He was also later involved in setting up the Department of Indian Affairs under Cardenas.[47] Moises's brother Aaron had been Obregon's chief of staff for many years. He later held many prominent posts, including minister of foreign relations and governor of the state of Nuevo Leon. In 1929, after

Obregon's assassination, it appeared for a time that Aaron would be nominated by Calles to be the next president. That he was not was in part due to fears that the public would react negatively to his Evangelical affiliation, even though he made a point of writing Evangelical leaders asking them to "make no mention of his 'former' Protestant affiliations."[48] Public acceptance of Evangelicals was still clearly limited.

Evangelical churches were inevitably affected by Calles's imposition of the religious restrictions of the 1917 constitution, but this was a war with the Catholic church, not Evangelicals. Calles admitted that "Protestant ministers ... have always adjusted themselves to the law."[49] Evangelicals were not really affected by state restrictions on the number of ministers, since each Evangelical denomination in a state was granted the full quota allowed the Catholic church. Of course, the complete banning of all ministers and/or church services in some states in the early 1930s had its impact. So too did the prohibition on foreign ministers, although its effect was mitigated by the apparent willingness of state authorities to allow missionaries to stay on, provided they did not preach or directly run churches.[50] Thus the 261 missionaries in Mexico in 1921 fell to only 233 by 1930, though they dropped further to 156 by 1935. In this latter year the total of 259 Evangelical Mexican ministers and 205 lay workers was not much lower than the estimates of their number in 1911. Had the religious upheaval not occurred, their number would surely have been higher, but their losses pale in comparison to those of the Catholic church, which saw the number of its priests fall from 4,492 in 1926 to 111 in 1935.[51]

Education was the one sphere where the church-state conflict left a permanent mark. The upheaval of the revolutionary years and the departure of most missionaries after the 1914 American invasion of Veracruz must have shaken the Evangelical network of schools. Yet by 1921 their 11,000 students were much the same as their numbers before the revolution.[52] After 1917 the constitution dictated that primary education was an exclusively state preserve, but this article was clearly not being implemented, since there were 8,704 students at primary level in Evangelical schools in 1921. When Calles applied the constitutional prohibitions after 1926, government officials encouraged Evangelicals to create non-religious civil associations that would enable the schools to continue as before.[53] In 1930 there were still at least 4,000 students at Evangelical schools, and the total number may well have been higher.[54] In Zitacuaro, for instance, the liberal and Presbyterian stronghold of the nineteenth century, a primary school was established in 1910, followed by an industrial school in 1923 and a secondary school in 1929,[55] the latter being the first of its kind in the municipio. Then, in 1934, the government introduced further constitutional changes, barring religious involvement in schools at all levels. This obstacle could have been surmounted with civil associations for secondary schools, but the constitutional changes also required that teaching in all schools "must be socialist and besides excluding all religious doctrine will fight fanaticism and prejudices."[56] In practice this meant that the teachers at the Zitacuaro school were obliged by government to sign a paper stating they had no religious commitment and would not attend religious services. This they could not do. Hence the three schools closed permanently, though Evangelical residences for older students at state schools were opened up later and continued for another thirty years.[57] Government pressure of this sort may not have been applied throughout the country, but within a few years there remained a very small number of schools, no longer under direct missionary or church control, with a total enrolment of about 2,000.[58] The old network had been broken.

Tables 2.1 and 2.2 show that, in this second phase of revolutionary struggle and church-state conflict, Evangelical growth continued, though the total Evangelical membership of 177,954 was still just under 1 per cent of the total population in 1940. In the stormy religious climate of this period the greatest growth occurred among those claiming to have no religion at all. Evangelicals grew by only a modest 7 per cent in the decade of the revolution, but Catholics saw their numbers decline by over a million as a result of the violence and social upheaval of the revolution. Evangelical growth was greatest in the 1920s, when their numbers grew by 76 per cent in the span of nine years, a growth rate almost five (4.7) times greater than that experienced by Catholics. Then in the 1930s, when anti-clericalism turned for a time into a more general, anti-religious climate, Evangelical growth halved, though they still grew by a fat third (37 per cent) in the 1930s. Tables 2.3 and 2.4 show that the Evangelical percentage of the population in 1940 was still higher in the north and the capital than anywhere else, though the proportion of all Evangelicals living in the former northern stronghold fell from 32 per cent in 1910 to 25 per cent in 1940. The remote south, which in 1910 was still largely closed to Evangelical advance, was beginning to prove more receptive. This was most evident in Tabasco, where Evangelicals in 1940 numbered 9,323, or 3.3 per cent of the total population. In no other state, including the former stronghold of the north, was the Evangelical proportion as high. In general Evangelicals in 1940 continued to be most numerous in the

Table 2.1
Mexican population by religion, 1910–90, national census

	Catholic		Evang.		Other		None		No reply	
	No.	% of total	No.	% of total	No.	% of total	No.	% of total	No.	% of total
1910	15,033,176	99.2	68,839	0.45	13,328	0.09	25,011	0.17	20,015	0.13
1921	13,921,226	97.1	73,951	0.51	22,718	0.16	108,049	0.75	208,836	1.46
1930	16,179,667	97.7	130,322	0.79	64,830	0.39	175,180	1.06	1,785	0.01
1940	18,977,585	96.6	177,954	0.91	49,925	0.25	443,671	2.26	4,417	0.02
1950	25,329,428	98.2	330,111	1.28	131,408	0.51				
1960	33,692,503	96.5	578,515	1.66	237,958	0.68	192,963	0.55	221,190	0.63
1970	46,380,401	96.2	876,879	1.82	199,510	0.41	768,448	1.59		
1980	61,916,757	92.6	2,201,609	3.29	639,928	0.96	2,088,453	3.12	86	0.0001
1990	72,870,369	89.69	3,969,858	4.89	1,242,307	1.43	2,634,926	3.24	532,185	0.66

Table 2.2.
Annual growth* rates by religion, selected periods, national census

	RC %	Evang. %	Other %	None %	Total %
1910–40	0.9	5.3	9.1	55.8	1.0
1940–70	4.8	13.1	10.0	12.1	4.8
1970–90	2.9	17.6	26.1	12.1	3.4

* Per annum growth = total percentage growth in time-period divided by the number of years.

peripheral regions of the country and in the more modern environment of the capital. In the geographic and cultural centre of the country, with the aforementioned exception of Mexico City, Evangelicals were thinnest on the ground. Whereas almost two-thirds (64 per cent) of Catholics lived in this still predominantly rural heartland of Mexico, fewer than half (44 per cent) of Evangelicals did so.

Missionaries continued to be an influential force in the Evangelical world in the 1920s and 1930s, though less so than formerly. As before, their greatest influence was at the administrative level within their respective denominations. Most withdrew from Mexico in 1914 in the face of growing violence and rising anti-Americanism, after the u.s. occupied the port of Veracruz for six months. In the same year they formulated what came to be known as the Cincinnati Plan, though it was not finally ratified until 1919. This wideranging scheme was designed to co-ordinate the activities of the eleven major mission boards then working in Mexico. Their aim was to avoid duplication and competition by allocating to each

Table 2.3
Evangelical and Catholic percentage of regions, selected years, national census

	Evangelicals %				Catholics %			
	1910	1940	1970	1990	1910	1940	1970	1990
North	1.3	1.7	2.4	5.7	97.1	95.6	95.7	88.1
Capital*	1.4	1.7	1.6	3.2	97.3	95.3	96.3	92.4
Centre	0.3	0.6	1.3	3.5	99.6	97.0	96.9	92.1
South	0.3	1.0	3.9	12.1	99.3	96.0	93.3	77.4
Nation	0.5	0.9	1.8	4.9	99.2	96.6	96.2	89.7

* Includes the federal district and the municipalities in the State of Mexico that were then part of Metropolitan Mexico.

Table 2.4
Regional distribution of Evangelicals and Catholics, selected years, national census

	Evangelicals %				Catholics %			
	1910	1940	1970	1990	1910	1940	1970	1990
North	31.9	25.1	22.2	19.6	11.0	13.4	16.5	16.4
Capital*	15.1	16.4	15.7	12.2	4.7	8.8	18.3	19.1
Centre	44.5	43.9	38.0	37.3	70.5	64.1	54.3	53.8
South	8.5	14.6	24.1	30.9	13.9	13.6	11.0	10.8
Nation	100%	100%	100%	100%	100%	100%	100%	100%

* Includes the federal district and the municipalities in the State of Mexico that were then part of Metropolitan Mexico.

board certain areas and regions as its particular preserve. In practice, this meant that Mexican congregations throughout the country not infrequently discovered that they were now attached to a new mission board and sometimes a new denomination. All this was done without consulting Mexican pastors and leaders, thereby causing considerable resentment and confusion.

The plans of the missionaries none the less proceeded because they continued to wield substantial economic power. In the later 1930s Davis's survey of historical denominations found that only 12 per cent were economically self-supporting. Dependence on missionaries was particularly marked in rural areas. At this time only one mission board had a concerted plan to reduce its subsidies, but it had been unable to meet its objectives in two of the three years in which the plan had been in effect.[59] Nationally, only 41 per cent of Evangelical laity contributed "more or less regularly"[60] to their local churches.

Despite their continuing economic and administrative powers, the missionaries' role in directing local congregations diminished. The immediate and most obvious reason was that their numbers fell from 300 to 159 between 1910 and 1935, while the total Evangelical community more than doubled, to 177,954 in 1940. Behind this was the constitutional prohibition on foreign ministers, which also caused the ever smaller number who remained to retreat further from the direct running of congregations. If the example given by Baez Camargo and Grubb of one mission board is any way typical, the influence of the missionaries must have been further reduced by the fact that "more than half ... spent less than 10 years in the field and nearly half less than five."[61] Few could have been proficient in Spanish or familiar with Mexican ways.

Particularly instructive is the rapidly growing Evangelical community in Tabasco in the 1930s, the early years of which have already been charted. Bennett's detailed study puts the Evangelical community at no more than 1,000 in the early 1920s.[62] Then followed the period of religious persecution under Governor Tomas Garrido, (1923–35), when all priests were driven out and their churches closed. In the second half of the 1920s there had been one missionary resident in the state for four years, but he was constantly harassed by the authorities. He and the last Mexican pastor were driven out by 1931. For the years 1930 to 1935 even the Evangelical churches were all closed. In the fifty years prior to 1935, in what Bennett describes as the era when missionaries and trained pastors controlled the Presbyterian church, fewer than thirty congregations had been established, the majority by lay workers. By 1940 their number had already more than doubled to seventy and continued to grow rapidly thereafter, even though there were no missionaries or Mexican pastors working in the state until 1943. Bennett's point is that rapid growth did not occur until the leadership of the Evangelical movement was left, by default, in the hands of local lay people. As long as the Presbyterian church was funded by missionaries and run by a small group of well-educated ministers, on an American model, there would be a shortage of leaders and a cultural gap between pastor and layman that would in turn block lay commitment and numerical growth.[63] Evangelical growth was also facilitated by the lack of organized Catholic opposition, by the anti-clerical sentiments of so many, and by the fact that the mainly poor and rural inhabitants of the state were little touched by secular indifference to religious solutions to life's problems.

The historical denominations in Tabasco and elsewhere remained the dominant force throughout the Evangelical world until 1940, but a major sea-change in the composition of the Evangelical world began to happen after 1910, with the emergence of Pentecostal churches. The modern Pentecostal movement erupted in California and Kansas at the beginning of this century, subsequently spreading through the south and west of the United States, where it had its greatest appeal among the poor, the uneducated, and the marginal.[64] Later chapters will deal with the distinctive characteristics of this religious world-view. For the moment I want to stress only that their newness and limited economic resources made it impossible for American Pentecostals to sustain missionaries and fund Mexican churches as the historical denominations were still doing. Their original concentration along the border and appeal to the poor and marginal combined to insure that the carriers of Pentecostalism from the United States were much more likely to be Mexicans, converted in the United States, who subsequently sought to share their new faith with their kin and neighbours at home. From the beginning Pentecostalism was an indigenous and autonomous movement. As Pentecostal numbers grew, missionary influences, which had always been limited, further diminished for Evangelicals as a whole.

The fragmentation of the Pentecostal world and their common disregard for written records have left us a less than complete historical account. The first congregation is thought to have been formed in 1914, in Villa Aldama, Chihuahua, the border state, by a woman and returning resident who had been converted two years earlier in a small Mexican congregation in Los Angeles. On her return to the u.s. she left her small congregation of twelve in the hands of a Methodist pastor whom she had also converted from his church in the state capital. From this foundation emerged the Iglesia Apostolica de la Fe en Cristo Jesus, which claimed 26 congregations by 1932 and 130 by 1944.[65] It has always been fully independent, never having any links or ties with an American denomination.

A similar pattern exists for two other notable Pentecostal denominations today. The Iglesia Cristiana Independiente de Pachuca was founded in the early 1920s by two brothers, both miners, who had worked in mines in Arizona, where they were first converted in a Methodist church. On their return to Pachuca they began to attend a mission of the Methodist church, where they were swayed by a visiting Mexican Pentecostal to embrace a Pentecostal style. They were for a time linked with a Swedish Pentecostal who founded a church in Mexico City, but the links were short lived; their own account gives no sense of any funding or leadership coming from the Swedish missionary.[66] By the early 1970s the Pachuca church was reckoned to be the largest Pentecostal denomination in Mexico.[67]

The Iglesia Cristiana Interdenominational was also founded and directed exclusively by Mexicans. In the early 1920s a group of Methodists, Baptists, and Presbyterians in Mexico City decided to form their own congregation because no Evangelical church was within easy reach. The driving force in the small group, Josue Mejia, had been converted in a Presbyterian church a few years before, but he was not prepared to take the lengthy seminary training asked of him by Presbyterian missionaries before becoming pastor. At first he said he followed the Presbyterian pattern of subdued worship combined with literary and musical evenings, but his small group did not grow. He then came into contact with other small Pentecostal groups, which caused them to pray more fervently so that "God filled us with His power."[68] Thereafter his group began to grow, spreading out to other parts of the city and then beyond, though he resisted all attempts to incorporate his group into other Pentecostal denominations. Since its beginnings it has remained an independent church with no foreign links, distinguished by its refusal to have any paid pastors.[69] In 1987 it claimed to have over seven hundred congregations.[70]

There are, of course, denominations like the Assemblies of God in Mexico, which have had links with the American mother church since their beginnings. Their first congregation was established in Tamaulipas, right on the border in 1918, just four years after the Assemblies of God had been created in the United States. The two founding preachers, an American black and a Texan Hispanic, were driven out in a short time, leaving the direction of the church to Modesto Escobedo, who subsequently founded many other churches in the area and headed the Assemblies of God district in the northern part of his state.[71] Other prominent leaders in northern Mexico, like Cesar Burciaga and Rodolfo Orozco, were converted in Hispanic-speaking churches of the Assemblies of God while working in Texas. Some then received training at a Bible school run by Henry Ball in San Antonio, but it was converted Mexicans, not missionaries, who returned to their respective communities to found churches.[72] Similarly, it was David Ruesga, a Mexican, who first started the Assemblies of God work in Mexico City, though he was soon joined, at his invitation, by the Danish Pentecostal Anna Sanders. Initially the fledgling collection of churches were part of the Latin Conference of the Assemblies of God with headquarters in Texas, but none of the pastors ever received salaries from there. In 1929 a separate Convention of the Assemblies of God in Mexico was formed in Monterrey, with David Ruesga as its head,[73] though personality conflicts caused him to break away the next year to

found the Iglesia de Dios en la Republica Mexicana.[74] Despite the
U.S. connection, here too the leadership and energy in church life
have been firmly in indigenous hands from the beginning.

1940–1970: MODERNIZATION AND RESURGENT CATHOLICISM

The period 1940–70 was one of unprecedented stability and prosperity, though the rate of social change accelerated. Tensions of various sorts were never very far below the surface. Cardenas's transfer
of lands from large landholder to peasant, in the form of commu-
nally owned *ejido* lands, slowed dramatically in the 1940s. The
strained relationship of the 1930s with the United States, after
Cardenas nationalized the oil industry, was substantially repaired by
co-operation in the Second World War and by the Mexican government's embrace of anti-communist rhetoric in the subsequent Cold
War years. Cardenas's far more conservative successor Camacho
(1940–46) stressed that his priority was "consolidation of the revolutionary conquests."[75] His successors shared much the same sentiments, which in practice meant that the government's main
concerns were economic growth and modernization rather than social reform. Under a policy of import substitution, whereby tariffs
were placed on foreign manufactured products and local manufac-
turing was encouraged, industrial production in Mexico for its expanding home market blossomed, reaching 8 per cent annual
growth in the 1960s. Accompanying the "Mexican miracle" of overall growth of 6 per cent per year was urbanization, which saw those
living in urban areas rise from 20 per cent in 1940 to 47 per cent in
1970.[76] The gap between rich and poor widened, but the middle
class grew. Throughout these years the now-established Institutional Revolutionary Party (PRI) was able to engineer or win the
votes of the great majority of the population, in the face of weak
political opposition.[77]

The same years saw a revival in the Catholic church and a
marked lessening in church-state tensions. Having failed to crush
the church, the state pursued a policy of reconciliation, though it
did so quietly and on its own terms. Cardenas had already signed
an uneasy truce, but Camacho went much further, declaring, "I am
a believer."[78] He was the first president since the revolution to attend mass. In return, the archbishop of Mexico, Martinez, advised
Catholics to give their support to Camacho and the PRI. Then in
1952 President Aleman publicly embraced Archbishop Martinez.[79]
The concrete result of these public gestures was that government

quietly suspended, though it never repealed, the most restrictive of the constitutional prohibitions on religious practice. Religious processions were quietly resumed throughout the country; the network of Catholic schools was revived and expanded;[80] and the number of foreign clergy grew, reaching some 17 per cent of the total in 1963.[81] The number of priests, which had already climbed back to 3,863 by 1940, more than doubled to 8,761 by 1970, while the number of parishes rose from 1,600 to 2,620 in the same time-span. Because of Mexico's rapid population growth in these years, the ratio of laity to priests actually rose from 4,912 in 1940 to 5,213 in 1970. The average size of parishes rose from 12,200 to 17,570.[82] By this last measure the situation had not appreciably improved since the 1940s, but the overall picture remains one of a growing and increasingly self-confident institution, with sufficient power that the PRI or the state was obliged to work quietly with the church in areas as diverse as changes in the educational curriculum[83] to the delivery of social services in the rapidly expanding cities.[84] By the later 1950s the Catholic church in Mexico was reckoned to be one of the strongest churches in Latin America.[85]

Evangelicals no doubt welcomed the government decision not to apply the constitutional restrictions on religion, but they cannot have been pleased at the rapprochement between the state and the Catholic church. Their worst fears seem to have been realized when, in 1944, the archbishop of Mexico issued a pastoral letter calling all Catholics to be more active in defending their nation and faith against the danger of Protestant heresy. Several bishops in the north also took up the call, leading to the boycott of the YMCA and Protestant businesses in some areas and to a general growth in hostility towards Evangelicals. In fact the episcopal campaign was soon called off when it was denounced as unpatriotic and contrary to the war effort by a group of revolutionary notables, "including a solid phalanx of former presidents."[86] The campaign fizzled, but the Department of the Interior refused to process some one thousand Evangelical applications to have their churches registered, as required by the constitution, during the presidencies of Camacho and Aleman.

Although the unregistered churches continued to function, Evangelicals were understandably worried. Around the same time locally initiated attacks on Evangelical churches and meetings also appear to have grown. Those recorded by the government averaged fifteen a year; the real number was probably higher.[87] One result was the creation of a Committee of Evangelical Defence in the later 1940s, which, from its base in Mexico City, marshalled evidence and presented the Evangelical complaint to the appropriate authorities.[88] Then, under the presidencies of Ruiz Cortines (1952–58) and his successor Lopez Mateos (1958–64), the hold on registration of Evangelical churches was removed. Government officials also began to take a more active role in protecting Evangelicals from Catholic persecution. Evangelical fears abated.[89] Persecution was still occasionally fierce, but it was locally driven in the face of government condemnation, and it affected only small pockets of Evangelicals.

Because of the generally accelerated rate of population growth throughout Mexico as a whole between 1940 and 1970, the annual rate of Evangelical growth, listed in Table 2.2, was almost three times greater than in the period of revolution and religious recession. The number of Evangelicals was also growing about three (2.7) times faster than that of Catholics, though this was actually less than during the 1910–40 period, when Evangelicals increased in number 5.9 times faster than did Catholics. The census listed Evangelicals as numbering 578,515 by 1960 and 876,879 by 1970. How much faith is to be put in this total number is difficult to ascertain, since other estimates differ substantially. A survey by the Evangelical Council of Mexico put the combined Evangelical community in 1961 at 356,972,[90] while calculations by American church-growth experts raise their estimate to 645,562.[91] Both these divergent estimates suffer from their reliance on data submitted by Mexican denominations, which measure membership in different ways, rarely pay much heed to systematic gathering of numbers, and sometimes simply guess. Yet it is generally recognized that these denominational surveys do not include a substantial but indeterminate number of Evangelicals attached to smaller denominations and independent churches. Outsiders like Father Rivera put the Evangelical community at 645,142,[92] while Penton raises the figure for 1960 to 1 million.[93] Though each figure has its problems, I am inclined to put greatest faith in the census because it is the only attempt at a direct enumeration of the population and because of the phenomenon of Evangelical apostasy, which will be charted in the next chapter. The denominational surveys agree that, by the 1960s, Pentecostals had come to be a majority of all Evangelicals. The latest of these efforts, for 1965, put Pentecostals at 64 per cent of all Evangelicals. The historical denominations of Presbyterians, Baptists, and Methodists, to name the largest, now accounted for only 24 per cent of the total. There were more Presbyterians than any other single historical or Pentecostal denomination, but they were now marginally smaller in number than the Adventists, who amounted to 8 per cent of all Evangelicals.[94] Even in Tabasco, still the state with the highest percentage of Evangelicals (8.3) in 1970, the historical denominations were losing their grip. In the latter part of the 1930s the Adventists had started to penetrate, followed by various Pentecostal denominations in the 1940s; by 1965 Presbyterians were 44 per cent of all Evangelicals, Adventists 30 per cent, and Pentecostals 24 per cent.[95]

Though no one estimate of the total population of Evangelicals is completely reliable, we can place greater faith in some of the trends over time revealed by the census. We see in Tables 2.3 and 2.4 that, after 1940, the initial Evangelical concentration in the north continued to fall. Though Mexico City grew enormously, the proportion of all Evangelicals living there remained relatively constant. The general growth among Evangelicals caused their percentage of the population in the colonial heartland to increase, but the actual proportion of Evangelicals living there fell from 44 per cent in 1940 to 38 per cent in 1970. Their area of greatest growth was the south.

The dynamism of the south is attributable in part to the penetration of Evangelicals into the closed corporate worlds of Indigenous peoples, who in both 1900 and 1940 amounted to approximately 15 per cent of the Mexican population.[96] This was a new phenomenon. Prior to the revolution there was "almost no mention of Indians"[97] in the voluminous reports and letters of the missionaries. Even as late as 1935, in their survey of the Evangelical situation Baez and Camargo admitted that "the accusation ... brought against evangelicalism in Mexico that it has done little to bring the Gospel to the Indian masses ... is true in the main."[98] One of the very few exceptions was the Mexican Indian Mission, consisting of three Presbyterian missionaries who began working in the Hausteca of San Luis Potosi in 1931.[99]

The largest and most controversial of the missionary agencies working among Indigenous people, then and now, is the Summer Institute of Linguistics (SIL). Its parent body in the United States is known as the Wycliffe Bible Translators (WBT). They reached their peak in the 1950s and 1960s, when they had some 250 "translators" working in Mexico.[100] SIL or WBT were typical of the new kind of interdenominational faith mission then emerging in the United States, which tended to be more evangelical and fundamentalist than the missions of the historical denominations. They represented one side of the great division slowly growing within American Protestantism between liberals and evangelicals. They recruited their support directly from individuals and congregations. Missionaries were attached to both WBT in the United States and SIL in the country where they worked. The ultimate goal of WBT was always evangelism of Indigenous peoples, but SIL's distinctive mission was the translation of Scripture into Indigenous languages as a means to this final end. Evangelism or church planting was to be pursued later by others.[101]

The WBT/SIL distinction evolved in the process of SIL's founding in Mexico. The institute's founder, Cameron Townsend, first worked in Guatemala, where he had completed translation of the New Testament into the Cakchiquel language by 1929. Not long after he met Moises Saenz, the Presbyterian under-secretary of education for Mexico, who invited him to pursue the same translation goals in Mexico. Saenz had long been committed to public education as a means of instilling a new sense of citizenship and common nationality to all Mexicans, particularly to the country's marginal and downtrodden Indigenous peoples. He had seen that his department's efforts to teach Spanish to Indians had met with little success: bilingual education seemed a more promising route. Townsend's descriptive linguistics and trained translators could be a great help in the pursuit of this goal. His scriptural aims no doubt added to his appeal to Saenz, though the latter had been forced to obscure his religious affiliation while active in politics.[102] Saenz's championing of the Indigenous cause led Cardenas in 1935 to establish INI, the Department of Indian Affairs. Cardenas's support for the same ideals also led him to meet and give his support to Townsend, who was content to present himself in Mexico as primarily concerned with the translation goals of developing written versions of the many Indigenous languages. Cardenas, the committed socialist, undoubtedly knew of Townsend's religious objectives, but they concluded a marriage of convenience on both sides that allowed each to pursue his separate goals while avoiding ideological differences and the constitutional prohibition on foreign missionaries. Thus, in 1936, SIL was born in Mexico, with government approval.[103]

Two of the earliest SIL teams to work systematically among Indigenous peoples did so among the Chol in Tumbala and the Tzeltal in Oxchuc. Both Tumbala and Oxchuc are "municipios," or county-like districts, located in the highlands of the southern state of Chiapas. By 1970 they had some of the very highest Evangelical concentrations in the country.[104] In Oxchuc's case there are a variety of first-hand accounts of the early years, from both anthropologists and missionaries, while for Tumbala there is only one source.[105] I have also had the opportunity to visit Oxchuc in order to talk to both missionaries and national pastors. The following therefore focuses on Oxchuc as a critical example of the role of missionaries in causing Evangelical growth. A fuller analysis of their impact in recent years is presented in chapter 7.

Marianna Slocum and her partner Ethel Wallis first attempted to enter the lowland Tzeltal community of Bachajon in 1941, but they were refused admittance by the local authorities because they were Protestants, despite letters of introduction from the Department of Indian Affairs. Not until 1944 did they obtain permission to settle in Yochib, Oxchuc, through the intervention of the prominent anthropologist Villa Rojas, who rented his residence there to them. Wallis soon left. Slocum was often on her own until joined in 1947 by a nurse, Florence Gerdel. During her five years in Yochib, Slocum learned the Oxchuc dialect and translated the Gospel of Mark, but she failed to make more than a very few converts because of the opposition of a prominent shaman and a schoolteacher in the area, who were eventually responsible for driving out her and her partner. However, her one successful convert, Martin Gourd, whose conversion was precipitated by the death of his wife and then his brother, travelled the surrounding area evangelizing and playing a victrola provided by Marianna. Through these efforts Juan Mucha, the first Evangelical in Coralito, heard of the new faith. An innovator, he was the first in his area to give up the old slash-and-burn form of agriculture for terracing. With relatives in tow he made two long trips on foot to Yochib to learn more of the Evangelical faith from Slocum. Not long after, he invited her to settle in Coralito, his home village. Faced with such strong opposition in Yochib, they readily accepted and arrived in Coralito for the first time in October 1949, to find that Juan Mucha had already drawn together seventy regular attenders for services in his home.[106] From this foundation the Evangelical movement in Oxchuc grew rapidly. According to Slocum, about 50 per cent of Oxchuceros were Evangelicals by the early 1950s.[107] Her estimate has been accepted by anthropologists,[108] but the census for the later date of 1960 puts Evangelicals at 34.7 per cent of the population.[109] In 1970 Evangelical numbers remained much the same, but they had fallen to 25.1 per cent of the population, apparently because of their greater willingness to migrate to the adjacent lowland municipio of Ocosingo, where land was more plentiful.[110] This remains a striking breakthrough, since Evangelicals were 4.2 per cent of the state of Chiapas's population, and only 1.8 per cent in all Mexico in 1970.

Three long-standing traits of the Tzeltal and Oxchucero world inclined them to look favourably on the new Evangelical tradition. The first and most obvious of these predisposing factors was their pervasive and deeply rooted religious orientation. Theirs was a world-view that took for granted the existence of supernatural forces. Evangelicals and other Oxchuceros were deeply divided in their views of the supernatural, but none doubted that it existed and that right relationship with it was the only solution to life's problems. Secondly, no Catholic priests had been resident in Oxchuc for many years prior to the arrival of the missionaries. Speaking no Tzeltal, priests passed through briefly but twice a year, baptizing children and blessing already consummated marriages. This neglect and institutional absence surely facilitated Evangelical advance, which was presented in the Tzeltal language by Oxchuceros.[111] Thirdly, witchcraft and shamanism were a major form of social control, whereby all who violated customary expectations were subject to the supernatural punishments of the shamans, who were deeply feared. This in itself did not cause conversion, since the old system had functioned for centuries. However, when additional forces, described below, threatened the traditional order, the practice of witchcraft seems to have grown, raising the general level of fear and anxiety to levels that may have inclined some to opt out by embracing the new faith.[112]

Apart from these predisposing elements, there were four precipitating factors that more directly caused the traditional order to change in ways that favoured Evangelical conversion. First, as Siverts stresses, land shortages, provoked by Mestizo invasion of Oxchucero lands after the revolution, created a growing state of economic hardship and social turmoil, which caused growing numbers to seek novel solutions to these ever more pressing problems.[113] There may be some general truth to this notion, but the Coralito base of Evangelical growth was in the highlands, where communal lands remained intact and Mestizos made no appreciable penetration.[114] Secondly and perhaps more pointedly, the marked population growth of these years, whereby Oxchuc's population grew by 239 per cent between 1940 and 1950, undoubtedly provoked some of the same dynamics stressed by Siverts.[115]

Thirdly, at precisely the time of the greatest Evangelical penetration (i.e., the early 1950s), the Department of Education (INI) initiated a "multi-faceted program" designed to bring Oxchuceros "into the mainstream of the national sociocultural system."[116] Roads were built, schools were established, new agricultural methods were taught, and modern medical centres and promoters were introduced.[117] Such developments were also behind the rise of a new political order based on municipal offices, existing everywhere else in Mexico, which were filled with younger bilingual men whose power lay in their ability to relate to the outside world. As this political transformation occurred, the old clan system of authority, which was intimately linked with the traditional religious system, become less influential and less capable of resisting Evangelical growth.[118] Evangelical success may also have been linked to the early sympathy and later conversion (1951) of an important tribal chief, Marcos Ensin, though there was sufficient opposition just prior to his conversion to cause the first Evangelical church to be burned to the ground.[119] When the old order is everywhere being questioned and new ideas introduced, the prospects for religious change are enhanced and the likelihood of sustained resistance diminished.

The fourth and most obvious cause of conversion was the arrival of the missionaries with their Evangelical faith. Yet Siverts rightly stresses that subsequent growth was linked to the fact that it was Oxchuceros, not Marianna Slocum, who did the evangelizing and preaching.[120] Recall, too, that when Slocum first arrived in Coralito there was already a body of seventy Evangelicals, recruited by Juan Mucha, who had himself encountered the new faith through another Oxchucero, Martin Gourd. The Presbyterian system of elders and deacons in the new Evangelical congregations also served as a familiar functional equivalent to the clan system from which they had detached themselves. Prior to 1964, when their first Oxchucero pastor was appointed, Evangelical leadership was firmly in the hands of the elders and deacons within Oxchuc, since their official pastor was a Mestizo from the city of Las Casas, who visited twice a year. By early 1957 Marianna had moved on to a new translation field. She was replaced by what came to be three missionary couples, who focused on leadership training and were never involved in pastoring or evangelism. Neither they nor Marianna ever funded pastors or church construction. Marianna was the original spark of the movement, but thereafter the missionaries played an advisory, supporting role. Their enduring presence, rarely achieved elsewhere, helped to nurture the new faith, but it did not cause it. Evangelical growth in Oxchuc was occasioned by the tensions engendered by rapid social change, by the continuing belief of Oxchuceros in the efficacy of religious solutions to life's problems, and by the freedom they enjoyed to mould a church consistent with their traditions and under their own control.

By 1970 the Evangelical presence in Mexico was a century or more old. Much had changed with nineteenth-century reform, twentieth-century revolution, a measure of urbanization and industrialization, improved communications, and the migration of so many Mexican workers to the United States to work. Mexico's links were greater than ever before with the great giant to the north, whence came the Evangelical tradition and with which it was still so firmly linked in public perception. Despite its former trials, the Catholic church and faith were still core elements of Mexican society and identity. Though social change and openness to new ideas were far more prevalent than ever before, the Evangelical community of approximately one million remained on the margins of Mexican society. Elements of the old legacy were still there: about five hundred missionaries were at work in the 1960s[121] and the mission boards of the historical denominations continued to dispense subsidies, though on a far smaller scale than before. Yet the now predominant and still growing Pentecostal majority had never been significantly reliant on foreign missionary support or direction. Everywhere, and as always, Evangelical successes and failures were primarily determined by internal, Mexican forces. On the edge of a society in flux, Evangelicals in 1970 faced a future with unprecedented opportunities for growth, but from a marginal status they had not been able to overcome in one hundred years of effort.

3 Gains and Losses: The Last Twenty Years

Whether one uses the disorganization or the deprivation approach to sectarian growth, Mexico in the 1970s and 1980s appeared to be an ideal breeding-ground for Evangelical advance. Discontent and uprootedness pervaded the lives of an ever greater swath of ordinary Mexicans. Inclinations to religious innovation were then fuelled by the continuing institutional difficulties of the Catholic Church in reaching out, personally and directly, to its ever expanding flock. After outlining this background to modern-day Mexico, I examine the extent of Evangelical growth over the last twenty years by looking at the census and the data I collected in the forty-three sample congregations. Careful attention will be paid to the extent of apostasy or drop-out rates, that other side of the ledger, which is so decisive in determining the long-term prospects of the Evangelical community. Even then, a full accounting of the causes of Evangelical growth must await the next chapter, where I explore the social background of converts and the various factors that help to explain their decision to embrace such a radically different faith.

SOCIAL AND POLITICAL CONTEXT

The "economic miracle" of the post–Second World War era was already beginning to unravel in the late 1960s. Economic growth began to slow, and the gap between rich and poor grew ever more marked. The great bulk of the population began to see its formerly rising standard of living stall and then fall. In the early 1970s Luis

Echeverria's government responded with increased government spending on medical and educational services for the poor. Subsidies for basic commodities like corn and beans were also greatly expanded. The cost was growing public-sector debt and rising inflation. In 1976 there was a major devaluation, an event that had not occurred since 1954. Under Jose Lopez Portillo, the incoming president, an austerity program sponsored by the International Monetary Fund (IMF) was introduced, which created rising unemployment and, in its first year, a 12 per cent fall in the purchasing power of the minimum wage, then earned by over half the population. However, recession was quickly replaced by rapid growth when massive reserves of oil were discovered in 1978. There followed a three-year honeymoon as government expenditures and the foreign debt soared, fuelled by the belief that such commitments would be easily covered by the vast patrimony to come from oil.

In 1982 "la crisis," as Mexicans have come to call it, hit with a vengeance, when world recession, falling oil prices, and rising interest rates created a situation where Mexico could not pay its $55 billion debt. The solution worked out at the time immediately eliminated the economic gains of the previous three years. The economy went into extended freefall, not experiencing any growth until 1989. Combined underemployment and unemployment rose to approximately half the labour force by 1986. The real value of the minimum wage fell by over 50 per cent, and some 40 per cent of the population were estimated to be suffering from malnutrition. To make matters worse, in 1985 Mexico City was hit with a devastating earthquake, and world oil prices again plunged, creating a further downward spiral of unemployment, inflation, diminishing living standards, and economic uncertainty.[1] A 1989 OECD study estimated that 28 per cent of households nationally were below the poverty line, which was calculated at twice the minimum salary set by the government.[2] A year later the census estimated that 63 per cent of working Mexicans had earnings at or below the poverty-line figure of double the minimum wage.[3]

These deteriorating economic conditions were compounded by Mexico's rapidly growing population. Between 1970 and 1990 the census recorded a 68 per cent growth in total population. Many experts, including the World Bank, would raise the census figure of 81 million in 1990 to 85 million.[4] Fertility rates and total population growth were even higher in the preceding period of 1950 to 1970, when the population grew by over 3 per cent per year. In the face of this cumulative pressure, the government committed itself in 1975 to family planning. By 1987 some 53 per cent of women were

estimated to be using contraceptives.[5] Fertility rates declined in the
1980s, but a 1991 estimate still put the annual growth of the population at 2.1 per cent, which, if continued, would lead to the dou-
bling of Mexico's population in thirty-three years.[6] With some
800,000 entering the labour-force each year throughout the 1980s,[7]
there was intense competition for those jobs and economic resources that were available. Such a rapid rate of growth, at a time
of fierce cutbacks in government expenditure, also put massive
pressure on health, education, transportation, and other social services just to maintain the inadequate standards of the past, let
alone improve them.

Uncertainty, scarcity, and disorganization were also impelled by
urbanization and the uprooting of millions of peasants from their
traditional villages. Again this process began well before the 1970s,
but the crucial threshold was passed in the last twenty years, when
the percentage of the population living in urban areas grew from 42
per cent in 1970 to 60 per cent in 1990.[8] The most dramatic example
of this trend is the phenomenal growth of Mexico City, whose population was estimated to be as much as 20 million in the early 1990s.
Monterrey and Guadalajara have also grown enormously, as have
the northern border cities, with their assembly-plant factories. In all
regions of the country, on the peripheries of the cities there has been
a mushrooming of poor neighbourhoods, filled with rural migrants.
In the city where I write, for instance, which lacks any manufactur-
ing base whatsoever, the total urban population has grown from
50,000 to about half a million since the 1960s, though many of the
latter are now dispersed through an outer ring of impoverished
neighbourhoods, with roots in the countryside as much as the city.
Fleeing from a traditional world that could no longer accommodate
them and cut off from many of the pressures and support networks
of family and community, the recent urban migrant, says disorganization theory, is far more open to embracing a new faith.

Given the above, it is scarcely surprising that the post-revolutionary political order saw its support and legitimacy questioned to
an unprecedented degree. This authoritarian system, centred on the
PRI, the revolutionary institutional party, harnessed for many years
the divergent interests of business, labour, peasants, and military.
Never completely without opposition, the PRI dominated all "elections" after the 1930s, supported by the great majority of voters,
though great numbers did not bother to vote.[9] The symbolic end of
this era is usually linked to the 1968 student massacre at Tlatelolco,
when security forces killed over two hundred demonstrators who
were protesting government repression of the student opposition to

the government's huge spending on the Olympics in Mexico City. Thereafter, political discontent grew, including a few short-lived guerrilla movements in the 1970s. However, electoral opposition remained slight because the opposition was divided, because the PRI retained its uncanny ability to co-opt its youthful leftist opposition, and because of its continuing stranglehold on the election process.[10] Electoral opposition grew, but abstention remained the predominant form of political protest. In the presidential elections of 1988 a moderate left coalition was led by Cuauhtemoc Cardenas, the once PRI governor of Michoacan. His father, Lazaro Cardenas, is the most revered of the revolution's presidents, for distributing much land to the peasantry and for nationalizing the oil industry. Anchored by this famous name, the Cardenas Front created the first ever real possibility of actually defeating the PRI on election day. In the event, the official results of the vote for president gave the PRI and its candidate, Salinas de Gortari, the barest of majorities, at 50.4 per cent of the votes cast. Since abstentions ran at around 50 per cent and many failed to get registered on the official electoral roll, it has been estimated that only 22 per cent of the potential electorate voted for Salinas.[11] Many believe that PRI's slim margin of victory was only achieved by electoral fraud. This complex political struggle is far from the central concerns of this book. Its importance here stems from its revelation of the deeply felt discontent of so many Mexicans with the existing social and political order. It is in this context of rapid social change and a deeply rooted lack of confidence in the political system that Evangelical growth must be understood.

THE CATHOLIC OPPOSITION

For a variety of reasons the Catholic church seemed unable to take advantage of the situation. In 1968, at Medellin, the Latin American episcopacy (CELAM) had embraced liberation theology and its "preferred option for the poor." Just prior to Medellin the Mexican bishops had issued a pastoral letter that condemned the injustices of the country's development strategies and broke the unofficial pact of non-aggression between church and state that had been forged after 1940.[12] Here and there around the country, most notably in the 1970s, radical priests and small movements embraced political action in the name of the oppressed, but they were typically short lived, culminating in episcopal oppression or their own internal dissolution.[13] Only in a diocese with a bishop sympathetic to liberation theology could the movement hope to prosper, but no more than five of the fifty-plus dioceses were headed by men so inclined.

In the face of papal opposition and the retirement of the "red Bishop" of Cuernavaca, Mendez Arceo, in 1982, liberationist influences went into further decline.[14] In 1993 the two major dioceses with a liberation theology thrust were San Cristobal in Chiapas and Tehuantepec in Oaxaca. Both areas in the 1980s had Evangelical populations significantly above the national average. It would be difficult to prove that liberation theology was the cause, but neither could it be described as a major obstacle to Evangelical advance.

After 1968, and particularly after 1981, the bishops adopted an increasingly independent critical stance towards the PRI and its policies. Their criticisms tended to be directed at electoral abuse and at the constitutional clauses described in the previous chapter,[15] which gave the state wide powers to restrict church affairs, though they were not enforced. The former body of objections was closely linked to the major party of opposition in the 1970s and early 1980s, the PAN. Since its foundation in 1938, the PAN had championed conservative Catholic causes. It was later embraced by large business interests, disaffected from Echeverria's populism.[16] Apart from a few northern bishops who openly supported the PAN, the great majority expressed no party preference, but the tenor of their criticisms has been rightly characterized as "not far from that held by the democratic right."[17] The Mexican left, by contrast, was marked by a deeply rooted anti-clericalism, shaped by the church's role in the revolution and by Marxist ideology, which precluded the possibility of a major alliance between Cardenas and the Catholic church.[18] Despite liberation theology, historically rooted animosities and current interests prevented or dissuaded all but a few fragments of the Mexican Catholic church from being the voice of the disinherited.

We saw earlier that the Catholic church had so revived itself after 1940 that it was reckoned to be one of the strongest, in an organizational or institutional sense, in Latin America. By any other standard it suffered from an endemic problem of clerical shortages, which seems to have grown more acute as the years have passed. Put simply, the church has not been able to grow as quickly as the Mexican population. Despite an increase in the total number of priests from 8,761 in 1970 to 9,602 in 1982, the number of laity per priest deteriorated substantially from 5,504 in 1970 to 7,286 in 1982. These ratios varied considerably from one part of the country to another in predictable ways. Thus one finds relatively low ratios in the heartland dioceses of, for instance, Morelia (4,100), Tacambaro (4,200), and Zamora (5,100), while the newer dioceses in the north ranged from 9,900 in Matamoros to 16,100 in Ciudad Juarez, one of the most rapidly growing border towns. Similarly high ratios also prevailed in the southern diocese of Tabasco (16,600), San Cristobal de las Casas (14,500), and Oaxaca (12,600). These differences, of course, correspond closely to the distribution of Evangelicals, charted in the last chapter and to be further described shortly. Where the Catholic church was institutionally weakest, the Evangelical presence was greatest. Given that a significant proportion of clergy were primarily involved in administration, teaching, or some other specialized ministry, the ratio of laity to pastoral clergy was undoubtedly higher in every diocese.[19]

There is every reason to believe that these high ratios and the challenges they provoke have grown more acute since 1982.[20] In the archdiocese of Mexico City, for instance, which covers the massive urban sprawl that envelops the capital, the ratio of laity to priests in 1993 was reported to be 17,112. Slightly less than half (46 per cent) the clergy were sixty years of age or older. Since the ordination rate was less than the death rate, the number of priests was expected to decline further.[21] Some sense of the difficulties the Catholic church encounters may be gleaned from the interviews I did with priests in each of my major research sites. In the northern border city of some 700,000, there were 17 parishes and but 25 priests, giving each a responsibility of some 28,000 laity. On a smaller scale, in one of the particular neighbourhoods where I worked, there were 6 Evangelical churches in the 5 neighbourhoods ("colonias") immediately surrounding the recently built Catholic church, run by 1 priest. He was also responsible for an additional 6 neighbourhoods on the same side of the city, as well as 17 rural settlements or ejidos further out. In the one of these ejidos, where I also worked, there were 3 Evangelical congregations and 2 full-time pastors; the priest's presence was confined to one service a week. Similarly, in the south, in the Chontalpa region of Tabasco, the town of some 50,000 where I resided was attended to by 7 members of a religious order, who were responsible for the mother church, 5 other chapels in town, and a further 102 chapels in the surrounding countryside. In the town alone there were 13 Evangelical congregations and 10 pastors. The numbers would surely have increased had I been able to survey the hinterland area containing the 102 rural chapels, which were typically visited by a priest once a month. Tabasco was, as we saw in the previous chapter, an old and exceptional example of Protestant concentration and Catholic neglect, but a comparable pattern also prevailed in the old southern city of Oaxaca. Here, its 29 parishes and approximately 40 priests in pastoral work were responsible for some 500,000 souls, who were being evangelized by about 70 pastors and 80 Evangelical congregations. Outside, in rural areas, and particularly in remote mountain areas, priests, I was assured, were much more thinly spread.

Only in the central region and in the city of Morelia did the Catholic church (with 50 churches, another 30 under construction, and about 100 priests) outnumber Evangelical pastors and congregations. In the older of the two neighbourhoods sampled for Mexico City, the 7 priests and 4 churches were only slightly outnumbered by 10 Evangelical churches and pastors, but in the far newer neighbourhood, in the mushrooming Neza area, the 3 priests in 2 churches faced 10 Evangelical congregations and pastors. Similarly, in one of the rural parishes I visited outside of Morelia, the lone priest was responsible for about 10,000 laity in a central village and seven adjacent hamlets, which together contained 3 Evangelical congregations, 1 resident pastor, and 2 others who visited. Here as everywhere else, Catholic priests were responsible for far more people, which greatly reduced their capacity for pastoral attention.

In the early 1970s over 90 per cent of Catholics were baptized, 80 per cent confirmed, and 72 per cent were married in a church.[22] When to this list are added burials as well as regular and special masses, a very large portion of the priests' time, they said, was taken up with ritual or liturgical responsibilities. The size of their parishes also meant that they could rarely know well more than a fraction of their more active parishioners, whose spiritual and other needs could easily consume all a priest's time. They had, in short, little time to reach out to the marginal or uninvolved. In all this the priest's situation was radically different from that of Evangelical pastors, whose congregations, we shall see, rarely exceeded two hundred.

Since 1970 two new movements deserving of brief mention have emerged within the Catholic church in Mexico. Both have the potential to affect the Catholic response to the Evangelical presence. The first is the world-wide growth of the Charismatic movement, which emphasizes the emotional, the ecstatic, and the miraculous aspects of Christianity and has the potential to serve as an alternative to Pentecostalism. Assessing the one research report done on this topic, Garma notes that it had its greatest appeal among the more privileged and was clerically controlled. The examples cited were all in urban areas.[23] My own findings confirm these observations. None of the six Catholic churches in the two Mexico City neighbourhoods where I worked had an organized Charismatic presence. Both were predominantly poor and/or working class, where Pentecostals abounded. In Mexican terminology, they were both "colonias populares." In every rural region of the country where I inquired, there was also no Charismatic presence. Charismatic activities in the northern city of Matamoros were centred in one of its seventeen parishes, while Oaxaca City has only recently seen a Charismatic presence, again in one city-centre parish, because of former episcopal opposition. Only in Morelia were Charismatic groups, of predominantly middle-class background, found in several parishes. The clergy kept a close eye on them, fearing their potential to become a parallel movement outside the church, while recognizing their appeal. Such sketchy evidence suggests that the Charismatic movement is not yet large in Mexico. It also addresses a very different constituency from that typically drawn to the Evangelical world.

Far more pervasive were the efforts to organize large parishes into small groups of lay people who would meet regularly without clerical guidance or supervision. This radically new conception of "Christian base communities" came out of liberation theology's dual conviction that the Catholic church should by lay led and committed to social action on Christian principles. When it was applied in Mexico, the radical theology tended to be downplayed or ignored, but the organizational form was embraced. Variously called "apostolic groups," "cells," "prayer groups," or "communities," they typically met in homes, small chapels, or the mother church itself. Bible study and worship were the most common activities, with the hope that this liturgical role would lead to evangelism. Most also professed some social-work or charitable goal, such as the guiding of the needy to a free doctor or to a parish dispensary, but this was the least developed emphasis in the parishes where I made my inquiries. None were involved in community-development projects or the like. It is likely that a more political thrust prevailed in the few dioceses where the bishop supported liberation theology.

In Tabasco the system of lay-led "communities" was implemented in the late 1970s to increase lay involvement and to reach out to the unchurched, particularly in the rural hamlets, where the presence of a priest was so infrequent. Priests were usually reluctant to specify numbers and proportions, but they all admitted that such schemes were least effectively developed in the countryside and encompassed only a minority of parishioners in urban areas. In Oaxaca and Morelia, ambitious schemes along these lines were being planned, but they were still very much at the planning stage. In Morelia's case, they were a direct response to the recent papal call to evangelize all of Latin America, which was driven not by liberation theology but by the need to counteract Evangelical growth. During the Pope's 1990 tour of Mexico, which included, by no coincidence, a visit to Tabasco, he called for a "a more solid training in the truths of our Catholic faith so as to form a front against the solicitations of the sects." "No Catholic in Mexico," he said, "can consider himself exempt from the obligations to bring defectors back to the church. I would like to meet with you one by one to tell you: come back to the fold of the church, your mother."[24] A few months later, the Tenth National Missionary Congress of the Catholic church in Mexico proclaimed, according to the president of the Mexican Episcopal Commission, that its chief aim was to "to contain the advance of the religious sects."[25] Only in Tabasco, and really only in one village, did I hear Evangelicals complain that their efforts to evangelize were now being countered by Catholic prayer groups, who followed up Evangelical visits with their own. More pervasive, however, were concerns that Catholics, to quote one pastor, were starting "to use our forms of evangelism. They read the Bible. They sing hymns. They say it is the same, but of course it is not." Whether the broad plans of apostolic or prayer groups will ever be converted into systematic action in Mexico is open to debate. They may brake future Evangelical advance, but their impact to date must be regarded as minor, since they have been so rarely and so incompletely implemented.

PATTERNS OF GROWTH

In assessing the demographics of Evangelical growth and the distribution of Evangelicals throughout the country, I am obliged to rely on a variety of sources of information. None is completely satisfactory. No fully complete or accurate census of Evangelicals has been conducted by myself or anyone else. Much can be gleaned from the forty-three congregations in which I worked, but questions about representativeness always exist with the non-random sampling technique I was forced to employ – in spite of my efforts to be representative. Denominational records are occasionally revealing, but they are often frustratingly incomplete and of questionable reliability, since Pentecostals attach little importance to accurate record-keeping. With more than eighty large Evangelical denominations, many more small regional groupings, and innumerable independent churches, it is simply impossible to identify all Evangelical churches and their combined membership.

This leaves us with the Mexican national census, from which were drawn the data enumerated in the tables of chapter 2. According to the 1990 census, there were then about 3,969,858 Evangelicals, who were then 4.9 per cent of all Mexicans.[26] The real figure is probably higher, since the census is generally recognized to underestimate the total population.[27] Every Mexican Evangelical leader with whom I spoke, from the head of the Bible Society to the leaders of varied denominations, large and small, insisted that their community was at least twice as large. In 1993 the most commonly cited figure, put out by the Foro Nacional de Iglesias Cristianas Evangelicas, put Evangelicals at 16 million, or 17.5 per cent of the total population.[28] It may be recalled from the previous chapter that some serious estimates of the Evangelical population in 1960 put it at roughly double the 578,515 recorded by the census. Yet this conviction that Evangelicals had already reached the one million plateau by the early 1960s was again refuted by the 1970 census figure of 876,879 Evangelicals, even though the director of the census in that year was an active Evangelical who had the census category changed from "Protestante" to the more familiar "Evangelica."[29] In 1990 some indirect support for the claim that Evangelicals were underestimated might be derived from the census finding in Table 2.1 that an additional 4.7 per cent of the population claimed an "other" or "no" religion, creating an avowedly non-Catholic population of 9.6 per cent.[30] Over two-thirds of this non-Evangelical, non-Catholic group claimed to have no religion. Speculation over how many Evangelicals might be hidden in the "other" and "none" categories is inevitably inconclusive and quickly proves futile. My own suspicion is that some – if by no means all – of these "others" and "nones" may have been Evangelicals, since the regional distribution of all non-Catholics was similar and differed markedly from the Catholic pattern. The safer conclusion is that no accurate figure exists for the total Evangelical community in 1990, or in any other year.

A brief digression is in order here on Mormons and Jehovah's Witnesses. They are not, as I pointed out in chapter 1, regarded by Evangelicals as part of the Evangelical world. Both reciprocate in regarding Evangelicals as in need of true conversion, but they and Evangelicals are linked together in public perception. For different reasons they are also sects in the technical sense of the word. The aggressive street evangelism of both often encourages the belief that they make up a larger proportion of non-Catholics than sober scrutiny warrants, though there is a dearth of information on both faiths in Mexico today.

According to official Witness figures, the number of Mexican publishers or active members grew from 30,261 in 1966 to 262,371 in 1989.[31] Using a multiplier of two to assess the total community, as others have done,[32] Witnesses numbered approximately half a million at the time of the 1990 census. Evangelicals were therefore roughly eight times more numerous. The controversy Witnesses generated was greater than either their size or even their visible street evangelism would seem to warrant. It was caused by their reluctance to salute the national flag and to stand for the national anthem. For Witnesses, such activities imply worship, which they are prepared to offer only to God.[33] The resulting charges of lack of patriotism or nationalism were then fuelled by the refusal of the Witnesses to involve themselves in politics and public life. Especially in rural communities, where voluntary public service has always been expected, Witnesses have provoked much passion and some persecution.[34] One of the major Witness leaders in Oaxaca told me that Witnesses were free to serve on school or other local committees "if they are nominated by others," but he also admitted that "it would be better not to," if this could be managed. Evangelicals, we shall see, do not share the same views, but it is often assumed that they do, much to their chagrin and despite their protestations to the contrary.

The Mormon presence in Mexico goes back to the last century, when American Mormons created colonies in Sonora and Chihuahua, fleeing what they felt was religious persecution for their acceptance of polygamy. There they lived in ethnically closed colonies until the revolution drove them back to the United States. Some later returned, but large-scale evangelism beyond their initial base in Chihuahua did not occur until the 1950s.[35] Thereafter, their numbers grew, as young American Mormons, on a two-year missionary program required of all members, fanned out over the rest of the country. Burly blond Mormon missionaries on bicycles, in ties, white shirts, and dark trousers, were and are to be seen in every part of Mexico. Their standard brick-built churches with railings, basketball courts, and paved parking lots reflect the intensely American style of Mormonism, though about two-thirds of the young Mormon evangelists, I was told, were Mexicans by the 1980s. Officially they claimed a baptized membership of some 617,000 in 1990,[36] but this figure must be treated with much caution. After six instructional visits in the home from missionaries with varying degrees of competency in Spanish, a convert can be baptized without ever entering a Mormon church or congregation, though most, I was told, do so once or twice before making their decision. Such a recruitment procedure does little to filter out the temporarily curious or simply the bored, who find a certain entertainment value in home visits from exotic young "gringos." In each of the four regions of the country the Mormon officials I met admitted, when pressed, that only about 30 per cent of their claimed members were still active, by which they meant at least monthly church attendance. The percentage of weekly attenders, they acknowledged, was even lower. Thus the real size of the active Mormon community is probably no more than a quarter of the official statistics cited above. Together with Jehovah's Witnesses, their combined numbers are probably less and certainly no more than the "other religions" enumerated in the 1990 census.

Tables 2.3 and 2.4 show that Evangelicals in 1990 were much more heavily concentrated in some parts of the country than in others. The Evangelical percentage of the population was lowest in Mexico City and in the centre, where Mexican culture and the Catholic church were most firmly rooted. This becomes particularly evident when one looks at the Catholic and colonial heartland of Mexico. Here in the large states of Guanajuato, Jalisco, and Michoacan, Evangelicals were still less than 2 per cent of the population in 1990, though they were 4.3 per cent of Puebla, and they had broken through to 7.5 per cent of the even larger coastal state of Veracruz on the Gulf of Mexico. Evangelical expansion in the rapidly growing metropolitan area of Mexico City more than tripled from 137,475 in 1970 to around half a million (483,783) by 1990, but its Evangelical proportion (3.2 per cent) was still lower than for the country as a whole (4.9 per cent). Table 3.1 further shows that the annual growth rate of Evangelicals here was less than in any other region of the country. Whether one speaks of the last twenty or fifty years, the proportion of all Evangelicals living in the capital has also declined. Though the differences are not so large, it is clear that the secular mega-city has not been especially open to Evangelical advance. Both here in the capita and in the central region as a whole Evangelicals continued to be underrepresented in 1990. Together these two regions encompassed half of all Evangelicals, which is no small amount, but it is still much less than the 73 per cent of Catholics resident at the same time.

In the northern states immediately adjacent to the United States, Evangelicals grew from 2.4 per cent to 5.7 per cent of the region's population over this most recent twenty-year period. Evangelicals were still more concentrated here than in the remainder of the country, but their annual rate of growth, a healthy 15 per cent, (see Table 3.1), was still below the national average. Thus the trend continued, going back to the beginning of the century, whereby the north was less and less the major Evangelical centre, containing 20 per cent of all Evangelicals in 1990.

Table 3.1
Average per annum growth* of Evangelicals and Catholics in regions, 1970–90,
national census

	North	Capital	Centre	South	Nation
Evangelical	15.0%	12.6%	17.2%	24.0%	17.6%
Catholic	2.8%	3.2%	2.8%	2.7%	2.9%
Ratio Evang./Cath.	5.4	3.9	6.1	8.9	6.1

* Per annum growth = total growth percentage over the twenty years divided by twenty.

By as early as 1970, and even more markedly by 1990, Evangelical concentrations were greatest in the southern states of Campeche, Chiapas, Oaxaca, Quintana Roo, Tabasco, and the Yucatan. Together Evangelicals accounted for 12 per cent of the population, while the Catholic share had fallen from 93 to 77 per cent in this twenty-year span. From 211,693 in 1970, Evangelicals expanded to 1,227,579 in 1990, which translates into a huge 24 per cent rate of annual growth. The initial breakthrough, it may be recalled, occurred in Tabasco between the 1930s and 1950s. Thereafter the greatest growth occurred in the more populous state of Chiapas, where Evangelicals grew from 4.8 per cent of the population in 1970 to 16.3 per cent in 1990, with Tabasco right behind at 15.0 per cent.

The simplest and most plausible explanation for Evangelical advance in the south is to be found in this region's long-standing isolation, politically, economically, and culturally, from the colonial heartland. Tabasco, we saw, was a liberal and then revolutionary bastion of opposition to central domination. It was also neglected by the Catholic church, which still today has proportionately far fewer priests here and throughout the south than it does in the centre or the nation as a whole. The Yucatan had its wars of independence in the last century, while the oppressive heat and absence of any noteworthy economic resource gave central Mexico little cause to involve itself in Tabasco, Campeche, and Quintana Roo until recently. Oaxaca, the home state of Juarez and Diaz, was a much more integral part of Mexico in the last century, but it has become one of the poorest and most politically marginal states in the country in this century.[37] Chiapas, which contained 43 per cent of all Evangelicals in the south in 1990, was part of Guatemala until the last century. It is therefore hardly surprising that a distribution of Evangelicals at 16 per cent and non-Catholics at 32 per cent of the total Chiapas population should be similar to the situation prevailing in Guatemala. But Guatemala's influence does not extend much beyond Chiapas or even throughout it; it cannot account for Evangelical growth beyond.

Evangelical success in the south is also linked to the presence of many Indigenous peoples in the region. The Yucatan, Oaxaca, Quintana Roo, and Chiapas were and are distinguished by their large Indigenous communities of 44, 39, 32, and 26 per cent respectively.[38] With their syncretic faith and long tradition of resistance to Mestizo hegemony, they have sometimes embraced the new Evangelical faith in large numbers. The most striking example is in the highland municipio of Oxchuc in Chiapas, which was analysed in the previous chapter. By 1990 the 36 per cent share by Evangelicals of Oxchuc's population was not significantly higher than their 35 per cent level in 1960, though their total numbers had almost tripled. Tumbala, in 1990, had the highest proportion of Evangelicals (45 per cent) in the state, and it too was overwhelmingly Indigenous. Despite these striking examples, it would be erroneous to suppose that Evangelical growth in the south was largely confined to Indigenous peoples. Tabasco is the clearest counter-example, with its tiny Indigenous presence of less than 1 per cent and its Evangelical community of 15 per cent. Further confirmation of this general rule is also to be found in Chiapas. In the 33 municipios where Indigenous people in 1990 were still a majority of the population (26 per cent of Chiapas was Indigenous), 22 per cent were Evangelicals. In the remaining 79 municipios of Chiapas, they were 14 per cent, which is not much lower than their total provincial share of 16 per cent. Thus the Evangelical presence was greater in Indigenous areas, but only 34 per cent lived in these Indigenous municipios in 1990. The majority of Chiapas's Evangelicals lived in Mestizo areas.[39]

Table 2.2 shows that, over the last twenty years, the rate of growth in the Evangelical population has been greater than at any other time in this century. Table 3.1 further shows that very rapid rates of growth existed in all regions of the country. A small part of the growth may be attributed to the general expansion of the Mexican population, but with an annual growth rate of 18 per cent versus 3 per cent, Evangelicals vastly outstripped Catholics. Since there is no reason to believe that Evangelicals have significantly different birth, death, or migration rates, the cause is clearly Evangelical conversion. To express this growth in slightly different terms, as is done in the last column of Table 3.1, Evangelicals were growing a little over six times faster than Catholics between 1970 and 1990. Not surprisingly, growth was highest in the south, both in absolute terms and in comparison with the local Catholic population. Even the historic heartland of Mexico was showing an unprecedented openness, so that Evangelicals were now growing slightly faster in numbers than in either Mexico City or the north, which had formerly been most receptive to Evangelical advance.

These figures by no means augur the imminent demise of Catholicism as the religion of the majority. High growth rates in small populations are always much easier to attain than in large ones, since small absolute increases in the former translate into large percentage increases, whereas the reverse is true of large populations. Evangelicals are still somewhere around 5 per cent of the national population. Breakthrough to the status of a sizeable minority remains a remote probability. If the census is to be believed, Evangelical growth slowed from an annual rate of growth of 15.1 per cent a year for the 1970s to 8.1 per cent for the 1980s. Since birth rates generally fell with the government's new pro-contraceptive policy, Evangelicals were growing about 4.5 times faster than Catholics in both decades. In other words, the relative difference between Catholic and Evangelical growth rates persisted, but the absolute level of Evangelical growth halved in the 1980s – though it was still a very respectable 8.1 per cent a year.

The most dramatic evidence of a huge growth potential in the Evangelical movement is to be found in the forty-three congregations where I worked. In each congregation I endeavoured to obtain as accurate a figure as possible of the number of baptized members and the number who had been baptized in the preceding year. Adult baptism is the ideal throughout the Evangelical world, since a child is not considered capable of making the personal decision to change and reform that is expected of any baptismal candidate. In practice baptisms occurred as early as twelve or thirteen years of age. Since a few pastors did not keep lists and some resisted my efforts to have them create a precise list or review an old one, the results must be regarded as rough and ready, though pastors usually knew their members intimately, since congregations rarely exceeded one hundred baptized members. I pressed and revised downward whenever it seemed warranted. In all, there were 441 newly baptized members over the previous year in the 40 congregations where I could obtain complete information. At the beginning of the same year, the combined membership in those congregations was 3,118. This yields a huge 14.1 per cent annual rate of potential increase, as can be seen in Table 3.2. It is this lived experience that makes Evangelical leaders so convinced that something must be wrong with the census. Over a ten-year period, to make a clearer comparison with the census, the compound growth rate was 274 per cent. This is a rate more than three times greater than the 80 per cent increase of Evangelicals recorded by the census for the 1980s.

Table 3.2 shows that substantial growth occurred in every denomination and in every region. A few distinctions are worth noting.

Table 3.2
Annual congregational growth potential,* congregational data

	Advt %	Hist. %	Pent. %	Total
Centre	n/a	13.7	19.8	18.9% (999)
Mexico	n/a	6.1	13.5	11.8% (432)
North	9.4	11.7	11.0	11.1% (587)
South	9.4	10.2	15.2	12.4% (1,100)
Nation	9.4%(149)	10.6%(961)	16.2%(2,008)	14.1% (3,118)

*Growth potential is calculated by dividing the total baptized population at the beginning of the
year by all newly baptized members. The bracketed numbers refer to all baptized members at
the beginning of the year in the pertinent cell.

Pentecostal predominance continued to assert itself in the 1980s,
with Pentecostals having an annual baptismal rate 53 per cent
higher than in the historical congregations. Within those congregations, Presbyterians, who thirty years ago were reckoned to be the
largest Evangelical denomination, now had significantly lower
growth (8.1 per cent) per annum than the Baptists (11.4 per cent),
who now were similar to the Pentecostals. Only in the south were
Presbyterians continuing to baptize at a rate similar to that in the
rest of the Evangelical world. Mexican denominations rarely gather
data that might allow for such calculations, but I did encounter one
exception to this general rule, which provides some independent
confirmation of my own data. According to the National Baptist
Convention of Mexico, which is by far the largest Baptist body in
the country, it baptized 74,192 individuals between 1981 and 1991.
As the total baptized community numbered 45,687 in 1981, the new
baptisms represent a potential increase of 162 per cent over the
decade. On an annual basis the Convention's statistics suggest that
Baptists were growing at just over 10 per cent yearly, which is very
close to my own estimate.[40]

APOSTASY

This highly impressive growth potential needs to be qualified by a
more pragmatic evaluation of the actual rate of increase at the end
of the year, after departures as well as new additions are considered. Table 3.3 attempts to do this. Besides growth through baptism,
pastors were asked to recall the numbers of already baptized members who moved into the congregation over the last year. They were
also asked how many baptized members left the congregation, for

Table 3.3
Annual net growth* of congregations by region and denomination,
congregational data

	Advt %	Hist. %	Pent. %	Total
Centre		8.2	15.4	14.4% (999)
Mexico		-3.1	6.3	4.2% (432)
North	7.8	3.6	4.6	4.6% (587)
South	7.1	6.0	5.1	5.6% (1,100)
Nation	7.4%	4.9%	9.6%	8.0% (3,118)

*Net growth is calculated by dividing the total number of baptized members at the beginning
of the year by the net increase in membership over the year, after departures as well as new
arrivals are taken into account. The bracketed numbers refer to all baptized members at the
beginning of the year in the pertinent cell.

whatever reasons, over the previous year. Not surprisingly, pastors
found it more difficult to recall losses than gains. It may be safely
assumed that pastors underestimated their losses, which they put
at 310, as against 441 newly baptized members and a further 119
formerly baptized individuals who moved into their congregations.
In sum, in the 40 of 43 congregations where such information was
available, the Evangelical annual growth rate was reduced to 8.0
per cent per annum. This is not a slow rate of growth by any
means, but it is little more than half the overall growth potential
recorded in Table 3.2. In the Baptist Convention's case their net
growth in membership at the end of the 1980s was only 49.9 per
cent, despite a 162.3 per cent increase in baptisms over the same period. This means that they were able to retain fewer than a third (31
per cent) of all the new members they baptized in the 1980s. If its
data is extended over the decade of the 1980s, Table 3.3 suggests
that Evangelicals grew by 117 per cent, which is far closer to the
census figure of 80 per cent, though there is still quite a gap. Part of
the disparity is due to my failure to ask pastors about the number
of deaths in their congregations over that same year. As a rough
correction for this deficiency, I have applied the crude death rate
for all Mexico to Evangelicals.[41] This produces a corrected net rate
of annual growth for Evangelicals of 7.4 per cent, which brings total
growth over the decade down to 104 per cent. Since pastors probably underestimated their losses, net Evangelical growth in the
1980s may not have been much higher than the census estimate of
80 per cent.

Average growth rates invariably mask considerable internal variation. The higher growth potential of Pentecostals vis-à-vis the historical denominations is transformed into an even greater difference

in Table 3.3's measurement of annual growth. Here, Pentecostals were growing at almost double the rate of the historical denominations in the 1980s, with the Adventists falling in between. When a relatively small sample like this is further broken down, it begins to produce anomalous results, as the effects of individual congregations come to dominate. The most striking example is the large 650-member neo-Pentecostal church in the central region, which experienced a net increase of one hundred in 1991 alone. At the same time these individual cases also reveal some of the diverse reasons why the marked growth potential of Evangelicals has sometimes been curbed.

In the north, Evangelical churches of all denominations did not grow as much as their potential might suggest precisely because they were located along the border. In the face of the economic crisis of the 1980s, legal and illegal migration to the United States soared to unprecedented heights. Northerners, it would seem, had more contacts "on the other side." They had the advantage of being able to commute back and forth far more easily, thereby maintaining longer terms of employment in the u.s. When the u.s. offered amnesty to illegals, as it did on a number of occasions, border residents were especially well placed to take advantage of the offer. Thus one Baptist church on the border found that its congregation of about thirty-five baptized members had not grown significantly over the previous ten years, despite seven or eight new baptisms a year. Two Pentecostal churches separately claimed that they had twice experienced losses of about a third of their members after amnesties; the remainder had all seen a steady trickle of members over the border. In Mexico City, by contrast, where two of my five sample congregations actually declined in size and another grew minimally, the pastors attributed their low rates of growth to the lack of housing in the immediate area, which obliged many of their young, newly married couples to move to cheaper, more distant neighbourhoods. How many would become members of new congregations was impossible to say. Similar problems plagued the rural areas in the centre and the south. In the latter region one small Pentecostal congregation had seen its membership balloon from fewer than fifty to over one hundred in a revival stimulated by some miraculous healings. But by the time I arrived the pastor was anxious, defensive, and confused, as his church now seemed to be in decline. By his own admission, ten recently baptized members had left; the commitment of others was clearly wavering, and a small group had broken away to form a separate group. Far from some sort of inexorable, monolithic movement of expansion, behind

Table 3.4
Current religious commitment of Evangelical childhood attenders, second-generation sample now twenty years of age or more

Same/Active	Same/Marginal	Other/Active	Sect	Nothing	RC	All
42%	9%	6%	0.4%	41%	2%	100% (1,132)

Nothing = all who attend any denomination less than once a month. Active = attend at least once a week in some denomination. Marginal = attend 1–3 times a month. RC = attend mass at least once a month. Same = attend same church as in childhood. Other = attend an Evangelical church other than that of childhood.

the overall figures of impressive growth was much fluidity, uncertainty, and fragility. Had Evangelicals been able to keep their many converts within the fold, their real rate of growth might have been three times greater than the census rate.

Had Evangelicals been able to retain the allegiance of a greater number of their children when they matured into adulthood, their growth rates would have been even higher. To test the degree of religious commitment of the second generation, I asked all in my major interview schedule to provide information on the current religious affiliation of any brothers, sisters, or adult children who had attended an Evangelical church regularly before the age of eleven and who were at least twenty years of age when the data were gathered. Table 3.4 provides the summary finding on the 1,132 individuals who fit this category. In all, 43 per cent of the second generation were no longer part of the Evangelical world, although hardly any had either embraced Catholicism (2 per cent) or taken up another faith (0.4 per cent). The great majority (41 per cent) were, in the expression used so frequently by Evangelicals themselves, simply "nothing" (nada), neither Catholic nor Evangelical. The empirical measure of those labelled "nothing" is less than monthly church attendance, though the vast majority in this category never or hardly ever attended. Another 9 per cent might be described as marginal, in that they attended one to three times a month. From the vantage point of North America or Europe, these may seem like excessively stringent standards, but by the criteria of sects everywhere and of Mexican Evangelicals in particular, persons attending but once a week would not be regarded as really active. People attending one to three times a month would be regarded as even more suspect. In all, just fewer than half, 48 per cent, continued to be active Evangelicals who attended a church service at least once weekly.

Denominational differences, summarized in Table 3.5, are again

Table 3.5
Apostasy among Evangelical childhood attenders, second generation sample now twenty years or more of age

	Advt*	Hist.*	Pent.*	Rural*	City*	Age** 21–30	Age** 31–40	Age** 41–50	All
Fem	20%	27%	37%	33%	29%	34%	26%	27%	29% (558)
Male	49%	57%	59%	61%	46%	57%	55%	59%	57% (574)
All	34%	42%	48%	48%	37%	45%	41%	45%	43%
	(150)	(570)	(412)	(599)	(309)	(435)	(352)	(173)	(1132)

Apostate = less than monthly attendance at an Evangelical church or attendance at a Catholic church.
* in childhood.
** current age.
Numbers in brackets in this and following tables refer to sample size.

evident, though not on a large scale. For reasons I cannot readily adduce, the small Adventist sector had the lowest drop-out rate and the highest percentage of strongly committed in the second generation. More certain is that the Pentecostals, who had the highest growth rates and most emphasized evangelism in their local church life, had the highest drop-out rate. Conversely, the Presbyterians and Baptists had lower growth rates and lower drop-out rates. Whereas Pentecostals in the second generation either remained highly committed or dropped out, members of the historical Protestant denominations displayed a more varied pattern, with a significantly greater proportion (11 per cent) showing signs of the classic denominationalizing tendency of continuing affiliation but reduced commitment in the second generation. Many more Presbyterians and Baptists (9 per cent) than Pentecostals (2 per cent) also switched, and when they did they almost always became active Pentecostals. This happened throughout the country, but the most extreme example is the large Neo-Pentecostal[42] church in the colonial heartland. Founded in 1984, its initial core group were largely second-generation Presbyterians and Baptists who were still some 30 to 40 per cent of the total membership in 1991. Not surprisingly, this development caused much bitterness and resentment on the part of the historical churches.

Regional differences are minimal and show no significant pattern, whereas rural-urban contrasts are more pronounced, though not in the way one might expect. As can be seen in Table 3.5, Evangelicals raised in cities were less likely to drop out than were Evangelicals with rural backgrounds. Further, though I do not present the figures in Table 3.5, those of rural background who remained in rural areas were just as likely to drop out (49 per cent) as Evangelical migrants to cities (47 per cent). Rural life has not insulated Evangelicals from the problem of second-generation commitment, nor has the city, as is commonly believed, proved to be a source of secularization and declining commitment. All that can safely be said is that Evangelicals in the city were more likely to switch denominational allegiance.

The most striking correlate of apostasy in the second generation is gender. In Table 3.5 it can be seen that 57 per cent of males but only 29 per cent of females raised in an Evangelical environment left in their adult years. In other words, 60 per cent of second-generation Evangelical women remained actively committed to their faith, whereas this was true of only 35 per cent of men. A full discussion of the various reasons for this state of affairs must await later chapters that outline the complex of demands, behaviours, beliefs, and practices making up Evangelical life. For the moment I wish only to stress the gap pervading all sectors of the Evangelical world. Table 3.5 shows it among Pentecostals, Adventists, and the historical denominations in roughly equal ratios, though the overall apostasy rates for these denominations differed. Similarly, the gender gap is evident in both rural and urban areas and at different age levels. The latter finding further suggests that dropping out was not just a temporary gesture of rebellious youth. Many now highly committed male Evangelicals of middle or advanced years told me they had gone through a period of rebellion, especially in their late teens and early twenties, when they "fell into the world." However, Table 3.5 shows no significant decline in apostasy rates for men as they advanced in years. Even in their forties and fifties over half of second-generation men of Evangelical background remained outside the fold.

Drop-out rates in the second generation are clearly linked to high mixed-marriage rates with Catholics, which, for the sample as a whole, amounted to a substantial 42 per cent (see Table 3.6). Here too there are significant differences in the responses of men and women to a mixed marriage. More married Evangelical women (45 per cent) had a Catholic spouse than did married Evangelical men (38 per cent), though the difference is not large. This may seem rather surprising, since married Evangelical men were much more prone to apostasy (58 per cent) than were married Evangelical women (31 per cent). Among men a mixed marriage was almost invariably associated with departure from the Evangelical world. Thus 93 per cent of male Evangelicals married to a Catholic had dropped out: only 4 per cent remained active church members. In

Table 3.6
Mixed marriages and apostasy, second-generation sample

	Married men	Married women	All marrieds
Drop-out rate	58% (436)	31% (440)	44% (876)
Mixed-marriage rate	38% (436)	45% (439)	42% (875)
Apostate among those married to a Catholic	93% (163)	48% (199)	69% (362)
Apostate among those married to an Evangelical	37% (271)	16% (240)	27% (511)
Active among those married to a Catholic	4% (163)	36% (199)	22% (362)
Active among those married to an Evangelical	54% (271)	77% (240)	64% (511)

Apostasy = person who attended an Evangelical church in childhood but now attends less than once a month or attending a Catholic church. Mixed marriage = marriage to a Catholic or member of a sect. Active = still attends at least once a week in denomination of birth or other Evangelical denomination.

contrast, only about half (49 per cent) of Evangelical women married to Catholics dropped out, and a full 36 per cent remained actively involved in their Evangelical church, despite being married to a Catholic. To put the same principle slightly differently, 97 per cent of religiously active and married male Evangelicals in the second generation were married to a fellow Evangelical, whereas this was true of only 72 per cent of religiously active, married female Evangelicals. In short, mixed marriages among Evangelical women did not invariably lead to apostasy, as was the case among Evangelical men. We must, of course, be careful about inferring causal trends, for it is not entirely clear whether mixed marriages led to apostasy or whether drop-outs were prone to mixed marriages. All that can be safely said is that the two are linked, though only partially, and that mixed marriages may help to account for the high rate of religious apostasy of second-generation Evangelicals, especially males.

In addition to this measurable loss through apostasy in the second generation, it should be recalled that Evangelical growth potential, as measured by their baptismal rate, was about three times greater than their actual growth rate. Data of this sort do not directly and exclusively measure drop-outs among converts, but high losses in the first generation are the only possible explanation for such a large gap between potential and net growth. Pastors in all denominations were agreed that a sizeable percentage of converts inevitably fell away. The effect of such losses clearly diminishes the growth potential of Evangelicals. It also insures that the very survival of the

Evangelical world depends to a unique degree upon the constant re-plenishment of new members through conversion rather than by natural increase – that is, the maturing of children born in the faith into adult membership.

Some sense of the relative mix of converts vis-à-vis subsequent generations may be obtained from the congregational sample. It may be recalled that I asked pastors in the forty-three congregations I surveyed for background information on all those baptized in the previous year. Similar background questions were also asked of a sample of the remaining congregational members, ranging from all members in some small churches to a one-in-five sample in a few larger ones.[43] Together these two samples produced a Evangelical population of 1,410. Just over a quarter (28 per cent) were born and raised in an Evangelical church, though not necessarily the one in which they were baptized. Another 9 per cent started attending an Evangelical church between the ages of one and ten, usually in the company of their converting parents. By any reasonable standard, children in this latter category are best viewed as born in the faith. The remaining 63 per cent might be described as converts, although one might well argue about how to define those who first started to attend an Evangelical church in their early teens. To be safe, I would prefer to regard converts as not starting to attend an Evangelical church until at least sixteen years of age. By this measure, a little over half (53 per cent) would still be defined as converts. My main sample, which was gathered in very different ways, provides striking corroboration for this finding, in that 52 per cent of the 485 Evangelicals I interviewed were also converts. Among adults, or those over the age of twenty in the congregational sample, converts rise to 62 per cent of all Evangelicals.

Given the greater conversionist thrust and higher drop-out rate of Pentecostals, it is perhaps not surprising to find in Table 3.7 that they had the lowest proportion of members born in the faith and the highest proportion of converts. The historical denominations, with their lower growth potential and greater success in retaining the second generation, had the lowest percentage of converts and the greatest reliance on natural increase. As always, the Adventists were strategically placed in between. Since Pentecostals were probably more numerous in the general Evangelical world than in my sample, the overall predominance of the first-generation Evangelicals was probably higher than my summary figure of 53 per cent.

Such a situation stands in marked contrast to the central issue posed by Niebuhr in his account of sect development. For Niebuhr,

Table 3.7
Prevalence of converts: affiliation age by denomination, congregational sample

	0–10	11–15	16–20	21–30	31–50	51+	Total
				Age (%)			
Advt	49	4	20	12	10	4	100% (116)
Hist.	49	8	10	15	15	4	100% (468)
Pent.	30	12	12	19	22	7	100% (826)
Total	37%	10%	12%	17%	19%	6%	100%
	(528)	(137)	(167)	(238)	(263)	(77)	(1,410)

the dilemma is that subsequent generations tend to lose the zeal and high commitment of the founding generation. In their so doing, the original sect tends to evolve into a more denominational or church-like institution. For Mexican Evangelicals, with their high rates of second-generation apostasy and a majority of members still converts after more than a hundred years of an Evangelical presence in the country, Neibuhr's forecast has proved largely irrelevant. Their "problem" might be better defined as that of a revolving door. In subsequent chapters I will explore the reasons for this state of affairs.

Though the evidence of a substantial measure of apostasy is clear, its significance for the future growth of the Evangelical community is less certain. Whenever there is rapid growth, it is probably inevitable that it be accompanied by a fair measure of loss. The fact still remains that Evangelical growth rates, whether measured by the census or by my congregational data, were higher in the 1970s and 1980s than at any other time in their history. Even when overall population growth finally started to slow in the 1980s, Evangelicals continued to grow at a rate 4.5 times faster than that of the Catholic population. There is also the question of whether and to what degree the census underestimates the Evangelical population. The claims of Evangelical leaders must be tempered by the congregational data showing that their net growth rate was very much less than their growth potential from the annual harvest of new converts. Until more information can be obtained, there is little value in speculating further about the absolute size of the Evangelical community. It none the less remains clear that the Evangelical community has gone through a remarkable twenty-year period of growth, vitality, and outreach. The nature and causes of this conversionist effort are the themes of the next chapter.

4 Conversion and Evangelism

Evangelism and conversion have long been the central preoccupations of Mexican Evangelicals. They take as a fundamental tenet of their faith the biblical injunction to preach the gospel to all nations. This "Great Commission" is one of the reasons they describe themselves as "Evangelicos" or "Gospellers." The distinctive conversionist orientation of Evangelicals, which is so evident in the high growth potential and baptismal rates outlined in the preceding chapter, is described in the following pages. The remainder of the chapter is devoted to an analysis of who is being drawn to this new faith and why.

For the moment the focus is on the conversion experience, or, to be more precise, on the decision to become a member of an Evangelical church through the ceremony of baptism. Such a decision, the neophyte is taught, ought not to be taken lightly, for it involves a total transformation of identity and lifestyle in which intense commitment to the new faith is expected to pervade all areas of the convert's life. The theological definitions and practical prerequisites vary from church to church, but the two universally cited requirements are that individuals genuinely repent their past sinful nature and that they "accept Christ as their only Saviour." From this point on they are to embrace him as their companion, mentor, and only guide in life. In so establishing a personal and immediate relationship with the divine or supernatural, Evangelicals believe they are "born again." This utterly transforming personal relationship with the supernatural is what Evangelicals mean by salvation. Without such a relationship, they believe, we are lost. Baptism, then, is the outward sign of this internal transformation, ceremonially performed before the community of believers and thereby recognized by them.

Pastors were uniformly agreed that evangelism should be the primary and unceasing goal of each congregation. Campaigns were the times, they recalled, when the church was most alive. All could remember one or another great campaign when a great harvest was gathered and many souls were won for Christ. The themes of evangelism, the setting of lofty goals, and the teaching of evangelistic methods were invariably stressed at annual denominational meetings and at many interdenominational conferences. The "Great Commission" referred to above was the doctrinal root of this emphasis. Pastors were also driven by economic or material considerations, since foreign mission-board support of local congregations and pastors was now only a historical memory.[1] Pastors survived on the givings of their congregations. The larger and more fervent a congregation, the more comfortable the pastor. Yet neither doctrinal nor economic considerations adequately account for the fascination of pastors with evangelistic work.

The "evangelist," or the person who "plants" or "raises up" churches, to use Evangelical terminology, has greater stature or prestige than the pastor, who is seen as performing the more mundane task of tending the work created by the evangelist. The true stars of the evangelical world, men like Luis Palau, Alberto Mottesi, or Billy Graham, were all evangelists; in every denomination and in every region there was a host of lesser-known acolytes. After weeks of preparation in the local church, town, or city, when the leaflets had all been distributed, the permission of the authorities arranged, the hall booked, and all the other arrangements made, the evangelist would arrive to packed and expectant meetings. A host of "decisions" would then usually be made during the campaign, which might last from a few days to several weeks. Then, when the evangelist moved on, as he inevitably did, it was left to the pastor and the local congregation to pursue those who had made their "decisions" in the heat of the campaign and to weigh the final harvest. Not all campaigns, by any means, were on such a grand scale. Most were two- to five-day affairs in a local congregation, with an outside evangelistic preacher invited from the surrounding area. But even on this modest scale the same dynamics were at work. To be invited regularly, especially outside one's own denomination, to preach at evangelistic services was an immensely gratifying recognition, by one's own community and peers, that one excelled at the essential task of one's profession and faith.

Pastors did not work alone in this endeavour. Especially in the period building up to and during a campaign, the lay members of the congregation were exhorted to distribute literature and to evangelize among their friends, neighbours, and relatives. In my major interview sample, 65 per cent of the 483 laity who responded said that they had made a concerted effort on more than one occasion to evangelize at least one person during the previous year. There were no significant differences among denominations, although women (61 per cent) and the second generation (59 per cent) professed to be somewhat less zealous than did men (71 per cent) or converts (also 71 per cent). Evangelistic fervour was probably more intense when campaigns were taking place, but only 4 per cent of those who did evangelize said their most recent effort involved door-to-door evangelizing of strangers. The vast majority did so quietly with friends, neighbours, workmates, and relatives, sometimes using the campaign as a pretext for inviting their contacts to a first evangelical service.

For any given year one could find examples of large campaigns in process in different parts of the country. David Barrett's *World Christian Encyclopedia* records several large campaigns during the 1970s, ranging from one by Luis Palau in eight Yucatan cities yielding 5,350 decisions to another in Tijuana with 930,000 attendance and 10,767 decisions.[2] Similarly, in 1990 and 1991, in Iztapalapa, a huge and rapidly growing delegation of greater Mexico City, a campaign was initiated by the Evangelism In Depth organization involving 86 pastors and 29 denominations or movements. On the "day of impact" there were plans for three thousand Evangelicals to disperse themselves through th streets of Iztapalapa, evangelizing with anyone prepared to hear their message.[3] The evidence from the forty-three congregations where I worked provides a similar though perhaps less dramatic picture. The congregations averaged 1.5 campaigns a year; one had as many as eight, though a quarter (10 of 43) had no campaigns at all. There were also on average 1.5 missions attached to each congregation; one had nine, though again twelve had none. In addition, over half (53 per cent) either had specific groups organized to evangelize on a regular basis from door to door and in hospitals, prisons, and the like, or they held weekly services in the homes of members as a means of evangelizing neighbours.

This picture of a vast and committed army of evangelists needs some qualification. The intensity of evangelistic effort varied enormously over time in any given area and from congregation to congregation – though it was still impressive. Periods of intensive activity were often followed by a fallow time. Among the ten congregations that held no campaigns, three different reasons for this lack were apparent. In one case a Pentecostal pastor in a poor neighbourhood in a big city was simply burnt out. Though he had conducted many campaigns in the past, his congregation had not grown substantially, as he was a poor preacher and there were many other Evangelical congregations in the area. In the end he devoted himself largely to the local Bible institute and was on his way out. This is an extreme example, but it would be fair to say that few pastors or congregations could sustain the radical commitment of unrelenting evangelism for extended periods of time.

In four other rural congregations, founded some years ago, pastors and laity could no longer see the point of evangelizing "non-believers" who had rebuffed many former approaches, who were neighbours and relatives, and who now grew angry at further evangelistic efforts. The lines were clearly drawn in such small communities. Though an occasional conversion might occur through personal contact, campaigns were unproductive and troubled local community relations. Indeed, it was my distinct impression that, throughout the country and for much the same reason, there was a measure of exaggeration in my survey's finding that 65 per cent had made repeated efforts to evangelize at least one person during the previous year.

In two other congregations, which were both large, lively, and growing churches, the pastors and lay leaders were convinced that formal campaigns were a waste of time and money. They produced many fleeting "decisions," it was said, but few long-term converts. Evangelism, they believed, most commonly occurred through the long-term personal efforts of their members with neighbours, relatives, and co-workers. This too was the widely shared belief in all three of the congregations in Indigenous communities. In the Presbyterian congregation I visited in Oxchuc, evangelistic campaigns had never been part of their substantial outreach. The idea of an organized campaign, with a "call" at the end for all non-believers to come forward and make a personal decision, was simply not part of their cultural traditions. Had such campaigns been implemented, they would have had little meaning, a perceptive missionary assured me, because any and all Oxchuceros, invited to a campaign, would invariably respond to the call as a matter of courtesy, regardless of their personal feelings. Such dynamics, we shall see, also occurred in the Mestizo world. The absence of campaigns, however, does not imply any rejection of the need to evangelize, only of certain methods. In all but the very first example the rejection of organized evangelistic efforts was a tactical, not a strategic decision.

PREDISPOSITIONS

Who then were the converts? What can be said about their background and the experiences that led them to be baptized? What follows will be based on two samples of Evangelical converts. The first includes the 745 Evangelicals from the congregational sample, who may be defined as converts in that they did not enter the Evangelical world until after fifteen years of age. This information, it may be recalled, is based on the census I took in the forty-three sample congregations.[4] The second population consists of the 254 converts I interviewed in a total sample of 485. Though their number is smaller, the latter sample provides a far richer and more detailed body of information, since it is based on the accounts of the converts themselves of their conversion experience.

The most frequently cited characteristic of sects in general and of Latin American Evangelical churches in particular is their predominantly lower-class origin. With some qualifications, Mexico appears to be no exception to this rule. Table 4.1 summarizes the occupational distribution of Evangelical converts in the labour-force from both the congregational and the main interview sample. The sometimes crude occupational categories in the table are used because they allow for comparisons with the Mexican work-force as a whole. Among the 376 working converts in the congregational sample, no more than 10 per cent could be described as either upper or middle class. They also tended to occupy the bottom rungs in these categories. In the managerial and director category, for instance, the four converts were a middle-level manager in the national oil company, an owner of three dry-cleaning establishments, the general secretary for a seamstresses' union, and a maintenance manager for a hospital. Similarly, among the 9 per cent in the next two categories, which roughly correspond to a professional class, three-quarters were nurses, teachers, or pastors, whose prestige and incomes are markedly lower than those of doctors, lawyers, and the like. The smaller sample of 143 from the interview sample, drawn in an entirely different manner, leads to similar conclusions, though the details are different. I have met and heard of a few converts with rather more wealth and political influence than Table 4.1 suggests, but no pastor would dispute the general finding of this table that Evangelicals have failed to reach, to any significant degree, the powerful and wealthy in Mexico.

Table 4.1
Occupational structure of converts and all Mexicans:* interview sample,
congregational sample, and census

	Nation** %	Cong. Sample %	Int. Sample %	Advt*** %	Hist.*** %	Pent.*** %
Manager/Direct.	2	1	2	0	3	1
Prof./Tech	6	5	2	6	8	2
Education	4	4	5	9	7	3
Supervisor/						
Inspector	2	2	2	3	2	2
Office workers	9	4	7	9	7	3
Storekeepers						
& workers	9	8	7	3	11	7
Agriculture	22	19	18	15	26	17
Other workers	46	57	56	56	35	66
All workers	100%	100%	100%	100%	100%	100%
		(376)	(143)	(34)	(134)	(351)

* = Students, retired people, and all not in the labour force are excluded. This particularly
reduces the number of female converts.
** = 1990 census.
*** = Combined interview and congregational samples.

There was also a lower-middle-class group of small shopkeepers,
office workers, and supervisors in factories or retail firms, who account for approximately 15 per cent of all converts. The remaining
three-quarters of converts were clustered in what might be described as the working, poorer, or popular classes. With the exception of two farmers who owned farms of less than fifty hectares, the
rest were divided between landless labourers and occupiers of very
small holdings on communal lands, or *ejidos*, where plots very
rarely exceeded five hectares. In the "other workers" category, in
which over half of all converts found themselves, about a third
were artisans or skilled workers employed as welders, carpenters,
plumbers, seamstresses, masons, bus drivers, or the like. The remaining two-thirds were commonly day labourers, domestics, construction workers, unskilled factory workers, street vendors, or taxi
drivers. Some of the artisans, skilled workers, and vendors might
better be put into the lower-middle-class category, but they were
probably counterbalanced by a comparable numbers of paid clerks,
sales assistants, and very small shopkeepers, who would more ap-
propriately be placed in a lower class.

Pentecostal converts were most heavily concentrated in the poorer
or popular classes. Fewer than a fifth could be described as lower
middle class or higher, whereas Table 4.1 suggests that this was true

of about twice as many converts (38 per cent) to the historical denominations. Adventists seemed to be in between, if any confidence can be attached to their tiny sample. However, the reach of the Presbyterians and Baptists into the middle classes should not be exaggerated, since it was primarily the lowest rungs of the middle class where they were successful. There has recently emerged a new style of Pentecostal church that explicitly reaches out to the middle class. It may alter future recruitment patterns of Pentecostals, but it is not yet large enough a force to make an appreciable difference.

The combined "agricultural" and "other working" categories in Table 4.1, taken from the 1990 census, reveal that about two-thirds of all Mexicans were outside the small middle and upper class. My two samples suggest that this was true of about three-quarters of Evangelical converts. Evangelicals, especially Pentecostals, were more concentrated in the popular classes than other Mexicans, but the difference should not be exaggerated, given the crude distinctions employed. Equally if not more striking is the fact that the class background of Evangelical converts does not greatly distinguish them from other Mexicans. Most converts were poor, but this was just as true of the population as a whole. The humble background of most converts undoubtedly shaped their needs and aspirations, but it does not explain why they in particular chose to embrace a new faith.

Apart from deprivation theory, the other major explanation of sectarian growth has been the disorganization theory, which, it may be recalled, focuses on how migration to the cities cuts urban peasants off from their traditional network of cultural restraints. They are then inclined to seek in Evangelical churches a religious substitute for the support network of their rural origins. Some solid evidence to support such a view can be found in Mexico, but it is far less widely applicable than commonly thought. As Table 4.2 shows, a clear minority (32 per cent) of Evangelicals were migrants, in the sense of having moved from the municipio where they were raised as children. A full two-thirds (68 per cent) lived out their lives in their place of birth. The same table shows that migrants were less prevalent in the rural Evangelical world, but only 40 per cent of urban Evangelicals were migrants. Even in Mexico City most Evangelicals, though not a large majority, were born locally. A similar situation also prevailed among Evangelical converts, who are the crucial group. According to Table 4.2, migrants remained a minority, albeit a substantial one – 44 per cent – of all converts. The majority of Evangelical converts continued to live in the place where they were born. Again, even when we confine our focus to Mexico

Table 4.2
Migrants among Evangelicals, congregational sample

All Evang.	Rural Evang.	Urban Evang.	Mexico City Evang.	All Convts	Rural Convts	Urban Convts	Mexico City Convts
32%	17%	40%	44%	44%	26%	53%	60%
(1404)	(493)	(911)	(214)	(739)	(234)	(505)	(133)

City, with its phenomenal growth, 40 per cent were born there, though the two "colonias" or neighbourhoods where I worked were very much part of this recent urban sprawl. According to the 1990 census, 17 per cent of all Mexicans and 40 per cent of all residents in the state of Mexico (into which the capital's recent growth most heavily extends) migrated from another state. Migrants were probably more prevalent among Evangelicals than among other Mexicans,[5] but the high birth rate of the cities and their many youth insure that almost half (47 per cent) of all urban Evangelical converts were born and bred there. Among the 120 urban converts in the congregational sample now in their twenties, only 38 per cent were migrants. Such individuals may have suffered from anomie, alienation, and despair, but it was not because they were recent rural migrants.

Lofland's widely applied model of conversion to new religious movements in the United States stresses that those who convert have a "religious problem-solving perspective" that disinclines them to seek the solution to their problems in political or other secular forms. Potential converts, according to this theory, are also dissatisfied with the faith they were raised in and typically show signs of being religious "seekers", who have already tried a variety of faiths.[6] Trying to pin down a "religious problem-solving perspective" is not that easy. There is the danger of falling into the tautological simplicity that the religious become religious. In Mexico we have already seen that there has been a strong tradition of anti-clericalism. The handful of Catholic priests I interviewed throughout Mexico estimated that 25 per cent or fewer of their flock attended weekly, though they were quick to add that attendance was far higher at the major festivals. Yet various opinion polls in the 1980s put Catholic weekly attendance at mass at about 45 per cent.[7] These figures suggest a relatively high level of religious commitment by the standards of all but Poland or Ireland. The pervasive folk Catholicism of Mexico and the still common custom of consulting traditional curers and shamans, especially among the less

Table 4.3
Frequency of regular Mass attendance before conversion, interview sample

	Advt	Hist.	Pent.	Male	Female	City	Rural	Total
Just before conversion	13%	18%	26%	18%	27%	25%	20%	23%
	(15)	(55)	(183)	(105)	(148)	(139)	(79)	(253)
Childhood	20%	38%	43%	35%	44%	47%	28%	41%
	(15)	(55)	(184)	(105)	(149)	(140)	(79)	(254)

The actual number of respondents here and in all subsequent tables varies slightly from issue to issue, as I neglected to put certain questions to a few respondents. A few questions were also added as my research progressed.

advantaged and less educated, all suggest a widespread and continuing acceptance of the power of the supernatural – and little secular cynicism. The generally low level of organized political opposition in the 1980s, when discontent was so massive, would seem to strengthen the notion that many Mexicans had little faith in political solutions to their problems.

Beyond such sweeping generalizations, which have, I think, a real measure of truth, the evidence becomes shakier. Among the converts I interviewed, 23 per cent in Table 4.3 defined themselves as active Catholics, in that they attended mass on a regular basis in the period before their conversion. The remainder were almost evenly divided between individuals who never attended (34 per cent) and those who did so very infrequently (43 per cent). Small but not especially noteworthy differences can be seen among denominations and between male and females. The childhood religious involvement of Evangelical converts was much higher, with 41 per cent saying they attended mass regularly. The difference, I suspect, stems from the higher rates of church attendance among Mexican women,[8] who brought their children along with them to mass. In either case, the pre-conversion religious involvement of converts appears to have been about the same or possibly less than that of other Mexicans. There is therefore no reason to believe that Evangelical converts had a distinctive and higher level of religious commitment than other Mexicans prior to their conversion that might account for their decision.

Religious seekers, or those who wander restlessly from one religion to another, may be found among Evangelical converts, but they are few in number. A classic example of such an orientation is to be found in the following conversion account from my interview sample of a middle-class educated couple who one day had a car accident with a fellow immigrant from Mexico City:

We began to chat. He said, "Do not worry. I fear God. We can fix it easily." Victor thought how is it fear of God? Does not God love you? We chatted a little and we thought we would like to chat some more. He invited us to a prayer meeting in his house and we went. I thought they were strange but at the same time I wanted to know more. Then Victor said let's not go again, but I said we have gone to so many places. Before we went with the Krishnas, Gnostics, with people with extraterrestrial studies. We had spent some time in a Catholic movement which ran retreats. He said, "OK." On Sunday we went to the church, and on this day we delivered ourselves to the Lord. We began to sing the hymns. The worship began and we began to cry. God definitely touched us both that day.

Such experimentation, especially such diverse experimentation is rare in Mexico. Only 6 per cent of the converts I interviewed ever explored a religious option outside of the Evangelical or Catholic worlds; for most this meant a dabbling with Jehovah's Witnesses. It is true that a quarter (26 per cent) had switched denominations in the Evangelical world since their conversion, but about half (52 per cent) of those who have ever switched joined their current congregation because they moved their place of residence or because they found it closer to where they lived. Among the remainder, who might be regarded as seekers, the most commonly cited motive (42 per cent) was a desire for a deeper or different religious experience, though such decisions were often fuelled by personality conflicts or by a chance encounter with a better preacher. Only a minority (6 per cent) cited doctrinal reasons. In sum, somewhat fewer than a seventh (13 per cent) of the converts I interviewed had histories that might be described as those of religious seekers.[9]

Of course the very fact of making the radical leap from the Catholic to the Evangelical world might be interpreted as *prima facie* evidence that all Evangelical converts were "religious seekers." A logical corollary of such a mind-set, one might reasonably presume, would be that such individuals might be inclined to grow dissatisfied with their new faith and then move on. Among the Tzeltal in Oxchuc, whose large-scale conversion in the 1940s and 1950s was described in chapter 2, the first convert and early leader in the breakthrough hamlet of Coralito, Juan Mucha, later dropped out.[10] So too did the first Chamulan convert, Domingo Hernandez, among the neighbouring Tzotzil, whose story of mass conversion

Table 4.4
Affiliation age of converts by denomination, congregational sample

16–20	21–30	31–40	41–50	51+	Total
22%	32%	23%	13%	10%	100% (745)

and persecution will be documented later.[11] Such a tendency to be a restless seeker and innovator may also help to explain my own evidence, presented in the last chapter, that many converts subsequently dropped out. Thus here too there is valuable insight to be gained from Lofland's model, despite its tautological tendency.

Youth was one of the more striking traits of Evangelical converts. Table 4.4 shows that 22 per cent of all converts became Evangelicals between the ages of sixteen to twenty. If the cut-off point for converts is put back to those who started to attend an Evangelical church at or after the age of eleven, as some would say is more appropriate, then the teenage proportion of all converts would rise to 34 per cent. This high figure is not really that surprising, since the teenage proportion of all Mexicans over the age of ten was a very similar 33 per cent in 1990.[12] In other words, Evangelicals were not disproportionately successful in recruiting Mexican youth. Converts were often young simply because Mexico was such a youthful society. Nevertheless, the presence of so many young converts, especially if those in their twenties are included, helps to explain the earlier indications of high drop-out rates in the first generation. Over and beyond any speculation about the depth and maturity of youthful commitment, young people in their teen and twenties are likely soon to have to move away from the church where they were converted, for reasons of work, education, and to find accommodation after marriage. Such a rupture after but a few years with the original locus of their commitment, where spiritual, emotional, and social attachments were first and most deeply rooted, must surely strain the religious commitment of many.

We saw earlier that there were conspicuous gender differences in the drop-out rates of the second generation. Gender differences also manifest themselves in a very similar and striking way among converts. Since the second-generation and congregational samples were gathered in entirely different ways, their common conclusions further underline the predominance of women in Evangelical life. Table 4.5 shows that females in the congregational sample were 63 per cent of all converts. They outnumbered male converts in all denominations, all regions, all age groups, in rural and urban areas,

Table 4.5
Females among converts, congregational sample*

Hist.	Pent.	City	Rural	21–30	31–40	41–50	Migrant	Not migrant	Total
66%	66%	64%	62%	62%	62%	59%	64%	62%	63%
(206)	(485)	(406)	(234)	(184)	(169)	(140)	(328)	(411)	(745)

* % female by region: north (68%); capital (59%); centre (67%); south (57%)

Table 4.6
Spouse's religion of married converts by gender, congregational sample

	Catholic %	Other/Evang.%	Same %	Total
Female	33	1	66	100% (294)
Male	7	1	92	100% (218)
Total	22%	1%	77%	100% (512)

Table 4.7
Marital status of converts by gender, congregational sample

	Sing. %	Marr. %	Common law %	Sep. %	Div. %	Wid. %	Total
Female	13	64	1	3	1	17	100% (466)
Male	15	79	0	1	0	5	100% (279)
Total	14%	69%	1%	2%	1%	13%	100% (745)

and among migrants and non-migrants – in roughly equal proportions. A very similar figure of 59 per cent also emerges from the 254
converts I interviewed, who were sampled in a very different way.
By any standard, female converts predominated throughout the
Evangelical world.

Like second-generation gender differences, the marriage patterns
of male and female converts are revealing. Among married converts,
virtually all males (92 per cent) had a spouse who was also Evangelical. However, Table 4.6 shows that a sizeable minority (33 per
cent) of married female converts had Catholic husbands. Some
would attribute the difference to the greater power of men over
women, whereby wives are obliged to follow the faith of their husbands. Dynamics of this sort undoubtedly were at work in some
marriages, but the same difference may also be seen as evidence of
the greater appeal of the Evangelical faith to women. Indeed, a full
third of married female converts were prepared to ignore and even
to defy their husbands' religious inclinations, despite the fact that pa-
triarchal assumptions abounded in the social strata from which
Evangelicals were drawn. Not only were Evangelical female converts

more likely to be alone in church because of mixed marriages, but Table 4.7 indicates that they were also more likely to be divorced, separated, widowed, and in common-law relationships. Only the proportion of singles was about equal for both males and females. Excluding the singles who had never married, the great majority of male converts over the age of twenty (86 per cent) were married to an Evangelical. In contrast, and again excluding the never married, just fewer than half of female converts over the age of twenty (49 per cent) were attached to an Evangelical spouse. In other words, a majority of adult female converts were independent women within their religious life, in the sense that they were not attached to an Evangelical male.[13] When combined with the low proportion of males among converts, the presence of independent women among Evangelical converts becomes all the more striking.

PRECIPITATING FACTORS

The above are the major predisposing factors linked to Evangelical conversion. There remains the question of what triggered or precipitated the conversion process. Among the converts I interviewed a full two-thirds identified a specific crisis or event in their lives as the immediate cause of their conversion. Lofland, in his often-used process model of conversion, speaks of the need for the potential convert to encounter a "turning-point" in life when "old lines of action were complete, had failed, or had been or were about to be disrupted, and when they were faced with the opportunity or necessity for doing something different with their lives."[14] Though most Mexicans may have been open to a religious solution to their problems, the idea of inevitability must be qualified here, in that not all are likely to define the same life experiences as crises necessitating radical personal change. Nor is it inevitable that those in crisis will seek a religious, let alone an Evangelical solution to their problems. Furthermore, some have noted that the conversion accounts, which Lofland and any observer must draw upon, are retrospective accounts that tell more about the current values and beliefs of individuals and their groups than about actual experiences.[15] There is some value in such warnings, especially in the case of Evangelicals, whose religious tradition emphasizes the need to experience a turning-point; this tradition may therefore hide more gradual processes of conversion. But beyond useful general warnings of this kind, such strictures are as futile as they are offensive, since they discredit *a priori* the only and closest observer of the conversion experience we are attempting to understand.

The following conversion experience illustrates these notions of crisis and of a turning-point in life. It concerns the conversion of a prostitute at the age of thirty-nine, when she could not reasonably have expected to pursue her former career much longer. Primly covered in a long dress and a shawl, she told me that she had been a convert for four years. Her story is undeniably coloured by her current convictions, but the lengthy sequence of events that led to her conversion remains clear. In her own words:

Before I was on the street. My life was like Mary Magdalene's. I was a sinner. I worked in cabarets and bars. I had four children. I had to work to support them and my mother. I fell into this type of life. But the Lord had compassion on me. He looked after me. I do not know why. Ten years ago one of my youngest brothers joined an Evangelical church in Mexico City. He told me to look for Christ because I was playing with danger. But I told him I couldn't look for Christ because I was bad. He told me if you ask God for a husband, he will look after you, because Christ is good and he supplies all our needs. Christmas was coming and I went to a temple. I liked it very much how they sang and praised God. I felt better than in the Catholic church. I felt something different. When I entered this church, all the world turned their heads to see me, because I was a very attractive woman. My hair was very long. I was perfumed, and my heels were very high. I liked to dress elegantly. The whole world admired me, men, women and children. I believe this is the day the Lord touched me. I told the Lord, if he would give me a husband, I would look for him. Years passed and I did not know when my husband would come. Then I met the man who is now my husband. We became friends and then we entered into a common-law relationship. He treated me badly; he was not responsible with me. I told him I was going to leave him for the bad way he was treating me. I had another pregnancy through him. When I had this pregnancy, I said I am going to leave. I called to the Lord, like I am talking to you. I said, "I do not want anything to do with this man you left me. I am going to leave him. If I live, I live, and if I die, I die. But I do not want this husband, and I do not want anything to do with your church. I have been to your temple, and I feel the same. I feel poor, I suffer hunger, I suffer many things and you do not help me." I packed my bags and I left my house. I was three weeks on the street. The Day of the Dead was coming up. A friend said, "Are you not planning to see your dead ones?" I told her, "You go because I do not have any dead ones." I passed on, without knowing that day I was going to have a dead one. They killed one of my sons so that I would come to the feet of Christ. They killed him in the street. They went looking for me. They said go to your house because there is a problem. I went. The street was closed. Among the people were my relatives. My house was open. I ran inside. I could not speak, and I saw my third son in a coffin. This is how I came to the feet of Christ. I lived near to this church [i.e., the church she now attends]. When we arrived at the cemetery, I said to my mother, "I want to go to this church," because my nephew was there. He told me much of this church. I told him, "One day I am going to come, but I do not know when." They brought me here to this church with my children. Omar, the pastor was here. He said, "Come in so we can pray for you because you are sad." I passed forward to the front. I felt touched by the Lord. I had a beautiful encounter with him. I told him the death of my son was not in vain. I said from this date, I am going to change. On this date, I bury my son, but on this date I bury myself. You are going to feed me. From this day forward, I am not going on the streets when I have no money to feed my children. I cried and cried and cried.

To provide some sense of order to the 254 conversion experiences I heard among respondents over fifteen years of age, I endeavoured to classify them by the type, if any, of crisis or turning-point that directly precipitated their decision to start attending an Evangelical church. For those accounts that might well fit into more than one category, I followed the predominant emphasis of the narrative. Table 4.8 provides the results in summary form, differentiated by gender and denomination. Strikingly, the largest single category consists of individuals who did not identify any specific experience, crisis, or event that triggered their conversion experience. I will return to this third of the sample later. The remaining categories are all quite small. They were not drawn up according to any general theoretical scheme. Rather, they closely follow the accounts of Evangelical Mexican converts in order to reveal the diversity and uniqueness of their experience.

Only two of the 254 converts identified economic difficulties as the reason for their conversion. In one case, a forty-two-year-old male from Mexico City, married to a Baptist, lost a secure middle-class office job, which eventually caused him to sell the family house and move in for a time with a brother in another city, where he and the family were tolerated but made to feel uncomfortable. He lost a great deal of weight. "It reached a point, I told my wife you are going to have to live with your mother and I with mine." He then acquiesced to the now twenty-year demands of his wife to attend a Baptist church, where he quickly converted. "I had a great need, an economic need. I found refuge in religion." When, not long after, he found a job and acquired housing through winning a raffle for an apartment, his faith was strengthened. In the second case, a young teenager in a small village in the north found herself

Table 4.8
Types of turning-point/crisis* in conversion, interview sample

	Fem. %	Male %	Advt %	Hist. %	Pent. %	Total
Economic	1	1	7	2	0	1
Addict	1	17	7	9	8	8
Legal	0	4	0	2	2	2
Family	5	6	7	7	4	5
Spouse	21	3	13	6	16	13
Widowed	3	0	0	4	2	2
Illness	23	16	0	11	25	20
Other	3	3	7	2	3	3
Kin	3	3	0	0	4	3
Marriage	11	8	27	18	6	10
None	29	40	33	40	32	34
Total	100%	100%	100%	100%	100%	100%
	(149)	(105)	(15)	(55)	(184)	(254)

* The first eight rows enumerate the percentage of converts who claimed that one of these problems/crises strongly influenced their conversion decisions. The kin row identifies teenage converts whose conversion was largely due to the conversion of kin. The marriage category consists of people who did not suffer any identifiable crisis but converted on marriage to an Evangelical. Nones are a residual category of all others.

caring for six brothers and sisters after her mother fled. "My two younger brothers used to work, but my father began to drink and gamble a great deal. The money earned by my brothers did not reach me. My father spent it. We used to eat chile and tortillas. Nothing more. When one has this kind of pressure, one is always looking for something. Through this I began to attend" a nearby Pentecostal church at the invitation of a relative. Such economic difficulties are, of course, widespread both within and without the Evangelical world. Economic deprivation may create a generalized sense of discontent, but when it is so pervasive it is rarely a turning-point or crisis in people's lives.

For men, a significant minority of converts came from destructive backgrounds, from which they escaped through conversion. The stereotyped picture of the Pentecostal church saving men and their families from alcohol and drugs has a substantial measure of truth to it, though it is far from a universal rule. It applies to 18 of my small sample of 105 men. As one rural Pentecostal of thirty-four years explained: "Six and a half years ago, I entered a church and came to know the word of God, but I left. I was a terrible drunk. Four years ago I had a hangover for three days. I felt the coldness of death – a cold sweat. I went away and hid myself to recover. On returning I could not handle it. It was a great struggle. I said, if I can do it I will deliver myself to the Lord. I said, 'Lord, raise me up like the prodigal.' From that day, I have not had a drop." Some of the converts in this category may not have been full-blown alcoholics, but all claimed to have had a serious drinking problem that disrupted their lives and caused them to seek in conversion a solution to their difficulties.[16]

For others the problem was the law. The most dramatic case involved a former policeman who had become embroiled in the labyrinth of police corruption in Mexico City. Captured by a rival police gang along with three others, the now-converted deacon was held for several days, beaten, and deprived of food and water. Terrified, he kept recalling his wife, who had converted to a Pentecostal church a year earlier, saying to the children, "The blood of Christ, whatever peril, will protect you." He thus resolved, "God, if you get me out of here, I will not return to this job, I will deliver myself to you." On being released, he fled home to move his family and find new employment. That first weekend, "I delivered myself to the Lord." For some men salvation often has a very this-worldly, specific, and concrete meaning.

For women, the proximate cause of their conversion was much more likely to be linked to tensions arising within the family. In Table 4.8 we can see that conflicts with husbands (spousal), problems with other members of the immediate family (family), and recent widowhood (widowed) lay behind 29 per cent of female conversions. The seven converts in the family category include three single mothers who, by their own accounts, were made receptive to evangelistic efforts by the burdens of raising a family on their own. Also included are the prostitute whose story is recounted above and a young unmarried mother who had just lost her first child. Similarly, a domestic in Mexico City, whose husband had deserted her, was driven to experiment with the Jehovah's Witnesses after the death of a daughter, though she subsequently joined a Pentecostal church to which other relatives were already attached. In the last case a widow who depended for her sustenance on a drunken son who beat her found solace in a Pentecostal church. As she explained, "Now I can put my problems on the Lord." The grief and anxieties of widowhood need, I think, no further elaboration. In all these accounts, conversion occurred not long after the loss of a husband and with the intervention of Evangelical kin or neighbours.

By far the largest category of female converts were those who had experienced spousal problems. In a few cases, desertion was the impetus. As one twenty-one-year-old recent convert to an independent Baptist church in the north explained: "I was not married to my husband. I had to share him with someone else. When I accepted Christ, it was the first time he left. It was a serious problem in my life." In the great majority of cases, alcohol abuse and violence on the part of the husband were the source of the problem. The following account of conversion through the influence of an Adventist neighbour is typical:

She began to talk to me. I had many problems with my husband. He drank a great deal. At times he hit me. When I had serious problems, she would come over. She would calm me. She would tell me things about God. I was a Catholic, but I hardly ever attended. She brought me pamphlets. I like to read, and from there I began to know things I used not to understand. She began to instruct me in praying, to ask God from the heart. From there I began to feel good. Then she invited me to go to church, if I wished. I felt something inside me that called me. So I went with my children.

Not all conversion accounts are quite so clear-cut. Among the 31 female conversion accounts identifying spousal abuse or desertion, in only 20 did women claim that the sole cause of their conversion was their problems with their husbands' behaviour. In the remainder, though they identified the husband as a source of real grief, they also explained their conversion in terms of how moved they were by the person who evangelized them or by the Evangelical services they attended. Furthermore, in all cases the abuse was of some years' standing. Family problems were therefore an important cause of female conversion, but only when they operated in conjunction with other forces.

Family problems were a less common cause of male conversion, as Table 4.8 shows. Their reasons were rather different. Only three claimed that spousal problems led to their conversion; two admitted that they were the cause of the problems. Among those with other family problems, the suicide of a beloved daughter, the death of a first child, the death of a mother, and home problems linked to an alcoholic father were each the catalyst of a conversion. In the last case, a twenty-seven-year-old balloon seller in Mexico City who drank heavily and dabbled in drugs was led to conversion after visiting his father, who was dying of alcoholism in hospital. There he met an Evangelical friend of his mother, who "told me I had to repent and that I must receive the Lord. It was the Lord talking. On this day my father died. They kept the body at the hospital and at night I went to the Centre of Faith, Hope and Love. They began to preach, and they said do you want to receive Christ. I could not bear it. I went forward. They prayed for me and the Lord did his work."

An acute illness in either the life of the convert or someone close to the convert was another major cause of conversion. Apart from the combined family set of problems, no other issue was mentioned more frequently by converts. Table 4.8 shows that a fifth of converts defined a serious illness as the major impetus behind their conversion. In a real minority of the accounts (7 of 51, or 14 per cent), the dangers and anxieties of illness caused converts to seek solace and meaning through the Evangelical faith. Thus a professional wrestler and market-stall owner in Mexico City converted to a Pentecostal church when his beloved mother died and then his wife came down with cerebral palsy. "I looked for refuge in something. I found it in alcohol. I abandoned my family." But within a year the wrestler was converted by a Pentecostal lady who owned a market stall next to his. "She spoke to me of Jesus Christ, because she saw the need in my life." Through this, he converted.

Far more dramatic events and claims were involved, however, in the remaining conversions linked to illness. In almost 80 per cent of cases a group of Evangelicals prayed over the sick person in his home or in church. As a result, 69 per cent of the 51 converts in this category were emphatic that a miraculous healing occurred, and another 20 per cent suggested, without saying so directly, that no other explanation was possible. Faith healing, or "divine healing," as Evangelicals would say, would appear from Table 4.8 to be more commonly experienced by women converts and to be more common in Pentecostal churches than in the historical denominations. However, we shall see that it is widely accepted and practised throughout the Evangelical world. In the next chapter I will examine in more detail the varied interpretations and implications that faith healing has for Evangelicals. For a substantial minority of Evangelical converts, it was the immediate cause of their conversion.

Each account of faith healing has its own particular emphasis, but the following, by a fisherman who converted at the age of twenty-eight into a Pentecostal church, reveals a number of common themes:

The pastor used to visit us. I did not want to have anything to do with the brothers. When he came around to talk to her [i.e. his wife], I would go around the back. But one time he arrived and I was seated. He used to come with his wife. We began to chat. I thought I am going to see what you do. I went as a critic. I saw that everything was good, that they were looking for God. So I began to attend. But the biggest thing that made me convert was my son. He was eight months old when he was very sick with dysentery. I brought him to various doctors, but they could not stop the dysentery. I went to some shamans (brujas), but they did nothing. The thing that gave me more confidence in God was that one night the pastor said that if any are sick, God will heal them. I passed in front and said my son is sick. He said do you believe that God can heal. I said I believe. The brothers put themselves to talking in tongues. I felt a confidence. The next day, my son began to eat and to be tranquil. Inside I rebelled. I said it was a pure accident, or rather it was the medicine that affected him. So He came. God touched my wife. She had a growth, here in the stomach. I could hear the throbbing. With my hand, I could feel it. One day she woke up and she said God healed me. I said you are crazy. She said I was sleeping and I saw a man in white. He entered, he took it out, and he left. Since this moment, I again began to have more confidence. But I had more confidence in God when I told him I had vices. I smoked marijuana. I had all the worst vices. I said to God, in truth I am yours. You have power over everything. I want to give up my vices. If I am going to serve you, take away my vices. So I began to centre more on the things of the Lord.

Despite the decisiveness of the single event of faith healing for so many converts, this account, like that of the former prostitute, again underlines how conversion is often a process of encounter and retreat, which only after some time culminates in conversion.

Altogether, 54 per cent of converts identified one or another crisis in their lives that significantly affected their conversion decision. Females would appear in Table 4.8 to be slightly more prone to such pressures than men, though it may simply be that males were more adamant about making an independent decision. The small size of the sample should not be forgotten, but Table 4.9 identifies some additional differences worth noting. Urban and migrant converts were more likely than rural and non-migrant converts to report that a specific crisis provoked their conversion. This surely reinforces disorganization theory's hypothesis that urban migration provokes problems that may cause conversion. Clearly that hypothesis is not the whole story, since 41 per cent of migrant converts to cities said that no particular crisis lay behind their conversion. Disorganization theory has equally little to say about the 33 per cent of rural converts who have never migrated but whose conversion was affected by a crisis in their lives. Table 4.9 also reinforces deprivation theory in showing that crises were more frequent in the accounts of urban working-class converts than among middle-class converts, though here too the differences are relative, not absolute. In short, Table 4.9 gives support to the two major sociological theories of conversion at the same time that it reminds us of how incomplete they are.

Marriage to a practising Evangelical proved to be the last major

Table 4.9
Converts with a crisis in conversion, interview sample

City Res.	Rural Res.	Migrant	Non-migrant	Urban Mid. Class*	Urban Work. Class*	Rural Work. Class*	Total
60%	42%	58%	48%	53%	61%	40%	54%
(140)	(79)	(141)	(113)	(36)	(82)	(25)	(254)

* The urban middle class collapses the first six categories in Table 4.1. The urban working class is based on the last category from the same table, and the rural working class is drawn from the second-last category in the same table.

Table 4.10
Religion of spouse of married converts at conversion, interview sample

	Envia* %	Evang. %	RC %	Total
Female	28	26	47	100% (109)
Male	42	39	19	100% (79)
Total	34% (63)	31% (59)	35% (66)	100% (188)

* Persons who converted at the same time as their spouse.

factor linked with conversion that I could identify, though it is slightly different in that it only emerged in my subsequent analysis of taped conversations with converts. As Table 4.8 shows, 10 per cent identified this as the major catalyst for their conversion. Here, gender differences were minor. In addition, another 3 per cent of the converts were teenagers whose conversion, they admitted, was directly precipitated by the conversion of their parents. In the marriage category are included only those whose conversion was directly a result of their marriage to a committed Evangelical. Table 4.10 shows that 31 per cent of the spouses of married converts at the time of conversion were already Evangelicals. The disparity between these 10 per cent and 31 per cent figures is due to the fact that some married converts, especially men, did not convert until some years after their marriage to an Evangelical. In other cases the converts were married to lapsed Evangelicals who played no significant part in their conversion. Another 34 per cent converted at the same time as their spouses, while the remaining 35 per cent were married to a Catholic at the time of their conversion. When gender differences in the same table are examined, a now familiar theme emerges. Almost half (47 per cent) of all married female converts had Catholic spouses at the time of their conversion, whereas this was true of only 19 per cent of married male converts. In other words, male converts may have been slightly more successful at inducing their spouses to join them in their conversion, but substantially more male converts were brought into the fold by an Evangelical spouse than was true of female converts. Female converts also showed a noteworthy determination to become Evangelicals, even when their spouses would not.

There remain, of course, the 34 per cent of converts in my interview sample who denied that any specific crisis or turning-point in their lives precipitated their conversion and who did not convert on marriage to an Evangelical. These are the individuals listed under the "None" category in Table 4.8. In a subsequent review of the Nones, I located another 14 converts who claimed that their post-marriage conversion was due to the persistent pressure of an Evangelical spouse. If these 14 are removed from the Nones, the category still represents a healthy 28 per cent of all converts. A few converts in this category echoed, but in a much more muted vein, some of the reasons we have already examined. Thus a teacher in a small town, whose wife was a Presbyterian by birth, converted to his wife's faith at the age of forty-nine. He explained:

I was in a bar one day with my friends. It seemed like someone said to me, "What are you doing here." When I thought about it, I got up from my seat. I said to my friends, "I've had it up to here." I never went back. First I went to the Catholic church here. I saw too many conflicts and divisions. Then I went to the Presbyterian church. I liked it. The religious person avoids problems. The religious person has to separate himself from the things that harm one. He has to adapt himself to a better way of living. I had many personal and family problems. It was my desire to attend.

When I pressed the teacher, he admitted that he had always liked football games, parties, and drinking, but he denied that he had ever had any acute addiction or problem. Rather, for him conversion was a process of maturation, albeit at quite a late stage, where he was seeking a more measured, tranquil, and cerebral life.

As for the others in the None category, their answers were far more unambiguously free of any implication of past problems. A small minority presented themselves as seekers going from church to church until they found the Truth. Most simply said that they started to attend out of curiosity, or because a mission was established on their street, or because of the persistent evangelizing efforts of neighbours or kin. Whatever the original reason, they found, as one convert put it, that "God touched my heart. I liked it a great deal and I never stopped going." Some said they were immediately

Table 4.11
Initial contact of converts with Evangelical world, interview sample

	Male %	Female %	Advt %	Hist. %	Pent. %	Total
Campaign	3	3	7	2	3	3%
Chance evangelism	3	2	0	2	3	2%
Door-to-door evang.	7	3	0	11	3	5%
Self	5	2	0	2	4	3%
Spouse	25	19	27	26	19	21%
Kin	28	45	27	29	42	38%
Neighbour	14	19	20	18	16	17%
Friend	8	3	20	6	4	5%
Co-worker	9	2	0	6	5	5%
Total	100%	100%	100%	100%	100%	100%
	(104)	(149)	(15)	(55)	(183)	(253)

drawn to the music. Others emphasized the sense of brotherhood. A few said they were moved to find "a living God and a close personal relation with Christ." Not all conversions, it would appear, can be attributed to the crises, problems, and turning-points in secular life emphasized by sociology. Some, it would seem, need no external impetus; they are naturally drawn to the message and way of life of Evangelicals.

Time and time again in the examples enumerated above it was somebody already known to the convert who initiated the conversion process, bringing the convert into first contact with the Evangelical world. Table 4.11 confirms this impression. In descending order of commonality, 38 per cent of initial contacts were through kin or relatives, closely followed by spouses (21 per cent) and then neighbours (17 per cent). When friends and co-workers are added to this group, over 85 per cent of conversions worked through pre-existing social networks. This does not, however, mean that social networks were the only really important cause of conversion. Rather these social networks were the crucial channels or links through which the various predisposing and precipitating factors described above function. Put differently, social networks alone, as the Nones indicate, sometimes led to conversion, but only among a minority of converts. By their very nature social networks of kin and neighbours usually existed for many years prior to the conversion and therefore cannot fully account for it. Conversely, a religious predisposition and one or more of the crises or turning-points in life mentioned above never of themselves led to conversion unless there was also some connection or channel by which the Evangelical message is conveyed to the person so predisposed. At least some of both factors were typically necessary if conversion was to occur. Even then, conversion was never certain.

The logical and empirical corollary of the foregoing is that the evangelism campaigns so dearly loved by Evangelicals were not in and of themselves an important means of conversion. Table 4.11 indicates that 3 per cent of the converts had their first contact with the Evangelical world through an evangelism campaign, by the invitation of a church member they did not know, or by reading a leaflet inviting all to attend. An acute crisis, illness, or additional prompting factor also played a major role in the conversion of all but one of those who accepted the invitation to the campaign. The following nicely illustrates how campaigns were more likely to lead to a conversion when other forces were at work. After seeing a leaflet advertising a Christian film during a campaign, a then thirty-seven-year-old lady in a new neighbourhood in Mexico City's sprawling periphery decided to attend

because I like films of Christ. The first time I went, there was not a film. I felt angry. I felt deceived. The pastor announced it would be postponed. The next time it was still not available. The pastor invited people to go forward to give themselves to Christ. I did not go. I was embarrassed. After the film next time, he also made the call. I felt embarrassed, but my sister went up, so, with my children, we went up and delivered ourselves to Christ. I did not know anything of Christ. I did not know how to study the Bible. After the campaign we stopped attending, but some brothers came to visit us to teach us. I said it was impossible for us to understand the word of God. Two weeks later I went to a service with my daughter who had a problem with her knee. All the doctor could do was give her medicine for the pain. When the X-rays were taken, he could see that the bone was deformed. The doctor said she would have to go to a specialist [the problem was not financial: the family had medical coverage through the husband's job], but I had heard that the sick were healed in church by prayers. My husband said take the child where you want, but not to the shamans. She was healed. When we returned to the doctor for an X-ray, there was nothing. This is when we came to know the Lord.

In addition to these few converts recruited through campaigns, another six were converted through chance encounters with an Evangelical who took the opportunity to evangelize. A further twelve converts were also evangelized by the door-to-door efforts of pastors and laity at a time when no organized campaign was in effect. In sum, only 10 per cent of converts were reached by the organized methods of street and church evangelism. Organized

Table 4.12
Years attending before baptism among converts,* congregational sample

	Male %	Female %	Advt %	Hist. %	Pent. %	Total
Less than 1 yr	30	27	6	22	34	28%
1–2 years	36	32	33	33	33	33%
More time	34	41	61	45	33	39%
Total	100%	100%	100%	100%	100%	100%
	(108)	(61)	(18)	(49)	(102)	(169)

* All converts baptized in previous year.

campaigns played a part in only a minority of these few cases. The only qualification is that some of those converted through the efforts of kin or friends may have been invited to participate in evangelistic campaigns that may in turn have shaped their final decision.

That pre-existing social networks should be involved in so many conversions should not be surprising. Despite the tendency of so many converts to recall a specific moment or event when they made a personal commitment, the whole process of conversion typically took place over an extended period of time. I have already alluded to this in some of the conversion experiences described above. Table 4.12 shows that only 28 per cent of the 169 converts baptized in the preceding year had been attending a year or less. No doubt many in this category attended for only a few months before being baptized, but the fact remains that more than two-thirds attended for at least a year before being baptized. Baptists and Presbyterians, it would appear, were less likely to make a quick decision than Pentecostals, but even among Pentecostals a full two-thirds attended for more than a year before making a final decision. It is therefore scarcely surprising that those with pre-existing social bonds with the Evangelical world were most likely to follow through a lengthy transition to full membership, with all its implications of a radical change in attachments, values, and identity.

Though Evangelicals were a real minority of the general population, few of the background traits of the converts clearly differentiated them from Mexicans as a whole. Their pre-conversion religious commitment did not distinguish them from other Mexicans. Impossible as it is to prove unequivocally, it is probably true that they had a "religious problem-solving perspective" on life, but there is every reason to believe that this was generally true of Mexicans. Similarly, the youthfulness of so many converts did not distinguish them from other Mexicans. Converts were typically drawn from the ranks of the less advantaged or from what might be described as the lower or popular classes, though again there was a significant number of exceptions. However, it must be remembered that the disadvantaged or popular classes were a huge swath of the population. Converts, then, were drawn from the largest social class. If deprivation is relative to others, as recent versions of the theory contend, then Evangelicals were not deprived. As for disorganization theory's emphasis on migration and uprootedness, Evangelicals and especially converts were probably more likely to be migrants than other Mexicans, but it would be well to recall that two-thirds of all Evangelicals and over half of Evangelical converts were not migrants. The most distinctive mark of the converts was the preponderance of women in their ranks, though here too one must avoid any caricature that ignores the third of converts who were men. The overall conclusion must be that Evangelicals were more typical than atypical of Mexicans as a whole. Though a clear minority, they were a mass or popular movement in that they stemmed from the ranks of the masses or popular classes.

In the accounts of the converts themselves of the precipitating factors that led to their conversion, what stands out is their emphasis on family and personal causes of conversion. Rarely if ever was mention made of the pressures, tribulations, and trials imposed by the wider society, to which sociology so frequently makes reference. In part this stems from the Evangelical outlook they were taught, which tends to define life's meaning and difficulties in personal rather than collective terminology. In part it may be because the converts were typically uneducated, disadvantaged folk who knew little beyond their immediate world and had never been provided with the education to analyse the social forces that shaped their circumscribed world. However, let me warn once again of the danger of dismissing converts' accounts out of hand by saying they suffer from false consciousness, which is really but another term for ignorance. Such a condescending dismissal leaves us with the explanations of deprivation and disorganization, which are inadequate, though not erroneous, since only a minority of Mexicans in these conditions were drawn to the Evangelical faith. We must also remember that only a minority of those who suffered from family violence, alcoholism, and so on became Evangelicals. An appreciation of the wider social context of Mexico today and of the pre-conversion life of converts enhances our understanding of their conversion, but there always remains an element of free will in their lives and of indeterminacy in our accounts.

5 The Evangelical World-View

In any account of a community one is always confronted with the issue of whether to begin detailed description with its organizational and structural aspects or with its characteristic beliefs, values, and world-view. Current sociological fashion emphasizes the former structural traits on the grounds that political and economic interests are the primary determinants of human behaviour. I see no value in taking a general stand on this issue, but in the specific case of a religious movement, where the primary goal of salvation is so clearly cast in non-material terms, the beliefs and values of Evangelicals are especially important in shaping their community today and their future trajectory. In this chapter I outline the distinctive values, beliefs, and emphases that come out of the religious tradition of Mexican Evangelicals and that shape their world-view. Specifically political issues will be left for chapter 7.

SALVATION

For Mexican Evangelicals, the essence of salvation is the achievement and maintenance of a personal relationship with the supernatural or God through the mediation of God's son, Jesus Christ. Salvation is achieved by faith, not right action, though the former is assumed to give rise to the latter. Salvation is available to all, despite the sinful nature of humans, by virtue of the payment or sacrifice paid by God's only son, Jesus Christ, through his death. Salvation is not guaranteed by baptism, but Christ's sacrificial death insures that, despite subsequent human failings, salvation can always be regained through genuine repentance and faith. In practice, all the Evangelicals I interviewed in my first two summers of research professed to be absolutely certain of their state of salvation. So unanimous were they that I subsequently deleted the question from my interview schedule. For reasons that will become apparent, I suspect that doubts and uncertainty were more widespread than such answers reveal. Nevertheless, Calvinistic angst was little emphasized by Mexican Evangelicals, who offered certainty of salvation for all prepared to make the leap of faith.[1]

For believers, salvation was not simply a promise of some desirable but distant future state. Salvation was more than an offer of heaven in the next world or life after death, though these were promised. Rather, there was a strong this-worldly emphasis, in that potential converts were assured that they would be immediately and utterly transformed in this world and blessed with a variety of gifts. The general promise was that the believer would have access to the unconditional love, care, and concern of God as a source of solace and strength. Through this special relationship with God, believers claimed that they received tranquillity, peace of mind, and a sustaining joy. For the more than half of converts enumerated in the last chapter who experienced a serious problem or crisis in their lives prior to conversion, this was a very powerful and specific promise. Evangelicals not only unburdened themselves to God through prayer, but they were convinced that God could and would answer their specific requests that a bad husband be reformed, a job found, or a sick child healed. These not-insubstantial promises can never be proved or refuted by sociology or any other empirical science. To the extent that such notions of personal transformation are believed, they may become real in their consequences. I can think of no satisfactory way of testing whether Evangelicals were really happier, more fulfilled, more tranquil, or better protected in the face of life's difficulties, but Evangelicals believed this to be true.

With the partial exception of the Adventists, who were regarded with some suspicion by many other Evangelicals, Wilson's concept of a conversionist sect, mentioned in chapter 1, identifies a key characteristic of Mexican Evangelicals. Evangelicals were all conversionist in the sense that they placed a high emphasis on recruitment, but this is not what Wilson is getting at. Rather, conversionist sects are distinguished by their insistence that salvation can only be gained by "a profoundly felt, supernaturally wrought transformation of the self."[2] Pentecostals, the great majority of Mexican Evangelicals, expressed this conversionist orientation most fully, but its essentials were to be found as well in the historical denominations in Mexico. What the Pentecostals and historical denominations had in common was their recurrent emphasis, in teaching and practice, on the need to achieve and then maintain this deeply felt, personal sense of profound emotional transformation. This born-again experience, alluded to so frequently in sermons and personal conversion accounts, was above all defined as a transformation of heart, of feeling, of direct emotional encounter and certainty rather than as an intellectual apprehension. It was not a one-time experience associated with the original conversion to be fondly recalled thereafter, as proof of an original initiation. Rather, for the faithful, like a fire or a flame, the experience of rebirth and the attendant sense of direct communion with the divine was something to be constantly fed and nurtured for fear that it might die out, and salvation's certainty recede. It was the key to salvation.

This conversionist emphasis on the importance of religious experience was evident in the huge amount of time devoted to church services and worship. In the forty-three congregations, each church had an average of 4.7 regularly scheduled services a week, over and beyond weekly Sunday school. At a conservative estimate this amounts to eleven hours of worship a week that a faithful member would be expected to attend, since a service was rarely less than two hours in duration and services of over three hours were not that uncommon. Such figures do not include extra services at the time of campaigns and the like, nor the frequent calls to members to attend a mission church. The devotional emphasis was more pronounced in Pentecostal churches, which averaged 5.3 regular services a week, but the historical denominations were far from laggards, averaging almost 4 (3.6) services a week. The three Adventist churches averaged 4.7 services a week. Of course, attendance was typically much lower during the week, but 69 per cent of the 1,076 in the congregational sample attended 2 or more services a week, and 87 per cent attended at least 1. Even more striking are the 479[3] respondents in the interview sample who insisted they attended an average of 3.5 services in the immediately preceding week, though it should be recalled that this sample tended to be drawn from the ranks of the more committed.[4] By this measure also, Pentecostals attended more services in the previous week (3.8) than did members of the historical denominations (3.0), but Table 5.1 shows that high attendance prevailed throughout the Evangelical world. Even the weekly meetings of the youth groups and women's associations, though they had their special agendas, devoted the bulk of their time to what was in effect a regular worship service.

Table 5.1
Average number of services attended per week, interview sample

Hist.	Pent.	1st gen.	2nd* gen.	Low** educ.	High** educ.	City	Rural	Total
3.0	3.8	3.6	3.5	3.5	3.8	3.7	3.1	3.5
(145)	(298)	(251)	(194)	(302)	(71)	(238)	(168)	(479)

* The first generation of converts started attending an Evangelical church after age fifteen; the second generation did so before age of eleven.
** Low education is completed primary or less, while high education is completed secondary or more.

No other activity involved in being an Evangelical, including evangelism or committee work, took up even a fraction of the time devoted to worship services.

Pentecostal churches expressed this conversionist orientation most clearly in the style and structure of their worship services. Wherever there was electricity, there was electrified music, with even very poor rural and urban congregations managing to find the resources for very loud sound systems, drums, electric guitars, and sometimes more. The quality of the usually teen musicians varied, but some were quite good. Everywhere the music was loud and catchy, often combining religious verses with very popular secular tunes. The same thirty to forty anthems were heard everywhere in Mexico, were known by all, and were sung with deep feeling, with arms outstretched.

Though the services had no formal agenda, they were clearly structured. Services started very informally with only a few in attendance, usually a small part of the band, and a young lay leader in front, who led the service for about a half an hour before turning its direction over to someone more senior. At first the service consisted mainly of music of a gentler sort, interspersed with an occasional exhortation or testimony. As the tempo quickened and the temple slowly filled, the leaders started to break into short bursts of loud, extemporaneous prayers of devotion through the microphone, often accompanied by tears. This was the sign for the remainder of the congregation to join in with their own audible and separate expressions of prayer, sometimes kneeling and sometimes standing. All followed in emotional intensity the leader, whose voice could be heard through the microphone above the babble. At first these episodes were brief and subdued, but they grew in intensity and duration as the service progressed, reaching a temporary peak with the arrival of the pastor. This first phase might take up as much as two hours, but it was typically between an hour and an hour and a half in length. By this point, most of the attenders had arrived, though small numbers continued to trickle in thereafter.

With announcements and then a sermon, the atmosphere settled for a while, but the preacher invariably grew more emotional as the sermon of about forty minutes unfolded, building to a peak when the call was made, asking all to come forward who wished to embrace the faith for the first time or to renew their commitment. The band started up again, people trickled forward to kneel at the front of the dias or raised platform, and the pastor continued his exhortation, ever more loudly, breaking into extemporaneous prayer and sometimes tongues. This was the emotional high point of the service. Anywhere between a third and two-thirds clustered together in front, surrounding those who answered the call, each praying loudly and independently. Some cried uncontrollably. Though the average service had about fifty to seventy adult and teen attenders, the combined effect of their voices, in a typically small, tin-roofed structure, was often very powerful. This is when the "in filling of the Spirit," as Pentecostals put it, was most likely to occur and was most strongly felt. The period varied in length from an occasional brief five minutes to ten or twenty or more, depending on the style of the church, the predilections of the pastor, and his judgment of how spirit-filled the congregation was that evening. Sometimes, when emotions were high and the presence of the Holy Spirit was strongly felt, this portion of the service could go on for over an hour, but usually the pastor led the congregation down with his voice much earlier, and people returned to their seats. The collection was then taken, a few hymns were sung, and the service ended. The whole structure of the service was designed to recreate and thereby renew the original profound and emotional encounter with the divine, when the person was first reborn. To the uninitiated there might appear to be a strong element of bedlam in all this, but in my experience all soon recovered their composure. All assured me that they were strengthened, renewed, and empowered by the experience.[5]

The historical denominations were very much opposed to this deeply emotional expression. Their services were far more measured in tone. Their singing, though spirited, was confined exclusively to traditional hymns, accompanied by no more than a piano or organ. They usually followed a set order of service. Even a raised hand during a hymn, let alone an electric guitar or collective extemporaneous prayer, would be greeted with horror. Nevertheless, the lengthy sermon in the second half of the service commonly dealt with the same themes of the saving power of a personal relationship with Christ. Here too, though less frequently, the sermon ended with a call to take up or renew the faith.

Though a religion of the heart was the dominant motif among Mexican Evangelicals, there was also what one might describe as an intellectual side, more pronounced among the historical denominations and Adventists but also evident among the Pentecostals. This strain stressed that theirs was the thinking person's religion. Their Catholic kin, Evangelicals said, were Catholics because of an unthinking obedience to tradition. Evangelicals, by contrast, insisted that they chose their faith after struggle and debate. Though the decisive event in their decision was often emotional in character, they were quick to assert that the only true source of religious knowledge was the Bible and only their faith was biblically based. They dismissed Catholics as uninformed and uncritical believers in superstition. This strain in Mexican Evangelicalism was most evident in the universal tradition of owning one's own Bible and bringing it to every service. When the pastor preached, he was constantly citing Bible passages for support, which all were urged to consult, to see for themselves that what the pastor said was demonstrably and unarguably true. There was also the tradition of the adult weekly Sunday school, typically of an hour's duration, before the morning worship service. Pastors admitted that half or fewer of their adult members now attended, but most had done so for a time in the past, and the mid-week services often had a straightforward biblical exposition as their theme. From my interview sample, 64 per cent of 447[6] said they read the Bible, apart from at church services, three or more times a week. A total of 88 per cent claimed they did so at least once a week. Pentecostals (63 per cent) were no less diligent in this regard than were members of the historical denominations (65 per cent). Even allowing for a measure of exaggeration, these figures suggest that the Bible played an important part in the daily life of many Evangelicals. When Evangelicals confronted Catholics, who rarely had any religious instruction beyond the catechism classes of their early youth, Evangelicals had the decided edge in biblically based debate. For not a few Evangelicals it was an appealing and reassuring notion that only their convictions had been reached by a careful weighing of the biblical evidence and that their faith alone was based on a provable, biblical foundation.

GLOSSOLALIA

Speaking in tongues, or glossolalia, was one of the more distinctive characteristics of Pentecostal religious practice. This vocal, often high-pitched, sing-song, pseudo-language was used as a form of prayer in both public worship and private devotions. Among tongues-speakers in the interview sample, a small minority (11 per cent of 147) usually spoke in tongues while alone in private prayer. Another 20 per cent normally did so in small devotional groups. By far the largest group (49 per cent) largely spoke in tongues during services. The remaining 20 per cent did so both publicly and privately. It was, then, most commonly associated with public worship, and it typically occurred at peaks of emotional intensity during the service, most notably in the period after the altar call.

As a tradition, speaking in tongues goes back to the Book of Acts in the New Testament and to the feast of Pentecost, just after the death of Christ, from which Pentecostals derive their name. Speaking in tongues is defined by Pentecostals as one of the "gifts of the Holy Spirit," granted to Christians after Christ's death as a means of sustaining a close relationship with God. Believers usually understand tongues to be a heavenly or spiritual language, though practitioners are sometimes said to speak a foreign language not known to them. This latter claim has never been confirmed by scientific investigation.[7]

Glossolalia was fervently rejected by the Baptists, Presbyterians, and Adventists I interviewed in Mexico. Adventist pastors were deeply opposed to its practice today, arguing on dispensationalist grounds that it was a practice suitable only for the early church. Presbyterians and Baptists were equally if not more opposed. Though they all acknowledged its biblical authenticity, they most frequently cited the requirements of Paul in 1 Corinthians that tongues were admissible only if practised in an orderly manner and only if accompanied by an interpretation. Since historical pastors dismissed speaking in tongues as inherently disorderly and gibberish, incapable of interpretation, they rejected the possibility of its ever being practised. Behind such visceral animosity lay their awareness of the appeal of tongues to not a few of their members (five of the Presbyterians I interviewed admitted that they had spoken in tongues, though none had publicly acknowledged it) and their resentment at having already lost members to the Pentecostals.

Pentecostals attached great importance to speaking in tongues because they believed it brought the believer into direct contact with the supernatural. In the words of the pastors, "It puts one in a deeper relationship with God"; "It is a sign that we have received the experience of being filled with the Holy Spirit"; and "It is important because it is direct communication through the Spirit with the Father." All the Pentecostal pastors I talked to denied that speaking in tongues was necessary to receive salvation, although 30 per cent said it was a sign of salvation. All agreed that glossolalia was something subsequent to salvation, which was marked by baptism with water. For the Assemblies of God, the largest Pentecostal denomination, speaking in tongues was the necessary sign of a second "baptism of the Holy Spirit," which was required of all pastors – though not of the rank and file. Other denominations said that this second baptism might occur without the outward sign of speaking in tongues, while a good number of pastors seemed to me uncertain of where exactly they stood on such theological details. All would agree that speaking in tongues was "a precious experience" that all should seek because it "brings one to God in prayer" and because it "edifies and strengthens" the believer.

Speaking in tongues was practised less frequently than one might think. A 1984 report on membership statistics for the Assemblies of God, for instance, listed only 38 per cent as baptized in the Holy Spirit.[8] Table 5.2, based on the 301 Pentecostals from my interview sample, reveals a higher percentage speaking in tongues, but here too the practice was far from universal. In all, 46 per cent had never spoken in tongues; another 7 per cent had done so only once; 34 per cent claimed they did so frequently.[9] Females, city dwellers, and the better educated appeared more likely to speak in tongues than did males, rural residents, and the less well educated, but none of the differences is especially striking. Equally noticeable is the lack of any decline in speaking in tongues in the second generation, which closely parallels the absence of any decline in church attendance over generations. Evangelicals dropped out in significant numbers in the second generation, but those who stayed remained highly committed. Like their pastors, the overwhelming majority (98 per cent of 160) of lay speakers in tongues denied that their gift was needed to achieve salvation, although here too 41 per cent saw tongues as a sign of salvation. Time and time again, those who spoke in tongues and made such disclaimers could not help but add that "Tongues are a sign of being filled with the Holy Spirit" and that they make one "feel more secure." Many of those who did not speak in tongues were vocal and emotional participants in extemporaneous prayer. All wanted to speak in tongues, but some had not been granted the gift. The many who lacked the gift of tongues were inevitably left with the nagging doubt that perhaps they lacked sufficient faith, or perhaps their salvation was less secure.

Only 9 per cent of tongues-speakers reported that they had first done so alone. Over half (61 per cent) said that their first experience occurred in a special service or smaller group designed to teach and

Table 5.2
Speaking in tongues among Pentecostals, interview sample

	Male %	Female %	1st gen. %	2nd gen. %	City %	Rural %	Low educ. %	High educ. %	Total %
Never	52	43	48	46	41	56	47	39	46
Once	6	8	10	4	7	8	9	0	7
Some	11	14	9	17	11	17	14	9	13
Often	31	35	33	33	41	20	30	52	34
Total	100%	100%	100%	100%	100%	100%	100%	100%	100%
	(106)	(195)	(183)	(98)	(165)	(106)	(201)	(33)	(301)

* The first generation of converts started attending an Evangelical church after age fifteen;
the second generation did so before age ten.
** Low education is completed primary or less, while high education is completed secondary
or more.

encourage tongues-speaking. The remainder (30 per cent) did so at a regularly organized service or small prayer group. Especially at the end of the service, when the altar call was made, the would-be tongues-speaker found himself or herself surrounded by practised speakers, who, by their demeanour and example, encouraged the breakthrough to tongues. It was very much a learned and taught practice, although the 46 per cent in the sample who did not speak in tongues, despite such aid and encouragement, indicate that not all could master the gift.

Pentecostals all agreed that, biblically, speaking in tongues might be accompanied by its interpretation, either by the speaker or by someone else. They rejected the Baptist and Presbyterian view that the two ought always to go together. They believed that tongues speaking without interpretation was for the personal edification of the speaker. When it was for the benefit of all, then an interpretation was thought to be appropriate. They also recognized as biblically sound the gift of prophecy, whereby a believer might receive a message from God to be shared with the congregation. In practice, pastors were extremely wary of these latter gifts, which they endeavoured to control whenever they could.[10] Only three of the twenty-nine Pentecostal pastors I interviewed allowed interpretation on a regular basis. In one case the main practitioner was the pastor's wife, and in another only a select group of trusted lay leaders were allowed to exercise the privilege without first informing the pastor of their message and gaining his approval. Another fifteen reluctantly and rarely allowed interpretations, while the remaining eleven said it was not a practice in their own church, despite the biblical foundation of the tradition. What they wanted to hear were interpretations of a general encouraging and uplifting nature. It was interpretations of a more specific nature, especially those involving the condemnation of individuals for wrong behaviour, that pastors feared. In the intimate atmosphere of the typical congregation the consequences of the latter type of interpretation could be extremely divisive. In one case the much-loved teenage son of the pastor was accused – falsely, I was assured – of causing a female member of the congregation to become pregnant. In another incident, a lady member of the congregation was moved in an interpretation to accuse the female pastor of undefined immorality. Since the pastor was unmarried and a young man was thought to be courting her, the disruption was considerable and several people left the church on this account. The damage caused by such incidents was all the greater precisely because the imputed source of the charge was God, not just the individual making the interpretation or prophecy.

The traditions of emotional fervour, speaking in tongues, and its related gifts are what might be described in sociological terms as mixed blessings for the Evangelical world. On the one hand, much of the energy, drive, and appeal of Pentecostalism derives from this ecstatic tradition. Pastors and laity alike stressed to me that speaking in tongues was an important ritual mechanism for reinforcing and refurbishing their strong sense of religious commitment. On the other hand, for the almost half of all Pentecostals who did not seem to be able to master the gift or technique, their failure left them with a general sense of anxiety over their religious status, and perhaps even a sense of failure. The gifts of interpretation and prophecy also tended to allow, if not actually encourage, the venting of many of the frictions, jealousies, and animosities that inevitably developed in such small, closely knit worlds. Perhaps these were some of the reasons for the higher drop-out rates in the Pentecostal world than in the historical denominations.

FAITH HEALING

Faith healing, or "divine healing," as Evangelicals called it, was another of the gifts of the Holy Spirit. Through prayer, it is believed, God enacts or causes miraculous healings to occur that cannot be explained by modern scientific medicine. Pentecostals gave faith healing far more emphasis in their preaching and teaching than did either the Adventists or the historical denominations. However, Evangelicals of all stripes placed great importance on the power of prayer in healing illness. As Table 5.3 shows, a full 84 per cent of

Table 5.3
Personal experience of faith-healing among Evangelicals, interview sample

Advt	Hist.	Pent.	Male	Female	1st gen.*	2nd gen.*	City	Rural	Total
77%	70%	91%	82%	85%	88%	78%	88%	82%	84%
(35)	(138)	(292)	(169)	(296)	(245)	(188)	(225)	(168)	(465)

* The first generation of converts started attending an Evangelical church after age fifteen; the second generation did so before age ten.

my interview sample claimed to have had a personal experience themselves or observed a divine healing in someone close to them. Males and females did not significantly differ here, while converts, who might have been expected to be more enthusiastic than those raised in the faith, were only slightly more likely to claim such an experience. Rural/urban and educational differences were of an equally low order of magnitude. Denominational differences were more pronounced, with over 90 per cent of Pentecostals claiming to have personally observed faith healing, while almost a third of the members of the historical denominations said they had not done so. It was also my impression from listening to their accounts that Presbyterians and Baptists were less likely than Pentecostals to describe their experiences in dramatic, emotional, and instantaneous terms. More concretely, Table 4.8 showed that Pentecostal converts were more than twice as likely as converts to the historical denominations to claim that a divine healing precipitated their conversion. The fact still remains that more than two-thirds of Adventists, Presbyterians, and Baptists claimed that they had personally experienced or observed God's miraculous healing power.

Laying on of hands was sometimes practised by church leaders during prayers for the sick. Some people were seen to have a healing ministry or to be specially blessed with the gift of healing. However, any tendency to attribute healings to humans was flatly denied by all the pastors I interviewed, including the Pentecostals. They were all adamant that only God heals and that God could work through the prayers of any believer. They rejected any magical notion that humans might control the supernatural or that any particular formula or technique might guarantee healing. Though God was seen as omnipotent and therefore capable of any healing, no matter how severe the condition, it was everywhere recognized that prayers did not always produce the prayed-for healing. When the illness was not healed, Evangelicals attributed this to three major causes. The first was lack of faith on the part of either the sick person or one of those praying. The second was a state of sin, and therefore of unworthiness, again in either the sick individual or among those praying. The third was that healing ultimately depended on the will of God. Sometimes healing was delayed or denied by God to lead a non-believer to conversion, or to test and thereby deepen a believer's faith, as in the classic case of Job. In other cases, pastors admitted, no discernible reason was apparent: even for the faithful, God's plans were sometimes a mystery. Moreover, neither lack of faith nor a state of sin were universal obstacles to healing, since it was recognized that the sinful and faithless were sometimes healed in order to bring them to conversion, or for reasons that only God understands. Within this framework, the absence of healing in the face of prayers did not disconfirm the believer's expectations. In other words, faith or divine healing, cast in these terms, could not be subject to empirical or scientific evaluation.

The above set of understandings was clearly and explicitly expressed by some pastors, but many others only came to it after my efforts to probe alternatives and logical consistencies. The explanations pastors gave to me and to their adherents often differed in emphasis from the account summarized above. This selective emphasis was then further magnified in the understandings of the laity. Table 5.4 shows that 40 per cent of pastors and 71 per cent of the laity said they were certain that a sick person with faith would be healed if prayers were conducted on their behalf. The tendency was much more marked among Pentecostals than in the historical denominations. This affirmation was not consistent with the above general account, but it does reveal the heavy emphasis all Evangelicals placed on the power of God and faith. Any other answer, they feared, might cast doubt on God's power and compassion. When asked (see Table 5.5) if lack of faith is always the cause of an illness that persists in a church member after having received prayers for healing, only 6 per cent of pastors agreed, but 28 per cent of the laity did so. In other words, few pastors thought that lack of faith was the major obstacle to healing, but their emphasis on the importance of faith led more than a quarter of their laity to think so.[11]

Only three of the forty-nine pastors had any reservations about making use of modern medicine or seeking the treatment of doctors. All were Pentecostals. Two expressed no more than a general warning that it would be sinful to resort first and only to modern medicine without seeking divine assistance, though they acknowledged that medicine could freely be made use of after prayer. Only one pastor actively discouraged the use of medical treatment, "unless their job requires medical proof of illness or if a close relative obliges them or their child to go. Anyone who goes voluntarily

Table 5.4
Faith-healing and certainty over efficacy*, interview sample

	Advt	Hist.	Pent.	Total
Pastors	0% (3)	20% (15)	53% (30)	40% (48)
Laity	72% (36)	54% (140)	79% (292)	71% (468)

*Percentage saying yes to the question: "If a sick brother or sister with faith receives prayers to be healed, are you certain the person is going to be healed?"

Table 5.5
Failed faith-healing and lack of faith,* interview and pastor samples

	Advt	Hist.	Pent.	Total
Pastors	0% (3)	0% (15)	10% (30)	6% (48)
Laity	33% (36)	16% (141)	33% (289)	28% (466)

* Percentage saying yes to the question: "If a member in full communion is sick and receives prayers to be healed, but the illness continues, are you certain that the person lacks faith?"

loses their right to attend the Lord's Supper." Among the laity, only 3 per cent defined it as a definite sin to seek a doctor's aid, while another 3 per cent said it might be under certain circumstances. All but one (of twenty-nine) were Pentecostals.

Evangelical acceptance of medicine was also to be found in the Indigenous municipality of Oxchuc, Chiapas, where Evangelical converts were one of the groups most open to the use of modern medicine and hygienic measures.[12] Even those who later dropped out of the Evangelical world did not re-embrace the magical healing practices of their former Christo-Mayan faith.[13] In a Mestizo community in the same state a decade later, Dirksen found that very few Catholics or Pentecostals expressed low confidence in modern medicine, but Catholics were significantly more likely to express high confidence. Dirksen saw this as evidence that Pentecostals were making an incomplete transition to a naturalistic view of illness. I am less certain, since Pentecostals resorted to doctors far more than they did to pastors, and the great majority expressed a moderate confidence in modern medicine. The mediocre quality of medical care in remote areas like this may have shaped some responses. Dirksen's data suggest to me that Pentecostals accepted modern medicine, but in doing so they did not wish to reject the power of God and their faith. Thus they expressed a moderate support for medicine in order to allow for their religious views.[14] It may not be a case of one or the other.

That Evangelicals so widely embraced divine healing should not be that surprising, since a religious problem-solving perspective, as I have already suggested, abounded in the popular classes from which Evangelicals were drawn. In the same poorer strata, chronic diseases of gastroenteritis, bronchitis, and the like were endemic, creating an abundant pool of sick in need of healing.[15] In rural areas medical services were sometimes not readily available. In urban areas the poor often could not afford them. The public medical clinics to which the poor sometimes resorted were typically overworked and staffed by young, inexperienced doctors.[16] I was often told that the medicines provided by such institutions were sometimes old and/or defective. Only in this context can the widespread acceptance of divine healing be fully understood, though such comments should not in any way diminish the influence of the central Evangelical belief that theirs is a God with power and a desire to heal his faithful.

Modern science and medicine now admit that ritual healing of this sort may work. Besides what scientists describe as spontaneous remission, the "placebo effect" is now a recognized, experimentally proven factor influencing healing outcomes. By placebo effect is meant "any therapeutic practice" that has "no experimentally proven clinical effect"[17] despite its demonstrable influence. Recent research shows that healing is most enhanced when there is strong faith by the patient in the healer, when the practitioner expresses deep confidence in the efficacy of his therapy, and when the situation is surrounded by uncertainty.[18] Such conditions surely apply to divine healings among Mexican Evangelicals, especially in those cases where medical treatment could not be obtained or had proved ineffective. Science and Evangelical Mexicans would thus concur that faith may sometimes produce healing among the sick. Science, of course, does not accept, though it cannot disprove, the assertion that God is the prime healer.

Very few of the Evangelicals I interviewed regarded recourse to doctors and medicine as sinful, but there was far greater uncertainty over the broader question of whether such practices signified a lack of faith. Table 5.6 shows that, among the Adventists and historical churches, only two of eighteen pastors admitted that recourse to a doctor might sometimes be a sign of a lack of faith, but approximately a quarter of their rank-and-file members thought it might be. Among Pentecostals, by contrast, only 42 per cent of pastors and 29 per cent of members were prepared to deny the possibility. The great majority of Pentecostals were roughly equally divided between those who thought recourse to medicine was always a symptom of lack of faith and those who thought it was only sometimes so. In short, popular conceptions of divine healing

Table 5.6
Use of medical services and lack of faith,* interview and pastor samples

	Pastors %				Lay members %			
	Advt	Hist.	Pent.	Total	Advt	Hist.	Pent.	Total
Yes	0	0	29	18	11	9	39	28
Maybe	0	13	29	23	17	15	32	26
No	100	87	42	59	72	77	29	47
Total	100%	100%	100%	100%	100%	100%	100%	100%
	(3)	(15)	(31)	(49)	(36)	(141)	(294)	(471)

* Percentage saying yes to the question: "Does a sick person who goes to the doctor lack faith?"

abounded that cast doubt on the depth and authenticity of the faith – and hence the salvation – of believers who turned to doctors, despite official teaching.

MILLENNIALISM

The doctrine that Christ will return was regarded as biblical by all the pastors I interviewed and was therefore defined as a central teaching. There were notable denominational differences. Since the total sample of pastors is only forty-eight and I did not question the laity on this topic, there is little point in putting what follows in table form. Baptists and traditional Pentecostals almost all agreed that the Second Coming was one of their most heavily emphasized teachings, while the Presbyterians and neo-Pentecostals downplayed its importance. The greater Pentecostal attention to this theme was reflected in the half (53 per cent) of their pastors who said they were certain or very hopeful that Christ would return in their own lifetime, though an equal number simply said they did not know. Baptists were slightly more hopeful (63 per cent), while five of the six Presbyterian pastors (83 per cent) stressed that they did not and could not know. The vast majority of Pentecostal pastors said that there would be a time of suffering or tribulation here on earth when Christ returned. Baptists agreed, while Presbyterians avoided the topic on the grounds that they did not know when and if a time of tribulation might come, or who might suffer from it. On the related doctrine of the rapture, which asserts that believers, and believers alone, will rise up to join with Christ in triumph on his return, it was once more the Pentecostals and Baptists who stressed this. They were almost unanimous in their conviction that the rapture would take place just before Christ's return, enabling them to escape the tribulation, the inevitable destiny of all non-believers.

These pre-millennialist doctrines had an obvious appeal for the poor and dispossessed. They offered the hope of an imminent end to the current dispensation and promised that only believers would share in the glory of a new world order with Christ, while all others would suffer the tribulation. Nevertheless, these beliefs were not, in my experience, key or central guides to Evangelical thought and conduct. Though Baptist and Pentecostal pastors said they were an important part of their teachings, it was my impression that they were rarely expounded in the complete form outlined above. They were a part of formal doctrine more than of living faith. Of the over fifty Pentecostal services I attended in Mexico over the last several years, only once did I hear such pre-millennialist beliefs clearly presented. This was in the weeks just following the Mexico City earthquake, when with well over a 100 per cent rate of annual inflation and devaluation added on, not only Evangelicals were inclined to think that the end was near. Only one Evangelical died in the earthquake, said the Pentecostal pastor, and he was the apostate son of a Presbyterian pastor. Christ's imminent return was frequently stressed as a source of hope and as a reminder of the need to live a fully Christian life. But the emphasis was primarily on the need to convert and to be saved now, rather than on the details and events of future last days and their consequences. Despite the presence of millennialist doctrines among many denominations, they were at best a minor element in the Mexican Evangelical world-view.[19]

The Adventist pastors I spoke to paid little heed to the tribulation and rapture, despite their formal adherence to the doctrine of the Second Coming. They did not profess any clear certainty or conviction that Christ would return in their own lifetime. They were distinguished by two other sets of belief, both related to their heavy emphasis on the importance of the Old Testament. The first centred on a strict adherence to the dietary laws of the Old Testament, which were interpreted and expanded to include prohibitions on coffee, tea, tobacco, and alcohol as well as pork and seafood. The other more distancing belief was their insistence that the Jewish Sabbath of Friday evening to Saturday evening be observed.[20] Thus Adventists seeking employment were sometimes severely restricted, for many Mexican employers expected their employees to work Friday evenings and/or part or all of Saturday.

ASCETICISM AND WORLDLY SUCCESS

Asceticism, or the rejection of worldly pleasures, was a central and pervasive preoccupation of Evangelicals of all denominations.

Though tobacco was a universal taboo, largely on health grounds, it did not provoke much passion. Consumption of alcohol in any amount was far more vigorously condemned by all the clergy. Over three-quarters (83 per cent) dismissed it as an unacceptable sin. The remainder, while admitting that an occasional beer might not be sinful in and of itself, still condemned the practice because of the former alcoholics in their ranks and because "the world is watching us, and we must give a good witness." So great was the taboo on drinking that it and sexual relations outside of marriage were the two grounds that all pastors identified as automatic grounds for excommunication or loss of membership. Pastors were equally unprepared to condone attendance at dances of any kind, though far more Pentecostal pastors (84 per cent) than Presbyterians and Baptists (64 per cent) defined this practice as an invariable and intrinsic sin. The latter were more inclined to stress that it was the environment of a dance to which they objected rather than the act itself. One lone liberal Presbyterian claimed he could not condemn a family dance, though he admitted that none of his elders would agree. Their lay members, judging by my interviews, concurred, as 77 per cent of the 461 who responded condemned all types of dances as categorically sinful. Only 3 per cent said they were not. Apart from the minority who objected to dances because of the attendant temptations of alcohol, drugs, and the like, the remaining great majority did so on three grounds. The principal reason was that dancing "provokes the flesh" and "awakens one's carnal appetites." It was therefore "contrary to spiritual life" because it was "a practice of the world and we have renounced them" after conversion and rebirth. Secondly, respondents condemned attending dances because "it gives a bad witness" to those whom Evangelicals were trying to convert. "If they see a brother at a dance, they say all dance, and there is no distinction between one and the other." Thirdly, as reborn people, not a few Evangelicals claimed that they were no longer drawn by "the things of the flesh," and that "now it has no appeal for me." To attend a dance was to admit to such earthly desires and to acknowledge that one's own salvation was in jeopardy. The unintended consequence was that Evangelical churches found it extremely uncomfortable and practically impossible to create social situations, and of course dances, where their young people might be encouraged to mix with matrimony in mind. Such opposition may partly explain why mixed marriages and drop-out rates in the second generation were so high.

Other worldly pursuits were judged less harshly, but here too there were many restrictions. A quarter (23 per cent) of the pastors and almost half (42 per cent) of the laity said that attending a cinema was allowable, depending on the film. Yet 93 per cent of the laity denied that they ever did so, and over half (58 per cent) condemned the practice under any circumstances. Not quite half (47 per cent) of pastors were prepared to condone a member of their congregation being a member of a local sports club or team. The figure rose to 53 per cent of the 415 lay members of the congregation who answered this question, though approval fell to 45 per cent of Pentecostals. A majority of both pastors and Pentecostals disapproved. They did so because they feared that the attendant social life, with what was invariably a largely Catholic team, would offer too many sinful temptations. Since Sunday was the principal playing day for most sports and leagues, there was the further concern that sports involvement would weaken religious commitment. Had I pressed this conflict with the lay respondents, the percentage condoning this pursuit would surely have diminished.

For women, questions of wearing make-up often provoked a blush when I asked. Almost a third (31 per cent) condemned any make-up as sinful, although an equally large segment (30 per cent) denied that make-up had anything to do with sin. The remaining 39 per cent, the largest single category, hedged their answers, saying it depended on the person and the amount of make-up, or that it was probably better not to use it, even if it was not a clear sin.[21] Only a minority of Evangelical churches in the 1980s insisted on veils, long dresses, and the uncut hair of the past. In some smaller and conservative denominations, most notably in the countryside, segregation of the sexes was still the norm. Here a bow in the hair was still regarded as rather daring. In general, female Evangelical attire continued to be governed by far more conservative and chaste rules than was evident in the general public.

When it came to watching television, again very few pastors (6 per cent) or laity (3 per cent) were prepared to say it was categorically sinful, but only 15 per cent of the former and 31 per cent of the latter said it was not. The great majority of the 454 surveyed expressed reservations about the sinful consequences of TV watching, depending on the program, the amount of time devoted to it, the maturity of the person, and whether it interfered with any church service or religious responsibility. Even with all these qualifications, the "telenovelas," or evening soap operas so devoutly and widely watched throughout Mexico, were condoned by only 48 per cent of the interview sample, though I suspect many more watched than this figure suggests.

The above was far from a complete list of earthly pleasures, but it encompassed most of those embraced by the classes from which Evangelicals were drawn. Drinking, gambling, social life organized around bars, avid pursuit of sports, and the frequenting of houses of prostitution were all predominantly male recreational pursuits. Among the 217 in the main interview sample who converted after the age of twenty, 92 per cent of the females said they drank little or not at all before conversion, compared to 40 per cent of the men. The remaining 60 per cent of men drank regularly most weekends, or to even greater excess. Similarly, 28 per cent of the women but 67 per cent of the men smoked before their conversion. Both practices now, of course, are utterly taboo. For men, conversion and commitment entailed a radical break with past behaviour and with the social norms of right and proper behaviour associated with their gender. Women, too, were expected to change, but the typical transformation was hardly on the same scale as for men. Nor were transgressions of the female pleasures of make-up and telenovelas treated with the same severity as the male sin of drinking, which was grounds for severe chastisement and loss of membership. It is hardly surprising that fewer men than women converted and that fewer males in the second generation remained committed.

These ascetic practices raise the related issue of whether and to what degree Evangelical affiliation led to material or economic improvement. Since most Mexican Evangelicals were Pentecostals, the details of Max Weber's original essay on the links between Calvinistic Protestantism and capitalism in Europe need not concern us here. Other investigators on this theme in Mexico have focused on peasant, rural, and often Indigenous communities. Though there were dissenting voices, the general consensus was that Evangelical conversion and commitment were linked with greater accumulation of wealth, increased literacy, and some upward mobility.[22] The crucial element, especially in Indigenous communities, was the Evangelical refusal to drink alcohol or to take part in the costly system of *cofradias*, which sponsored religious festivals, where copious amounts of alcohol, incense, and fireworks were employed, leaving many peasants in an indebted, impoverished state. Evangelicals also made no use of the services of the shamans, whose services were expensive.[23] Annis estimates that, in the socially and culturally similar Guatemalan highlands, at least a quarter of Indigenous household income was devoted to traditional Catholic ritual expenses; such calculations did not include the additional costs of shamans or taking on a leadership position in a religious festival.[24] Even assuming 10 per cent tithing by Evangelicals, conversion freed a significant amount of wealth for other investments. In comparing

Evangelicals and Catholics, Annis also shows that Evangelicals put a greater stress on education, were more likely to innovate by pursuing "higher-paid, upwardly mobile occupations that lead to small businesses," and had higher agricultural incomes, even though "most Protestant converts" had formerly been "dispossessed peasants."[25] No hard data comparable to that of Annis exist for Mexican Evangelicals, but the more impressionistic accounts for Indigenous Mexicans do not differ in any substantial degree from his conclusions.[26]

My own information, drawn from the interview sample, is confined to Mestizo communities for all but one congregation. To assess whether conversion made an economic difference, I asked converts whether their living standard and income had improved since conversion. Upward mobility was evaluated by comparing current with conversion occupation. Recorded answers were confined to converts with five or more years in the Evangelical world on the rather arbitrary grounds that this was the minimum period of time needed for conversion to make a difference. Of this sample of 184, Table 5.7 shows that 55 per cent of men but only 29 per cent of women said that their living standard had improved. For a time-span sometimes as short as five years, this is an impressive figure for men, but the far lower level for women equally stands out. They differed because female converts were much more likely to be out of the labour-force and/or economically dependent on someone who was not an Evangelical convert.[27] In contrast to male converts, far fewer females controlled their own economic destiny. Many lacked the power to convert any changed attitudes they might acquire into real economic improvement.

Though the same table shows that 40 per cent of all converts claimed their living standard had improved, a much smaller proportion (21 per cent) said that their income had grown. The disparity is attributable to the 19 per cent in the sample who said that they or their converted husband earned no more money than formerly but now devoted their wages to the family rather than to drink, extramarital sex, or a host of former vices. Almost half of the overall improvement had nothing to do with an increase in economic resources but rather with a better use of them. In the other cases, the converts said that their own or their spouse's income had increased because they were more diligent, hard working, organized, or focused in their post-conversion occupation. Approximately a seventh (14 per cent) experienced some degree of upward mobility, in the sense that they acquired a better job or shifted from being an employee to owning their own small business. Though I

Table 5.7
Economic changes among converts with five or more years in the faith,
interview sample

	Advt	Hist.	Pent.	Female	Male	Total
Better living standard	36%	56%	34%	29%	55%	40%
Higher income	36%	42%	13%	15%	31%	21%
Upwardly mobile	27%	31%	7%	10%	20%	14%
Total no.	11	45	128	108	75	183

Table 5.8
Occupational trends over generations: Evangelicals aged 20–50 in labour force,
congregational sample

	Hist. %		Pent. %		Total %	
	Convt*	2nd gen.*	Convt	2nd gen.	Convt	2nd gen.
Manager/director	4	1	0	1	1	1
Professionals	18	34	4	11	9	22
Shopkeepers/						
supervisors/clerks	21	35	12	21	15	27
Trades/skilled	10	7	30	24	23	17
Unskilled	31	16	44	26	39	23
Agriculture	17	6	11	16	13	10
Total	100%	100%	100%	100%	100%	100%
	(83)	(82)	(183)	(87)	(285)	(184)

* The first generation of converts started attending an Evangelical church after age fifteen; the
second generation did so before age ten.

have no available basis of comparison with Catholics, in the economic chaos of the 1980s this seems an impressive achievement, especially for the 20 per cent of men who claimed to have done so.

Equally if not more crucial is the question of whether Evangelicals rose on the social ladder over generations. Table 5.8 provides
some insight by comparing the occupational distribution of converts with that of the second generation, raised in the Evangelical
faith. To reduce the impact of the older age structure of converts, I
confined analysis to those in the labour force between the ages of 20
and 50.[28] Following the format of Table 4.1,[29] the occupational categories are again broad and rather crude, but the general patterns
seem clear. From first to second generation, the proportion of unskilled workers fell from 39 per cent to 23 per cent. The proportion
of Evangelicals in higher management and administration remained insignificant in the second generation, but the white-collar
sector of shopkeepers, office workers, and supervisors rose from 15

per cent in the first generation to 27 per cent in the second. Even more striking is the growth in professional occupations, from 9 to 22 per cent, though in both generations well over half the professionals were in the lower strata of teachers, nurses, technicians, and the like. Overall, Evangelicals experienced a widespread though modest measure of upward mobility over generations.

Marked denominational differences may also be discerned in Tables 5.7 and 5.8. Leaving aside the Adventists, whose very small numbers make generalization problematic, we can have rather more confidence in the consistent differences between the larger group of Pentecostals on the one hand and Presbyterians and Baptists on the other. By all three measures in Table 5.7, economic advance was more prevalent in the historical denominations, where 31 per cent of converts were upwardly mobile, as opposed to 7 per cent of Pentecostals. Not surprisingly, Table 5.8 reveals that the typically poorer and lower-class background of Pentecostals in the first generation persisted into the second. Material advance, it would seem, was more prevalent in the historical churches. Since Pentecostals were probably more numerous in the Evangelical world than these samples indicate, the overall rate of Evangelical advance was probably more modest. Nevertheless, 34 per cent of Pentecostal converts said their standard of living had risen since conversion, and their proportion of professionals tripled from first to second generation, while those in unskilled occupations fell by almost half. Asceticism may therefore be a cost or price that erodes the commitment of some, but it reaps benefits for others over the long haul, which may enhance commitment.

THE STATUS OF WOMEN

Attitudes towards women were another crucial and, some might say, perplexing element in the Evangelical world-view. The centrality of this issue stemmed from the simple fact that so many Evangelicals were women. In previous chapters we saw that 63 per cent of converts were women and that the drop-out rate for males in the second generation (57 per cent) was almost twice as high as it was for women (29 per cent). The result, seen in Table 5.9, was that females were 64 per cent of the 1,410 members enumerated in the congregational sample. Table 5.10, which summarizes my headcount of males and females actually attending the major Sunday service in twenty-three congregations,[30] indicates that females were even more prevalent, accounting for 67 per cent of attenders. The same table shows that this pattern extended throughout the

Table 5.9
Females across Evangelical world, congregational sample

Advt	Hist.	Pent.	1st gen.*	2nd gen.*	Rural	City	Total
61%	67%	63%	63%	67%	67%	64%	64%
(116)	(468)	(826)	(745)	(528)	(493)	(684)	(1,410)

* The first generation of converts started attending an Evangelical church after age fifteen; the second generation did so before age ten.

Table 5.10
Female attendance at main Sunday service

Advt	Hist.	Pent.	Total
67% (140)	65% (452)	68% (922)	67% (1,514)

Evangelical world.[31] It has also existed for a very long time; a national survey of Evangelical churches done in the late 1930s found that 65 per cent of the members were women.[32] The Evangelical world then was predominantly female. During mid-week, when outside work caused many men to arrive home late, the preponderance of women was even more striking.

Table 4.8 shows that over half of female converts (56 per cent) were led to their conversion by their desire to resolve acute problems of illness, widowhood, desertion, or abusive husbands. We will see in the next chapter that Evangelical churches sometimes served as a haven or refuge for women, but the Evangelical world was no defender of female equality. Male power in the Evangelical world was absolute. Hardly any pastor thought it should be otherwise. Among the historical denominations, the Presbyterian church barred women from being pastors, elders, and deacons.[33] The Baptist insistence on congregational autonomy meant there was no official policy, but I was unable to find any instance of a female Baptist pastor in Mexico. Pentecostals had a long tradition of female pastors, but they were very much an occasional exception to a general rule of male hegemony. In the large Assemblies of God, for instance, women were allowed to become licensed ministers with the right to preach and lead services, but a prayer of dedication at the end of a service could only be done by a male pastor or deacon. Women were also barred from higher ministerial office, and they could not administer the sacraments of the Lord's Supper, marriage, or baptism. One of the Assemblies of God pastors I interviewed was a woman with her own congregation, but she admitted she was a rarity, and she chafed at the need to import a male pastor for any important religious ceremony. The preferred pattern was for the Bible-institute-trained woman to serve in a supporting role to men, either as a missionary or as the co-pastor, with her husband in charge.

Of the 20 Pentecostal pastors I queried on attitudes to female pastors, 14 said a man was preferable, 5 said women were unacceptable under any circumstances, and only 1 (5 per cent) claimed no gender preference. In the historical denominations, only 1 of the 6 felt gender should not be an issue. On the related issue of whether females should be deacons or senior lay leaders within the congregation, a majority still expressed a preference for men; 42 per cent here professed no gender bias. Only in the lesser leadership posts of running the youth group, Sunday school, or the like did a majority feel that gender should not be a consideration, though more than a third (37 per cent) still preferred male leaders. At this third tier, pastoral inclinations were least strongly expressed, but the overall bias for male leadership was clear. Besides the doctrinal arguments drawn from Paul and examples of the all-male apostles, pastors justified their preference on the basis that "emotionally she is weaker," that "we are more responsible," or that, for a male leader "there is more respect and authority."

Table 5.11 shows that the lay members of the congregations were rather more open to female leadership, though they also reflect the teachings of the pastors and probably the general assumptions of Mexican society regarding the status of women. Only on the issue of pastors did a clear majority (60 per cent) either reject a female categorically (29 per cent) or express a preference for a man (31 per cent). Opposition to female deacons dropped to about a quarter of those questioned, while 89 per cent felt that gender should not be a factor in choosing other congregational positions of leadership. Denominational differences were small or non-existent, though in fact women in leadership positions were more common among Pentecostals. For no reason I can discern, rural folk appeared to be somewhat less biased against female leaders than were city residents. Predictably, women were more open than men to female leadership, but a 54 per cent majority of the 148 Evangelical women I polled still expressed a preference for a male pastor. Those women who were categorically opposed produced many of the same explanations as their pastors and husbands, arguing that "we have a temperament different from men" and that "the man is the head of everything, and he can handle things better." Only a quarter of women (25 per cent) agreed with such opinions. In clear disagreement were the almost half (46 per cent) of all Evangelical women who firmly denied

Table 5.11
Lay attitudes to female church leadership: percentage support no gender bias,
interview sample

	Hist.	Pent.	Female	Male	City	Rural	1st gen.	2nd gen.	Total
Pastor	41%	39%	46%	26%	34%	48%	33%	46%	40%
	(61)	(156)	(148)	(69)	(102)	(104)	(116)	(89)	(217)
Deacon	66%	77%	77%	68%	71%	80%	75%	72%	74%
	(62)	(150)	(146)	(66)	(101)	(99)	(110)	(90)	(212
Dept/	89%	89%	95%	77%	88%	90%	86%	92%	89%
Head	(63)	(158)	(152)	(69)	(102)	(107)	(117)	(92)	(221)

any preference for male pastors and claimed that "in the eyes of
God there is no distinction between man and woman." The remaining third (30 per cent) who said a man was preferable as a pastor
tended to do so rather reluctantly, pointing to the greater freedom of
men to answer calls late at night, or simply shrugging and saying
"we are accustomed to always having a man."

Many of the above opinions would make a feminist convulse, but
it must be remembered that these were overwhelmingly poor, uneducated women, of whom two-thirds (69 per cent) were outside
the paid labour-force, with little experience of the world beyond
their immediate homes and neighbourhood. Many of the converts
in their ranks were also tough, independent women who typically
met with much criticism and opposition from Catholic husband
and relatives in the face of their decision to convert.[34] Brusco, who
writes of Evangelicals in Colombia, suggests that women were
drawn to the Evangelical world because it cured their husbands of
their former vices, turning them into model family men who thereafter devoted their money and energy to the care of children and
spouse.[35] One female convert told me that life was better since her
husband converted because "he no longer beats me." Almost all
claimed that family life was more harmonious. Faced with these
circumstances, many Mexican Evangelical women would prefer, it
seems, a responsible if authoritarian husband to an abusive or absent one. Herein lies the essential appeal of the Evangelical doctrine
that the man is to be the head of the household, just as the pastor
guides his church and a male God wisely and justly rules over all.

The dilemma for women was that ascetic, puritanical, and pro-
family values were one of the major obstacles to male conversion.
It may be recalled from the last chapter (Tables 4.6 and 4.7) that 33
per cent of married female converts still had Catholic husbands.[36]
When the widowed, divorced, and separated are added to their

ranks, less than half (49 per cent) of once-married Evangelical women had an Evangelical spouse. Perhaps most aspired to one, but the practical prospects were generally slim. For this majority of Evangelical female converts without spouses, the doctrine of a paternalistic family ideal had little relevance. They accepted it because it was biblically based, because it might be better than what they had, and because of the sexist notions that pervaded Mexican society. In practice if not in doctrine, what they found in Evangelical churches were many other women like themselves, without males and in need of mutual support.

EXCLUSIVISM AND CATHOLICISM

The last and most fundamental characteristic of the Evangelical world-view to be addressed here is their exclusivism. By this I mean their conviction that their faith is the only true faith and that all others are therefore false, heretical, and dangerous. Respect for other religions and faiths was not a part of their lexicon. This exclusivism was sometimes extended inward. Thus 27 per cent of Pentecostals (206) said they had doubts about whether members of the historical denominations were "true Christians," while 18 per cent of the latter (96) said the same of Pentecostals. As for Adventists, 26 per cent of all other Evangelicals questioned the authenticity of the Adventist faith. About half of Adventists felt the same about Pentecostals, Presbyterians, and Baptists. Mutual suspicions of this sort may be the inevitable consequence of the extreme seriousness with which Evangelicals regard their faith, but this exclusivism also contributed to the deeply divided state of the Evangelical world, which I explore in the next chapter.

Exclusivism was most clearly and forcefully directed against Catholicism. Evangelicals believed that Catholics were not real Christians. Doctrinally, most Evangelical pastors said that only God knew if a person had been saved. In theory, they accepted that even Catholics might accept Christ as their personal saviour and thereby attain salvation. Yet in my interviews with pastors, only one, a rare liberal Presbyterian, was prepared to affirm that Catholics were true Christians and part of the body of Christ. Another 44 per cent professed grave doubts, and the remaining 54 per cent flatly rejected the possibility. As for the lay members of their congregations, they were even more emphatic: 79 per cent denied that Catholics were true Christians, while just 3 per cent were prepared to embrace them as equal partners in the Christian world.

It would be fruitless to review an Evangelical critique of Catholic doctrine, for this was not their fundamental objection, though Evangelicals were convinced that Catholicism distorted basic Christian truth. Given the opportunity, Evangelicals were happy to tell one of the corruption, avarice, and other failings of the Catholic clergy, although they were reluctant to raise this at first for fear of alienating potential converts. The core objection of Evangelicals was that Mexican Catholics "practice idolatry" by "worshipping images" rather than God and Christ. Catholics, said the pastors, "do not have a personal relationship with Jesus Christ," which for Evangelicals was the *sine qua non* of salvation. Evangelicals focused their condemnation on the religious practices, customs, and traditions of the mass of the Catholic population, claiming Catholics worshipped dead representations rather than a living God. Catholicism they dismissed as a pre-Hispanic vestige dressed up in Roman error, which was as pagan as it was heretical. In the adversarial language of not a few Evangelicals, Catholic Mexico was a "nation of virgin worshippers."

Less partisan observers would agree that Mexican folk Catholicism is distinguished by its focus on and devotion to a variety of saints, some of the most notable of whom are female.[37] The best-known example is the dark-skinned Virgin of Guadalupe, sometimes known as the Mother of Mexico, who appeared before Juan Diego, an Indian, in 1531, just twelve years after the conquest. When Diego was not believed by his sceptical bishop, he was told by the Virgin to gather roses in his cloak and bring them to his bishop, who found the cloak to have an image of the Virgin pressed upon it. A shrine was built in her honour on the former site of the temple dedicated to Tonantzin, the Aztec mother of the gods. The image of the Virgin of Guadalupe now hangs in the homes of many Catholics. Each year millions make pilgrimage to the vast basilica erected on her behalf, to pay homage and to make sacrificial offerings for answered prayers.

Scattered throughout Mexico are a host of local virgins and saints, each with her or his separate festival, shrine, and devout following. In a village near where this was written, an annual festival had just been held to honour the patron saint of the community, the Virgin of the Nativity, as the local posters proclaimed, though a more intellectual and centralized Catholicism would say that she was but one manifestation of the Virgin Mary. In the church she occupied the central place above the altar. Prior to the celebration of the festival's mass, regional folk dancing was performed in the atrium of the church, including the pre-Hispanic dance of the plumes. After the mass, accompanied by a band and fireworks, a procession of some sixty Zapotec women in traditional dress toured the community, each carrying on her head a large, now-laminated representation of her own or another Virgin, surrounded by a platform of flowers. Despite official Catholic teaching, each Virgin had her own devout following. All were convinced that their Virgin was different and endowed with a special power.

The syncretic folk Catholicism, so briefly described above has long been the religious expression of the majority of Mexicans, be they Mestizo or Indigenous. In condemning this tradition, especially the Virgin of Guadalupe, Evangelicals were rejecting a core – some would say the central – element in Mexican national identity, which endeavours to integrate, in the same syncretic fashion, the Hispanic and pre-Hispanic elements of Mexico's heritage. Chatinos, Criollas, Mayans, and Mestizos have never held much in common other than their Catholic faith. Even when the Catholic church flatly condemned the war of independence, the insurgents still marched into battle behind the banner of their Virgin.[38] Thus, religious and national identity have become synonymous, fused through the central symbol of "Our Mother," the Virgin of Guadalupe. It follows from such a world-view that the Evangelical tradition could not be truly Mexican and must, by its very nature, be destructive of all that is distinctively Mexican. Despite the organizational weakness of the Catholic church, it has been these deeply rooted cultural definitions and practices, infused with Catholic symbolism, that have been the major obstacles to Evangelical advance.

All the above reveals how very much Evangelicals were members of a "high-tension" faith that put them in opposition to many elements in the popular and Catholic culture of modern Mexico. From condemnations of the Virgin of Guadalupe, alcohol, dancing, and fiestas to varying degrees of reservation about football, telenovelas, and make-up, this sectarian stance of Evangelicals set them apart from the rest of Mexican society. Where there were abuses in and victims from the pursuit of these cultural practices, there were potential recruits to the Evangelical world. These victims, most notably women, were drawn by the restorative, redemptive aspect of the Evangelical faith, evident in both the tradition of faith healing and in the broader emphasis on a personal, loving God who responds to the needs of his faithful. But if conversion was facilitated, long-term commitment was made more difficult, because it entailed such a radical change in former lifestyle, especially for men, and because such a focused, ascetic lifestyle might be difficult for some to sustain over an extended period of time. Not surprisingly, the drop-out rates, calculated in chapter 3, were greatest in Pentecostal churches, where the faithful were expected to devote about eight hours weekly to attendance at highly emotional services and where the floater, the sleeper, or the spiritually exhausted was soon visible.

Evangelicals, and especially Pentecostals, we saw, stressed the centrality of a profound emotional transformation of heart as the core religious activity and as the key to salvation. Doctrinally, salvation was "by faith alone." Through the sacrifice of Christ's death, Evangelicals were assured of forgiveness for their sins, despite subsequent lapses, provided they truly repented and had faith. Having sufficient faith was the key to salvation's security, but no objective, clear standard was proffered to the faithful by which they might be reassured that their faith was sufficient to be or to remain saved. It may be recalled that, in the early stages of my research, I stopped asking Evangelicals how certain they felt of their salvation, since all replied so positively and categorically. I had doubts then about how honest their replies were, and my doubts have grown. This is particularly true of Pentecostals, who, in two central practices of their faith, were often obliged to question its depth. In the case of speaking in tongues, about half of all Pentecostals could not master the practice, which their tradition taught was the mark or sign of being filled with the Holy Spirit. In the sphere of faith healing, more than two-thirds of Pentecostals felt that going to the doctor was or might possibly be a sign of a lack of faith, while a quarter believed that unanswered prayers for healing were a sign of a lack of faith. Since recourse to doctors was widespread and not all prayers were answered, the grounds for doubting the depth of one's faith were widespread. It seems to me that there was a greater edge, uncertainty, and anxiety over salvation among Evangelicals than either they or their doctrines admitted. Such common, built-in grounds for questioning faith may help to explain both the intensity of Evangelical religious commitment and their high rates of apostasy.

6 Community Life

The bulk of Mexican Evangelical religious life is enacted in local congregations. Two contradictory aspects of this small world soon became apparent during my research visits. On the one hand there was much evidence of brotherhood and mutual support, but so too were there many signs of lack of co-operation, of schism, and of great resistance to efforts at local, regional, interdenominational, and national co-operation. In exploring why this is so, I pay particular attention to the social background, activities, career needs, and lay expectations of the pastors, who were the leaders of the Evangelical world. Here our concern is with the organizational and belonging dimension of Evangelical life.

The primary concern in chapters 3 and 4 was the theme of conversion, but here as in the previous chapter our focus shifts to the issue of commitment, particularly long-term commitment. The two concepts should not be equated, for conversion, as the high apostasy rates in chapter 3 demonstrate, does not necessarily lead to long-term commitment. As we examine the various dimensions of commitment, attention must and will be paid to the psychological, social, and material rewards of membership that may strengthen or reinforce commitment, though such rewards cannot be regarded as the original cause of the conversion. Equal attention must be paid to the costs of commitment, which vary from group to group and may help to account for the distinctive Evangelical patterns of high drop-out rates as well as high growth. However, the intuitive appeal of such notions of rewards and costs is less clear-cut than is at first apparent. The giving of time, money, or energy to a movement would for many be a clear "cost," yet for some Evangelicals the giving of time and money to their church is a reward in and of itself, in that they will incur costs in order to secure their definition of rewards.

CONGREGATIONAL DYNAMICS AND COMMITMENT

With few exceptions, belonging and commitment took place within very small congregations, where the opportunity and potential for intimacy were great. Like the Jehovah's Witnesses and the Hutterites, who have both established a tradition of splitting congregations when they much exceed 150 members, Evangelical congregations remained within the familiar confines of the typical band of our hunting and gathering past. It would be ludicrous to impute any calculated anthropological intention to this state of affairs, though the consequences may be real enough. In the specific case of the forty-three Evangelical congregations, thirty-four (79 per cent) had fewer than 100 baptized members; 86 per cent had fewer than 150 members. Only the neo-Pentecostal churches have explicitly rejected this custom, though the one example in my sample, with 650 members, endeavoured to compensate for any resulting anonymity by organizing weekly prayer and study groups of five to twenty members to which about half the total congregation were affiliated. The other larger congregations were all older churches affiliated to the historical denominations and drew their membership from an entire town or city. In the typically small congregation the Evangelical sense of intimacy was further enhanced by the majority of members' living within walking distance of the church. Except for some rural areas, there was usually the option of two or more Evangelical churches in any given residential area, which insured that the intimacies of brotherhood or of a fictive kin network were combined with the appealing option to pick and choose one's "kin."

The "costs" of commitment were considerable and varied, as might be expected in any sect in high tension with its surrounding society. In the previous chapter reference was made to the varied prohibitions on traditional recreational patterns, from dancing to alcohol to movies. Despite Evangelical protest that such activities no longer interested them, the loss of any or all may reasonably be regarded as a "cost" of commitment. The same also applies to the huge amounts of time that members were expected to devote to attendance at church services. Attendance at a minimum of three services a week, consuming about seven hours of time, was expected of committed Pentecostals, while members of the historical denominations might scrape by with two services. These were the minimum expectations. In fact, as I documented at the beginning of chapter 5, average attendance was significantly higher. The most devoted were women, who were much more likely to attend mid-week services as well as those on Sunday. The cost of lost time was considerable to the many housewives with numerous children and few labour-saving devices. For the 30 per cent of married female members whose husbands were Catholic,[1] the potential cost of marital strife was especially potent when husbands found themselves deserted for considerable periods of time on their one day of rest, or came home at night during the week to a deserted kitchen and home.

Financial costs were also often substantial. Pastors of all denominations taught that tithing was the duty of all good Christians, though the emphasis they put upon it varied. Leaving aside married women with Catholic spouses, Table 6.1 shows that 52 per cent claimed that either they or their spouses tithed. No means of independently checking this claim is available, but my estimate for the historical denominations is broadly similar to data from the National Baptist Convention, indicating that between 37 and 47 per cent of its members tithed in the 1980s.[2] These are strikingly high figures, since so many were poor and a substantial number who did not tithe were widows, unemployed, students, and the like. Those who said they tithed may not have given a strict 10 per cent of their pre- or post-tax income, but they did give, or claimed to give, a regular and predictable amount in a separate envelope, apart from the collection at every service. The greater proportion of men in the labour-force undoubtedly accounts for their higher rate of tithing. Adventists appeared to be the most steadfast tithers, though as always their small numbers make such a conclusion especially tentative. Pentecostals, despite being poorer than the members in the historical denominations, tithed more frequently, though the difference was not that great. In rural areas tithing was episodic, confined to the harvest and the sale of cash crops. In urban areas, or where wages were the predominant form of sustenance, the tithe was collected monthly in a special envelope. Between first and second generation there was again no sign of diminished commitment. Since the tithe in Pentecostal churches was typically for the sustenance of the pastor, there were frequent calls for additional donations to building funds and a host of other special causes. Those who might wish to escape these burdens were

Table 6.1
Evangelicals who tithe or whose spouse tithes, interview sample*

Advt	Hist.	Pent.	Female	Male	1st gen.	2nd gen.	City	Rural	Total
70%	45%	54%	48%	59%	54%	52%	63%	40%	52%
(30)	(119)	(245)	(238)	(156)	(206)	(165)	(174)	(15)	(394)

* Excluding married females with Catholic spouses.

placed under considerable pressure not to do so. Monthly donations were sometimes posted, and tithing was usually a prerequisite for holding leadership positions. Converts may have recouped
a portion of their donations through their newly ascetic lifestyle,
but for all Evangelicals, financial contributions were a recurrent
cost linked with commitment.

On the other side of the ledger, the major "benefit" was salvation,
but here I want to focus on the often unintended psychological and
social rewards associated with membership and commitment. At
the most basic of levels, members of the typically small Evangelical
congregations, whose lives were so consumed by church life, were
never lonely or without something to do. Except for a few large
urban congregations, all knew each other intimately by virtue of sit-
ting side by side for several hours weekly, sharing a common and,
for Pentecostals, a deeply felt emotional experience. Before and
after services, and even during long services, people gathered outside the church to chat. Their sense of community, however, was
largely centred on their immediately church-related experiences.
Only 14 per cent from the interview sample often visited or social-
ized with other members of the congregation in each other's homes;
the rest (86 per cent) did so very occasionally or not at all. Only
among the young and unmarried was there significantly more socializing. Since weekends were short, the work day was long, and
so much time was devoted to services, there was little opportunity
for visiting with one's "brothers and sisters in the faith."

In poorer neighbourhoods and the countryside Evangelical
churches did provide the young with one of the few places, apart
from the street corner, where they could regularly congregate outside the home. On weekends, youth clubs were a popular focus for
youthful energies. The program always had a strong religious
component to it, but there were usually a few games. Sometimes
there was the adventure of a visit to another youth group, or a musical group was formed to evangelize in the market, the park, or a
prison. Most importantly, the young were together and away from

home. Pentecostal churches, with their electric music and contemporary melodies, offered a measure of real entertainment, a chance to clap and sing and even to play a musical instrument, all in a style quite similar to modern popular music. This was a far gentler and safer atmosphere than public dances, which may explain the preponderance of females, who were brought up to have little interest in the organized sports activities that drew males away from the Evangelical world.

Congregations also provided their members with an opportunity to share their burdens and triumphs with others. In both the historical and the Pentecostal churches, most services set aside a time for those who wished to come forward to share publicly their prayers of thanks or petitions to God concerning events that had affected them personally and recently. The microphone was usually passed round to each in turn. All eyes typically rolled when a few old ladies came forward without fail every week. The other, less frequent participants usually dealt with the routine events of birthdays, anniversaries, successful completion of a year at school, or a new member of the family. The fact remains that all now knew of the event, and its importance was enhanced. Less frequently, but still regularly, there were much more personal, emotionally wrought accounts of illness, a lost job, a frightening accident to a child, or a husband who wanted the speaker home rather than in church. Whether women suffered more or whether they were more willing to share their innermost feelings in public would be difficult to say with certainty, but women made up the great majority of those wishing to share their troubles with their new family. In their account of their tribulations, the speakers usually described both their fears and the sustaining strength of their faith, thereby reinforcing and sharing their commitment with all and finding real catharsis. In Pentecostal services, where emotions were given freer reign, the catharsis was all the more complete when the sister with the burden was approached, touched, and prayed over by fellow members of the congregation during the altar call at the end of the service.

Congregational support for members at times of emotional stress was evident not only at funerals, when all rallied round, but whenever there was major illness in the family. All were informed of the illness during services, and prayers were said. More importantly for the unintended kinds of rewards deriving from membership, 82 per cent of respondents in the interview sample said that the pastor had visited during the last serious illness in the family, to pray over the sick person and to see what the congregation could do.[3] This figure rose to 88 per cent for Pentecostals. Such visits occurred less frequently among Adventists (68 per cent) and Presbyterians (55 per cent), but only because their few pastors typically had responsibility for several congregations, which made it impossible for them to attend to all who were ill. With almost no variation across denominations, 87 per cent of respondents said that they or the sick member of the family were also visited by one or more lay members during the same illness. Such attention at a time of need, especially for believers in the power of prayer, surely strengthened commitment.

Evangelical congregations, no matter what their denomination, offered many opportunities for leadership and personal development, which may be thought of as another of the benefits or rewards that indirectly derive from membership. Pastors set the agenda during the service, and they usually took on the prime responsibility to preach unless there was a special guest. They otherwise looked to a variety of members of the congregation to lead prayers and certain portions of the service. Since congregations were small and there were so many services, anyone with aptitude or interest was given considerable opportunity to become a fledgling leader. Lacking a written liturgy, lay leaders soon learned the art of extemporaneous speech and prayer in front of an audience. The strongly evangelistic thrust of most congregations, their heavy stress on the born-again experience of conversion, and the attendant sense of personal transformation and internal elation – these influences together combined to create an abundant pool of neophytes eager to share their own experiences and to win more souls for Christ. The aspiring leaders had a rich array of positions in the congregations, ranging from deacon, secretary, and treasurer to director of the Sunday school, women's group, youth group, and evangelism committee. Since the directors often had a committee under them, there were almost as many positions as there were active and willing laity. In theory, appointment to a position was usually determined by the vote of all active members, but in practice people were urged by the pastor and a few other key leaders to accept nominations in an elaborate ritual of musical chairs, controlled by the pastor, where hardly anyone was left out and where the able slowly rose. Technically open to all, this structure insured that each new level of commitment made by the faithful was rewarded by greater degrees of prestige, authority, and the satisfaction of honed leadership skills.

Pastors, we saw earlier, favoured men over women for leadership positions. This bias was least pronounced when it came to appointing the heads of the various departments. Their preference for male deacons was much stronger, but they often appointed women, for three reasons. First, with so many committees and so few male members, pastors often had little choice but to seek women. Secondly, since most married women were either housewives or worked at home, they were much more likely to be available than their menfolk, who returned from work each day late and tired. Thirdly and relatedly, pastors admitted that women tended to be more responsible and diligent in the performance of their duties. Thus women were subordinate to male pastors, but many were able to carve out their own niche, from Sunday school, the women's group, or the evangelism committee to leading services before the pastor arrived, preaching when he was away, and visiting and consoling as a deaconess the many female members in need of a woman's touch. No other institution among the popular classes, apart from the spiritist halls, provided women with so many opportunities for independence, leadership, and personal expression outside the home.[4]

Economic benefits or rewards have sometimes been thought to be a primary reason for Evangelical commitment. In the last century, when missionaries were very much in control of the Evangelical movement, converts were derided as "corn Christians," though Bastian's research suggests that the missionaries "had neither the economic means nor the desire to buy clients."[5] Still today, almost all the Catholic clergy I interviewed suggested that American largesse, channelled through the pastors, was one of the major reasons for Evangelical success. I will deal with American financial support for churches and pastors in the next chapter. On the narrower theme of direct aid to members of the congregations, I found the practice to be almost entirely confined to the distribution of second-hand clothing in a few congregations right on the border, which very occasionally received such assistance from a sister church on the other side. Elsewhere, among the seventeen missionaries I interviewed, four occasionally distributed a few bags of clothing to needy pastors. Only one, an Ecuadorian running a weekend Bible institute for fledgling pastors, filled a school bus once a year with clothing from his home church in New Mexico, for distribution through the pastors to needy congregations. The remaining twelve gave nothing whatsoever directly to the members of local congregations. In part this was because of the distance and cost involved in transportation. It also reflected the conviction of most missionaries that material aid to congregations fostered local attitudes of dependency that would hinder future church growth. Almost all felt compelled to offer an occasional gift to a maid, neighbour, or pastor who was sick or in dire need, but this was the extent of their material aid. In the forty-three sample congregations, direct aid to the laity occurred in only one case. This involved the donation of one or two bags of clothing by a missionary, and his provision of building materials for twenty-five outdoor latrines over the previous four years, amongst the approximately one hundred families that made up this Indigenous congregation. In the remaining forty-two, or 98 per cent of congregations, including those in the north, none during the previous twelve months had received any money or material goods from American or any other foreign source for distribution to congregational members.[6] Missionary largesse was not on a sufficient scale to affect in any meaningful way Evangelicalism's appeal.

On converting, Evangelicals not only distanced themselves from their Catholic relatives but were expected to terminate their relations of *compadrazgo*, or god-parenting, previously contracted with Catholics. Besides the baptismal godparents, most Catholics had additional godparents for confirmation, first communion, and marriage; some had even more. The more socially important relationship here was not between godparents and godchild but between parent and godparents, who become co-parents, with lifelong obligations to one another. Some students of this pervasive Catholic Mexican practice stress how *comadres* and *compadres* with greater economic influence were chosen in order to secure a future supply of fictive kin to whom one might turn in times of material need.[7] Others stress the ways in which *compadrazgo* was used to affirm and strengthen mutual obligations with people within one's own social class who were not kin.[8] In either case, *compadrazgo* created an extended network of fictive kin. Such bonds were broken at conversion. The prospect undoubtedly deterred some conversions from occurring at all. It was surely a cost for all who persevered. In the interview sample, only 9 per cent of Evangelicals had Catholic *compadres* with whom they maintained social contact of anything more than the most passing nature;[9] none suggested that this involved the obligations of the past.

Whenever Evangelicals looked for employment, church and fellow Evangelicals were an obvious source for aid and information. As they typically referred to each other as "brother" and "sister," one might think the practice was widespread. In fact, only 11 per cent of the forty-nine pastors characterized such assistance as an integral part of their ministry; 61 per cent said they were able to help very occasionally; and 29 per cent said they never did so. One pastor defined the limitations of many others when he claimed that "all I can do is pray for them," since he had no personal contacts in the labour-force. However, pastors could and sometimes did work

through the other members of the congregation, who were likely to
have such contacts. In all but the largest of congregations, most
would soon hear that a particular brother or sister needed work.
Yet of the 175 in the interview sample who obtained a job when
they were Evangelicals, only 14 per cent said they received help
from another Evangelical who was not a relative; another 10 per
cent said a relative and fellow Evangelical provided assistance. One
might conclude that religious contacts were more useful than family, but the fact still remains that the remaining 76 per cent obtained
their varied jobs without any assistance from either family or
church. Religious contacts were thus an important source of employment for no more than a minority of Evangelicals.

In both rural areas and in the poorer urban strata where Evangelicals were concentrated, home construction and repairs were typically done by the family in piecemeal fashion, as resources slowly
accumulated. Traditionally people turned to neighbours and kin for
aid when needed. This still seemed to be the case for Evangelicals.
Only 9 per cent of 384[10] in the interview sample said they had received any help from a fellow member of their congregation who
was not a relative the last time their home had been enlarged or repaired. Even in rural areas, where the tradition of mutual aid was
more deeply rooted, only 13 per cent said they had received such
support. Apart from their own personal experience, 78 per cent denied that this was a practice in their particular congregation. Another 5 per cent said it happened occasionally, and 9 per cent said
it was confined to help for widows without kin to assist them, or to
a real case of emergency, such as the destruction of a home by fire.
Only 8 per cent said it was a common practice in their own particular congregation. Co-operative home-building was not an Evangelical tradition.

I also sought to explore the degree to which Evangelicals gave
preference to other Evangelicals when shopping, when hiring the
services of a plumber, electrician, or carpenter, or when seeking
medical treatment. Here one sees somewhat greater signs that it
would be a good idea to give preference to Evangelical "family,"
but such notions and practices were hardly pervasive. In Table 6.2
it can be seen that 18 per cent said that the last tradesman they had
hired was an Evangelical; 8 per cent said they shopped at an Evangelical grocery store; and 12 per cent said they had an Evangelical
doctor. Approximately a third in each case opined that it would be
a good idea to give preference to Evangelicals, but they did not do
so, they said, because they could not find or did not know an Evangelical with the appropriate skill or service. In fact, this was not

Table 6.2
Economic co-operation: extent of preference for Evangelical services, interview sample

	Tradesmen %	Grocery Store %	Doctor %
Yes, give preference	18	7	12
No, but is preferable	35	29	30
No preference	47	63	59
Total	100% (380)	100% (324)	100% (323)

always true. Had they looked further afield, even a little, almost all could have found an Evangelical doctor, grocery store, or plumber had they been really interested in doing so. In all three cases a majority claimed that they did not and would not give preference to Evangelicals. Brothers they were in the faith, but a sense of practical obligation and mutual aid in such areas simply did not exist for most Evangelicals. Only in a very small minority was it strong enough to be translated into action.

The one area where Evangelicals believed mutual aid in practical or material form should be exercised, and would be available, was for emergencies or those in great need. Should a serious emergency arise in their lives, 83 per cent of 328 in the interview sample were confident that members of their congregation would rally round with food, clothing, and other practical necessities, though I am not entirely clear how deeply rooted this confidence was in all cases. A full 92 per cent also pointed out that their congregation did give to the truly needy at times of real emergency. Most could recount specific cases. In the forty-one congregations where I gathered such information, only two small Pentecostal churches had made no organized effort in recent years. Twelve (29 per cent) had monthly collections of foodstuffs, clothing, and the like, which were then distributed by the pastor and a committee to those deemed to be most in need. In the remaining two-thirds of congregations, collections or requests were made episodically in response to the needs of particular individuals or families. At one service I attended in the countryside, for instance, the congregation dug into their pockets for a brother who was in need of hospital treatment following a work-related accident. Donations of money, however, were rare. Especially in the Pentecostal churches, where so many were poor, donations were confined to the very basics of oil, beans, and corn. Only in a few prosperous historical congregations, and only a minority fit this description, were regular donations made to a few elderly widows. Elsewhere, the support was short-lived, sufficient it was hoped, to tide over a family without any other resources until the breadwinner recovered from illness or found new employment.

The amounts involved in the donations were by most standards meagre, and they did not occur frequently in most congregations. Yet such qualifications must be set against the backdrop of the limited resources congregations typically had and the virtual absence of a government welfare net. Evangelicals did have the reassurance that should a crisis arise, when their own efforts and the support of family were inadequate to sustain them, they could look to their brothers in the faith with some confidence for a minimal level of material aid as well as understanding and concern. Without their church and pastor, they would have felt far more alone and insecure. This was the bedrock of Evangelical brotherhood, which, like the cathartic sharing of difficult times during services, strengthened religious commitment.

Evangelicals, then, were not like an ethnic group in the sense of feeling themselves part of a naturally closed community, within which all bonds of responsibility and obligation were confined. Nor can the congregation be reduced to a functional equivalent of *compadrazgo,* though mutual aid was sometimes present. Evangelicals did have a special sense of brotherhood with each other, but as members of an Evangelical religious community they could not ignore their religious injunction to love those outside as well as inside the faith. Further, as Evangelicals, who prized so deeply the call of evangelism, they were all the more driven to reach out in all spheres to non-believers. This is why, apart from all the more mundane considerations of cost and convenience, so few were willing to seek only Evangelicals as their grocers, plumbers, and doctors. In their limited charitable activities, no congregation was prepared to stipulate that charitable giving be confined to Evangelicals alone. For all practical purposes, charity was confined to the faithful in 11 per cent of the congregations. In all others, pastors pointed proudly to examples where they had reached out to a non-Evangelical, though here too the majority of giving was kept within the fold. They were inclined to give to those whom they knew and trusted most, but very few were willing to embrace this as a general rule. Set apart from the world, they certainly felt, but they could not and did not look only inward.

This outreach had once been most evident in the network of schools and hospitals established by the historical denominations, which had the dual purposes of social service and evangelism. We saw how Evangelical-run schools had largely collapsed in the post-revolutionary period. Here I want to focus on the hospitals that remained in this depleted network in the modern era after 1970. The number of institutions was very small, but their recent history tells us much about the Evangelical world.

After the Cincinnati agreement of 1919, Presbyterian medical missionaries established themselves in Morelia, Michoacan, where they founded a hospital, La Luz, with the dual objectives mentioned above. With the financial aid of the mission, prices were lower than at many other hospitals, and a certain proportion of beds were reserved for the indigent. A nursing school was established that recruited heavily, but by no means exclusively, from Presbyterian congregations. Evangelism was pursued within the hospital and through an outreach program to former patients and the relatives of the nurses, which led to the founding of one of the rural congregations where I worked. The prestige of the hospital grew after the Second World War, when one of its doctors, a Mexican Presbyterian, became president of the state university and mayor of the state capital.

Problems arose with the departure of the missionaries. Because religious bodies could not own property, a civil society of prominent lay Mexicans was the nominal owner of the hospital, though they met infrequently The missionaries really administered the hospital. In 1964 the largely inactive civil society was reconstituted by the missionaries when they gave up complete local control, but it too soon subsided. After the final departure of all Presbyterian missionaries from Mexico in 1972, the Mexican Presbyterian director of the hospital was left in charge. In subsequent years evangelistic and social-service outreach diminished. By the early 1980s growing concern by the other Presbyterian doctors that the then director was corrupt led to the revival of the civil society. A nasty struggle culminated in the ouster, though not the prosecution, of the director. Not all my varied informants were certain that the director was corrupt, but all were agreed that the hospital had become run down and was driven solely by a profit motive.

After the coup, an again reconstituted civil society set up a new bureaucratic level of an administrative society of local Presbyterians. The latter body was to oversee and implement a plan to restore the Presbyterian, social-service, and evangelistic character of the hospital. The idea was to revive the founding principles of the hospital. The new director was an avowed atheist from a Presbyterian background. He was appointed, I was variously told, because he was the oldest in the group and because he had the best medical reputation. He was regarded as a bit of a rogue, but all professed to have a certain affection for him.

For a few years in the mid-1980s the hospital revived; profits were channelled into reconstruction, and it began to pay rent through the administrative and civil society, to be given to the national Presbyterian church as a form of tithing. However, in 1988 the administrative society became concerned at its increasing inability to obtain a full accounting of the budget from the director. They were also worried by the growing number of his relatives in high administrative posts. The director responded by charging the head of the administrative society with embezzlement and mismanagement of funds. He further claimed that the civil society, the technical owners of La Luz, no longer existed, after what he described as its illegal reconstitution in 1964. He therefore concluded that ownership of the hospital now naturally devolved upon its workers and staff, whose rights he was defending against the avarice of the administrative society. On these grounds some doctors, many nurses, and the workers' union were persuaded to lock out the administrative society. In 1992 the director was still in control and the case was before the courts. The director was said to have much political influence. Without a judicial decision, the director remained in control. I cannot explore here the labyrinth of counter charges, but even former supporters of the lockout agreed that the Presbyterian chaplain had been fired, all the plans of social service and evangelism dropped, and the nursing school reconstituted, its Evangelical character removed. Charges of corruption, bribery, and nepotism were rife. La Luz was no longer a Presbyterian institution.

The experience of La Luz was not unique. The Pan American hospital in Guadalahara, for instance, had long been the pride of the Baptist church. In 1993 it remained under the nominal control of a civil society whose members were elected by the Baptist National Convention, but it was no longer reputed to put any significant emphasis on social service or evangelistic outreach. Here too, former directors had been removed for suspicion of corruption. Rumours of this sort were current in 1993. The missionaries who worked there until the second half of the 1980s had all withdrawn, through concern that the hospital no longer had a religious focus. When to this is added the previously cited evidence of the collapse of Evangelical schools attached to the historical denomination, it seems clear that the missionary legacy of institutional social service, and the kinds of rewards and attractions it might entail, had disappeared from the Mexican historical denominations. For Pentecostals, of course, such structures never existed.

Adventists were the one exception to this general inability and/or lack of interest among Evangelicals to provide institutional services beyond the congregation. Far from suffering from any millennialist apathy about the future, Adventists have had a long and rich tradition, especially in their missionary work, of stressing the establishment of schools, hospitals, and clinics.[11] By the mid-1950s Pedro Rivera, a Jesuit, had published figures suggesting that half of all the Protestant primary schools and medical institutions in Mexico were in Adventist hands.[12] In Linda Vista, Chiapas, and Montemorelos, Nuevo Leon, Adventists had their major centres, each with its hospital, schools from primary to senior secondary residences, and a growing number of programs at the college level. An Adventist spokesman claimed in 1990 one hundred educational centres through the country as a whole .[13] I have no comparable figures for medical services nationally, but every Adventist congregation where I worked had an Adventist hospital or clinic no more than an hour's drive away. All had access to at least an Adventist primary school. Foreign and particularly American aid had undoubtedly been involved in providing some of the capital costs at such places as Linda Vista and Montemorelos, but its significance should not be overstated. As early as the 1960s, Adventists were distinctive for the degree to which they ran and funded their own affairs.[14] In the later 1980s and 1990s the schools supported by the Adventist congregations where I worked were all built and maintained with entirely Mexican funding and direction. More to the point, despite a long history of direct missionary support for the schools and hospitals of the historical denominations, this legacy had been entirely squandered by the Presbyterians and Baptists, while Adventists had seen theirs grow. The key to the latter's success seems to have been their tradition of tithing and a centralized organizational structure, built around sixteen regional conferences. With its own legally constituted civil association and head office, each regional conference had the funds, the authority, the staff, and the local knowledge to administer this network effectively.[15] In contrast, the regional Baptist associations and Presbyterian presbyteries lacked both the financial resources and the experienced permanent staff to oversee such activities, if they could ever have agreed to implement them. Again the Pentecostals lacked the resources as well as the will to follow in the Adventist path.

PASTORS: LEADERSHIP DILEMMAS

Evangelical leadership was not only largely in the hands of Mexican nationals but was very much a leadership deriving from the rank and file rather than one imposed from above. Table 6.3 shows that half of the forty-nine pastors I interviewed were converts,

Table 6.3
Social background of pastors and laity, pastor and interview samples

	Pastors			Laity		
	Pent.	Hist.	Total*	Total*	Hist.	Pent.
Convert	61%	33%	51%	52%	38%	61%
	(31)	(15)	(49)	(485)	(146)	(303)
Rural	29%	40%	33%	35%	34%	35%
	(31)	(15)	(49)	(485)	(146)	(303)
Primary school or less	48%	33%	43%	62%	54%	65%
	(31)	(15)	(49)	(468)	(146)	(286)
Less than secondary	77%	53%	67%	84%	77%	89%
	(31)	(15)	(49)	(468)	(146)	(286)

* Includes Adventists as well as Pentecostals and members of the historical denominations.

which is virtually identical to the 52 per cent of converts in the interview sample of lay members. So too is the proportion from a rural background almost identical. When such a small sample is further broken down, we cannot place much confidence in any one number, but the overall pattern is revealing. Compared to the Presbyterians and Baptists, Pentecostal pastors, like their laity, were more likely to be drawn from a humble background, in the sense of being less well educated. Excluding the two neo-Pentecostal pastors, who were both raised in historical denominations, only three of the remaining twenty-nine Pentecostals were from what might be described as middle-class backgrounds: the father of one was a pastor, while those of the other two were the owners respectively of a bus and a truck. The parents of the remainder were all peasants, unskilled workers, street vendors, and the like. Among the fifteen pastors in the historical denominations, by contrast, five of the parents were professionals, though two were pastors like their sons and another four were skilled tradesmen; the others were all of humbler backgrounds. Similarly, pastors were better educated than their lay members, though not by a great margin: 43 per cent of the former but 62 per cent of the latter had a primary school education. Among Pentecostal pastors 48 per cent had no more than a primary school education. Among pastors of all denominations, 67 per cent had not completed secondary school, while 77 per cent of Pentecostal pastors had not. Especially for Pentecostals, this is the profile of a clergy who understood and spoke the language of the members of their congregations, since they shared so much with them.

Despite their humble background, over half (58 per cent) of Pentecostal pastors had attended a Bible institute full time for two or three years; another 13 per cent had attended for the same length of time on a part-time basis.[16] The level of instruction was restricted by their low level of secular education, but this was no disadvantage, given the educational level of their future congregations. Besides doctrinal and pastoral instruction, typically provided without charge by local pastors, students learned, if they were to survive, two related skills. The first was to live very frugally. Fees were usually very low, but these, plus room and board, had to be paid. Most students were poor converts with limited family backing. The institutes sometimes had the resources to assist a few especially needy and worthy individuals, but most supported themselves through a combination of loans, donations from friends and sympathizers, holiday employment, and weekend visits to nearby churches, where the collection was passed after the visiting student gave the sermon. Since congregations were almost all poor and small, and the pastor had already taken his tithe from the more faithful, the donations were rarely generous. Those who survived, and many did not, perforce learned the second crucial skill, which was to preach and pastor well enough to eat.

The high commitment of so many Pentecostals, their strong emphasis on evangelism, and their many opportunities for lay leadership created an abundant pool of pastoral candidates and Bible institutes. The Assemblies of God, for instance, saw the number of its Bible institutes rise from 5 in 1963[17] to 23 in 1984. In that latter year alone there were 390 new graduates for 1,489 Assemblies of God churches and 625 missions.[18] By 1990 the number of their Bible institutes had risen to 30,[19] and I was told that by 1993 they numbered 38. Since even small denominations quickly looked to establish an institute to train pastors, it would be impossible to calculate their total number at the national level. Some idea of their prevalence may be gained from the city I studied in the colonial heartland, where its forty-plus churches had three and possibly more Bible institutes, all Pentecostal, which produced about twenty-two graduates a year. Only a minority could expect to find an established church willing or able to offer them a position with an income sufficient to support a pastor and family.

To serve as pastors, all but a few were obliged to evangelize in an area without an established church. The most common pattern was to be given responsibility for a small mission attached to an existing church, with the goal of building up membership sufficiently so that the mission could support a pastor financially and thereby become a church. Almost all the pastors I interviewed started this way, though many subsequently moved on when the mission failed to grow. In fourteen of the twenty-six Pentecostal churches where I worked, the current pastor either founded the church or took it over as a small mission and built it up to the status of an independent church. At first, a Bible institute graduate might be given free room and board by the pastor or by a sympathetic member of the mission, but there was no centralized denominational support. If recent graduates wished to move beyond this hand-to-mouth existence, they had to enlarge their membership. Typically, they started with a nucleus of two or three families and perhaps a vacant lot. First, a crude, temporary structure of cardboard, wooden slats, and corrugated iron was built as a church, with one or two small rooms behind for the pastor. If the pastor was successful in enlarging his flock, a more permanent structure of brick or concrete might be built, but this too was done step by step, as resources slowly accumulated. When construction occurred, some of the men in the congregation would help out at the weekends, but during the week it was usually the pastor alone who continued the work. Thus many pastors had constructed a fair portion of the churches in which they held nightly services. During the day, apart from building, they devoted their time to visiting their small congregation and seeking out Catholic neighbours and relatives of existing members who were ill, in distress, or otherwise open to their efforts to evangelize. This system induced a certain entrepreneurial and proprietorial style in the pastor's approach to church growth, with some being far more visibly successful than others.

The usual practice in Pentecostal churches was for the tithe to be set aside for the sustenance of the pastor. It was usually given monthly, either directly to the pastor or earmarked in the general collection by being put in a special envelope. In the twenty-six Pentecostal congregations I studied, six did not follow this custom. In two cases, including the large neo-Pentecostal church, with 250 tithing, the pastors received a set salary, though I am told that the pastors of some large Pentecostal churches received all the tithe. In a northern congregation, an unmarried pastor with an ambitious building plan tried to encourage more giving by limiting his income to a fixed amount, equal to a typical factory wage. In another very small church in the south the pastor, who was obliged to support his family through construction work, put all meagre contributions he received into a general fund, from which he received any surplus after the costs of light, church upkeep, and the like were deducted. The fifth church was effectively dominated by one layman who kept a succession of young pastors subservient by limiting them to a small salary that he set. In the last case, after the former pastor had run off with a member's wife and many bad debts, the two co-pastors who took over agreed to take no salary so as to restore the lost confidence in the leadership, which had caused membership to fall from one hundred to thirty. In the seventeen congregations where the tithe went exclusively to the pastors,[20] they received an average of fifteen tithes a month from people who earned an income. If all had tithed fully, which was doubtful, the typical wage for pastors would have been 1.5 times the average wage in their congregations. Seven pastors received ten or fewer tithes a month, which left them in an extremely poor state, while five earned over twenty tithes, the highest being twenty-eight. As this last pastor resided in a northern city, where wages were relatively high for Mexico, he was quite comfortable and able to run a car, but he was far from affluent. With few exceptions, pastors were in tight and uncertain economic circumstances, heavily dependent on the giving of a few of their more affluent members, whose hurt feelings or thwarted desires could have disastrous economic consequences. Larger congregations would appear to have been the answer to this dilemma, but very few congregations were able to grow beyond one hundred baptized members.

At the other end of the spectrum were the Seventh-Day Adventists and Presbyterians, who suffered from a marked scarcity of pastors. In between were the Baptists.[21] Adventists and Presbyterian pastors received regular salaries from their presbytery, association, or local church, which provided a standard of living substantially higher than all but a very few Pentecostals, though their standard of living would best be described as modestly middle class. The chief cause of the shortage was the requirement of completed secondary school for admission to theological college and then completion of a rigorous four-year training at the Presbyterian seminary in Mexico City, or at Montemorelos in Nuevo Leon for the Adventists. These high academic standards effectively disqualified the vast majority of members in both denominations. For those who did meet these standards, other occupations offered better salaries, while the high cost of completing the program and the great distance from home deterred others. Presbyterians in the provinces found that the young they sent away sometimes did not return after four years of exposure to the cosmopolitan life in Mexico City. Not a few congregations also became disturbed at what they regarded as the liberal, ecumenist, and even liberationist style of Presbyterian intellectuals in the capital. As a result, regional seminaries were established in the later 1980s,[22] but the shortage of pastors in the early 1990s remained acute outside the major cities. In the two Presbyterian congregations where I worked in Tabasco, the pastor in each case was responsible for at least twenty other congregations,[23] while the Adventist pastor was obliged to spread his time between fifteen congregations. Most of these congregations, both Presbyterian and Adventist, saw their pastor for one or two days a month. Under these conditions pastors could not visit and know intimately all members of their congregations, as did the Pentecostals. In the cities, however, where Presbyterian pastors were more plentiful, they were expected to visit more frequently, and they could not ignore the expectations of the elders and deacons who set their salaries.

The common consequence of clerical shortages among Adventists and Presbyterians, particularly in rural areas, was that the laity often ran the local congregations. At times this may have fostered church growth, in that leadership was open to all and all were expected to be active participants. On other occasions the absence of a pastor allowed one lay person to run the congregation as his own personal fiefdom. Mexicans referred to such individuals as *caciques*, borrowing this originally Indian word for chief, which was widely applied in Mexico to local political and economic bosses. It did not take me long to discover that I could do nothing without the approval of the *cacique*, who was quick to point out that "we do not depend on the pastor." The seventy-year-old Adventist *cacique* and patriarch quoted here, who was still active on his *ejido* allotment, had built the church on land he provided. Over half the congregation were his children, grandchildren, and their spouses. In Pentecostal churches, too, in both town and countryside, it was not unknown for one lay member, usually with a prosperous business, to dominate the congregation and pastor through the power of his financial generosity. These were extreme cases. Far more common was the tendency for a small number of families to regard the church as theirs and to be very quick to make their views known to the pastor should he, by either omission or commission, fail to meet their expectations. Everywhere the often authoritarian and paternalistic style of pastors was curbed and counterbalanced by the unconstrained power of the laity to withdraw their support, to drop out, or to shift allegiance to another church and pastor.

SCHISM

The organizational precariousness of Evangelical congregations was also enhanced by their typically small size of fewer than one hundred baptized members. Pastors usually attributed this pervasive and distinctive trait to the costs and difficulties of travel and hence the desire of their members to have a church within walking distance of home. There was an obvious measure of truth to this claim, but the actual number of churches in many areas greatly exceeded such needs. In each of the two Mexico city neighbourhoods where I worked, for instance, there were ten separate Evangelical churches while a small town in the south where I spent a summer contained four Presbyterian, seven Pentecostal, and two Adventist churches. With few exceptions, the churches in all these three areas were small, competing directly for members with at least two or three highly similar churches in the same few streets or catchment area. The intimacy proffered by such small congregations may partially account for their appeal. At the same time, one might reasonably have expected to see countervailing forces at work to reduce competition, such that those remaining might have had a more secure economic and numeric footing. That rationalization of this sort had not occurred to any appreciable degree was in large measure due to the highly schismatic character of Mexican Evangelicals, which they shared in common with other Latin American Evangelicals[24] and with Pentecostals elsewhere in the world.[25]

The fissiparous tendency of Mexican Evangelicals was evident in the schismatic creation of the Iglesia de Dios en la Republica Mexicana in the 1920s from the still nascent Assemblies of God movement. In the 1940s another schism in the former denomination created the MIEPI (Movimiento de Iglesias Evangelicas Pentecosteses y Independientes),[26] which claimed to have five hundred congregations by the middle of the 1970s.[27] Then in the later 1970s an endeavour in the northern region of the Assemblies of God to revise their constitution led to the breakaway of some seventeen pastors, who formed a new denomination, the Fraternity of the Assemblies of God, which claimed to have over two hundred congregations by the end of the 1980s. Doctrinal matters were never an issue. Rather, there were disagreements over fixed pastoral salaries, the use of tithes, regional reorganization, and other administrative matters. There were so many contending coalitions and positions on all the issues that the seventeen breakaway pastors were rarely united in the positions they held. Personal animosities, power struggles, and the heavy-handed treatment of the most vocal of the dissidents by the Assemblies of God leadership appear to have been the most important causes of the schism. None of the most controversial proposals, most notably the setting of pastoral salaries, was ever implemented by either side. The subsequent growth of the Fraternity has since been due to the evangelistic efforts of its founding group in the North and to the periodic adhesion of disgruntled congregations from the mainstream Assemblies of God. A scattering of independent churches, looking for the respectability of a denominational label without much denominational control, also contributed to the Fraternity's growth. For the mid-1970s, Barrett's Encyclopedia estimated that there were some 240 Evangelical denominations in Mexico.[28] The total number of denominations has surely grown since that date, especially if the multitude of independent churches and loose regional affiliations are considered.

Apart from the proliferation of new movements and denominations, there was a parallel and more frequent tendency for local congregations to experience their own splits, divisions, and breakaways. Not part of a wider schismatic movement, they were every bit as much a schism in that internal congregational conflicts caused a portion of their members to leave, affiliating elsewhere or establishing a new congregation. In the forty-two sample congregations,[29] twenty-five (60 per cent) had either experienced a schismatic breakaway or were themselves a product of one. None of the twenty-five was part of a wider schismatic movement. Nineteen of the schisms led to the founding of a new congregation,[30] of which fifteen came to be affiliated to a different denomination. Schisms seemed to be somewhat more frequent in Pentecostal churches (68 per cent) than in the historical denominations (50 per cent), though the small sample size here, as always, diminishes the reliability of the finding. Since sixteen of the twenty-five schisms occurred over the last ten years and more distant conflicts may already have been forgotten, schisms were a very pervasive experience in the Evangelical world.

Like the rest of Latin America, doctrinal issues were not the major cause of schism.[31] Only six of the twenty-five schisms might be loosely placed in this doctrinal category in that they involved conflict over a Pentecostal style of worship in historical churches. In one case some fifty years ago, Presbyterian missionaries established a mission in a rural hamlet in the colonial heartland through contacts made when a resident of the hamlet was treated in their medical clinic. One of the missionaries visited a number of times, but his other commitments obliged him to hand over weekly visits to the mission to an Evangelical hospital orderly, who turned out to be a Pentecostal. When the missionary discovered his "error" and withdrew the orderly from the mission, a schism erupted, which led to the creation in an adjacent hamlet of a Pentecostal church that was three times larger than the Presbyterian church in 1991. In another Presbyterian church, which had formerly seen a number of its active female members desert to aid in the founding of a neo-Pentecostal church, the issue came to an ugly confrontation in 1990. The immediate impetus was a newly appointed pastor with

Pentecostal leanings who caused a group of active women members to make public display of their own charismatic leanings, which till then had been held in check by their disapproving husbands. The new pastor denied that he actively encouraged the women, but relations none the less soured between those for and against the new style. The waters were further muddied by the presence of the former pastor, who did not move on when his expected new appointment fell through and who was openly opposed to charismatic tendencies. After rancorous charge, countercharge, and public confrontation, the new pastor was pushed out by the enraged husbands in the consistory or leadership of the church before his contract had legally expired. In the aftermath, approximately 10 per cent of the Presbyterian congregation shifted to the neo-Pentecostal church, which offered the ousted pastor temporary aid and then a full-time position, thereby confirming the worst suspicions of the remaining Presbyterians.

Students of schism elsewhere have noted that pre-existing social, class, and ethnic divisions frequently underlie and are the true impetus to the subsequent division.[32] Only one schism in the sample congregations could be placed in this category. In the highlands of Chiapas an intense political struggle between conservative and progressive factions at the municipal level so deeply divided a Tzeltal Presbyterian church that the disaffected minority broke away and established its own congregation while remaining within the same denomination. The schism was undoubtedly aided by the growing rivalry between the pastor and a very active younger elder who led the schism and brought many of his relatives along with him, though he did not become the pastor of the new church. More broadly, the deep Mestizo-Indigenous division of Mexico had not produced a formal schism between the two in the Presbyterian church, which still held the allegiance of the majority of highland Indigenous Evangelicals in the early 1990s. A presbytery or regional governing body for Indigenous Evangelicals was formed in the early 1970s, thereby enabling them to escape Mestizo domination. In the later 1980s the growing body of Indigenous Presbyterians further split into Chol and Tzotzil presbyteries, while the highland and lowland Tzeltal each formed their own presbyteries. Growing rivalries, diverging agendas, and increasing problems in co-operation, I was told, fuelled this later institutional separation. In 1993 it had not yet erupted into formal schism at a regional level.

Dissatisfaction with leadership and struggles for power together constituted the major cause of schism in the sample congregations. Put in statistical terms, 72 per cent (18 of 25) of schisms were caused by discontents of this sort, which occurred in 43 per cent of the forty-two congregations I surveyed. Not only, therefore, were schisms a pervasive feature of Evangelical life, but highly divisive struggles for leadership and power were an almost equally characteristic trait. Each incident had its own distinctive colouring, but it seemed to me that the various cases might be usefully differentiated according to who led or initiated the revolt, though here as elsewhere there were often compounding factors.

In five of these power-driven schisms discontent centred on perceived failings in the existing pastor or leader. Presumably some generalized degree of discontent must exist in any rank and file for a schism to occur, but in the other two types it was the emergence of an alternative leader that was the crucial event. Here the decisive factor was simply a generalized sense of discontent with the existing leader on the part of the rank and file. In a colonial heartland city, for instance, the Second Baptist Church was formed by a splinter group from the First Baptist Church. The schism was engendered by resentment at what was seen as the overly authoritarian ways of the pastor, who was condemned for being particularly harsh with young couples who sometimes chatted or courted in church. When a younger and more sympathetic layman offered his house as a mission, the split occurred, though the young layman did not himself seek to become leader or pastor, as so often happened elsewhere. In the other four cases the outrage was directed at rumours of sexual misconduct and/or theft of church funds. In three congregations the membership plummeted as the discontented reaffiliated elsewhere, though a substantial number of those who left were rumoured to have simply dropped out, so disillusioned were they with the failings of their spiritual leader. In the remaining congregation, a young assistant pastor had an affair with the head and founding pastor's wife while the latter was away. When the founding pastor returned, he divorced his wife. The incident seemed to unhinge him. Though he was in his fifties and affiliated to an extremely puritanical denomination, he openly courted and later made pregnant a seventeen-year-old member of the youth group. Rumour then became public knowledge and scandal when the enraged Catholic brother of the pregnant teen drunkenly accosted the pastor during a service, waving a pistol and publicly condemning the pastor for violating his sister. In the aftermath, 90 per cent of the congregation fled. In this case, however, a recent convert from an acutely alcoholic background gathered together a substantial remnant of the disaffected to form a mission loosely attached to another denomination, which he has since ruled with an iron hand, as a *cacique*, with a succession of pliant young pastors.

In the second type of power struggle, which includes only two cases, the crucial impetus to the schism was what can best be described as the poaching efforts of an outside person or group who induced a segment of an existing congregation to affiliate to the new work or church. In a small, newly founded church on the northern border, which must suffice as the one example here, the pastor was forced to leave his church and neighbourhood for several months in order to find secular work, since his congregation could not afford to support him fully. In his absence a mission, supported by an American Hispanic church, was established a few blocks away, which at first offered the relatively rare inducements of free food and clothing, though the practice later stopped. When the absent pastor returned, he had lost half his congregation, who became the founding core of the new mission and subsequent church. In 1989 the congregations still lived side by side, each maintaining about the same number of members.

In the remaining eleven schisms, the struggle was directly between an established pastor and a contending layman seeking to enhance his power and pastoral functions. The typical pattern was for the layman to found a new church or mission around a group of supporters who preferred his pastoral style to that of the incumbent pastor. In one contrary case it was the pastor who was obliged to leave after coming into conflict with a lay *cacique* who had founded and built the church and drove the pastor out through withholding his substantial tithe. The more typical account outlined below, which is based on interviews with pastors and lay members in both the mother church and its schismatic offspring, reveals the extremity of the passions, the extravagance of the charges, and the underlying resilience that often accompany such conflicts.

The contender returned to his home town three years before the schism occurred, after a stint in Mexico City, where he had built up a successful construction company and converted to the Baptist faith through the influence of his Baptist-born wife. Tall, university educated, and handsome, with bright eyes and the strong evangelistic fervour of the convert, the recently arrived contender stood in marked contrast to the older, smaller, and darker incumbent. Now in his fourteenth year as pastor, even his supporters admitted that he was not a strong preacher or very hard worker. Over the next few years the contender honed his leadership skills by devoting much time and energy to the revival of the church's neglected missions, where he showed films and preached. By the year of the schism he had established himself as an active, respected member of the congregation. His mission work was beginning to gain him a reputation in the regional Baptist association. His core supporters were, like him, converts and successful business people who admired his energy, drive, and entrepreneurial style, while they had diminishing patience with the incumbent, who showed no signs of mending his ways.

At a monthly business meeting of the church, the contender's supporters were able to pass a motion calling for the incumbent to step down. The more established members of the church, who still controlled the church executive, responded by declaring the vote invalid, citing by-laws that such a motion had to be made public prior to the meeting and that it had to be passed by a two-thirds majority. In the subsequent months, factional positions hardened as relations between them deteriorated in the increasingly stressful context of joint services. Fearing the factions might come to blows, and after efforts at reconciliation by the regional Baptist association had failed, the pastor closed and locked the doors of the church. The contender's supporters then held services on the church's steps for a time before breaking into the church, arguing the incumbent had now clearly abrogated all pastoral responsibilities by failing to hold regular services. Around the same time an article was published in the city's newspaper claiming the incumbent was negligent in his duties, had stolen church funds, and was a proven devotee of Satan. The contender's supporters denied any connection with the article; no one else believed them. Representatives of the National Baptist Convention intervened but to no avail. The contender's faction claimed that they could not get a fair hearing before the regional association and that only legalistic manoeuvring denied their just, majority decision.

In the end the federal government intervened as the legal owner's of the church's property. Rumours of bribery were spread on all sides. At the membership meeting overseen by federal officials, the incumbent's supporters won, flatly rejecting the losers' claim that the pro-incumbent executive had stacked the voters' list with their own supporters. The regional Baptist association responded by ejecting both sides of the schism from its ranks for besmirching the reputation of all Baptists. When I arrived ten months later, the approximately 40 dissidents had formed an independent Baptist church of some 55 members, had acquired a large property, and were ensconced in a temporary structure. The original Baptist church still retained its former pastor and it was putting 11 new baptismal candidates through a three-month course. The regional Baptist association, for its part, was hinting that the original Baptist church might be reincorporated into its ranks, though no such prospect seemed forthcoming for the dissidents.

Disputes over religious practice and power struggles both enhance our understanding of schism, but these factors, which I have stressed up to this point, do not fully explain it. As Roy Wallis perceptively observed, leadership ambitions and power struggles are to be found in all religious organizations, but schisms are far more prevalent in some than in others.[33] What, then, were the predisposing factors that so inclined Mexican Evangelicals to schism? I would argue that their "propensity to schism," to use Wallis's phrase, was to be found in four related characteristics of their Evangelical world.

First, the sectarian tradition of "the priesthood of all believers" and the attendant notion that educational or other formal qualifications should not be a prerequisite for leadership positions insured that few were barred from contending for the pastorate. This characterization did not, of course, apply to the Adventists and Presbyterians, but none of their nine congregations in my sample experienced schisms induced by power struggles.[34] Secondly, the highly decentralized decision-making structure of the Evangelical world, especially in the appointing of pastors, provided very few external constraints on local power struggles. In part this derived from the strong tradition of congregational autonomy, which was most fully expressed by the Baptists, who believed that the local congregation alone should govern its own affairs. This principle was much less widely held in the Pentecostal world, though practical considerations caused it often to be practised. The Assemblies of God and MIEPI, to cite two of the larger and more dynamic Pentecostal bodies, had the authority to veto, though not to impose, a congregation's choice of pastor. It was, however, my distinct impression that they were reluctant to exercise this privilege. They could and sometimes did intervene in unresolved local power struggles, but they were inclined to delay in the hope that a local decision might be found. Their caution stemmed from their awareness that an unhappy congregation might well reaffiliate to one of a host of doctrinally similar denominations, happy to accept whatever pastor the congregation chose. The fragmented character of the Pentecostals, with their many independent churches and many small, loosely formed coalitions, heavily circumscribed whatever centralized authority officially existed. Such conditions did not of themselves cause schism, but neither did they hinder local power struggles in any way.

Thirdly, rather than looking to centralized offices for appointments, preferment, or salary, Evangelical pastors, and Pentecostals in particular, were obliged to build up their congregations and personal livelihoods in direct competition with all other pastors, apart perhaps from those in their own denomination in another catchment area. Such pragmatic considerations often lay behind the poaching or sheep-stealing kind of schisms referred to above. The entrepreneurial style of pastoring produced by this competition was officially sanctioned by the Assemblies of God and MIEPI, who curtailed the power of local regional bodies to remove founding pastors. For precisely this reason the divorced pastor referred to above was not removed by his denomination, despite his affair with a teenage member of the congregation. The denomination did not cause the subsequent schism, but it did nothing to prevent it.

Last and most importantly, there were a variety of consequences that flowed from the conversionist orientation of Evangelicals, to which reference was made at the beginning of chapter 5. Just as the key to salvation was a deeply felt apprehension of the supernatural and a consequent sense of transformation or rebirth, so the primary task of leadership was to nurture it among the faithful and engender it in others. This skill or gift was, in theory and practice, available to all. It could not be bestowed, withheld, or exclusively claimed by any denominational authority. This was the theological basis of the doctrine of the priesthood of all believers. Intimately linked to it was the equally central doctrine of the "Great Commission," which so emphasized the constant need to evangelize. Together these two doctrines and their attendant expectations made it extremely difficult for incumbent pastors to suppress an effective preacher and/or lay evangelist who might in the end steal their job or a portion of their flock. The wise incumbent shunted younger, neophyte leaders off to Bible institute and mission field, but this was far more difficult with older men, whose jobs and financial responsibilities tied them to local neighbourhood and church. The emotional fire of this conversionist orientation produced an endless supply of future competitors with the incumbent. If the incumbent became tired or burned out, his flock might soon grow receptive to other leadership candidates, since all were agreed that deep conviction and evangelistic fervour were the only true signs of right leadership and secure salvation. Over the years, familiarity could breed a measure of indifference among the laity, but the Evangelical world rarely possessed the institutionalized or centralized structures that might rotate pastors and thereby avoid this dilemma. In short, an abundance of potential leaders, a further element of precariousness in the career of pastors, and a measure of schism were the fruit of this conversionist orientation.

CO-OPERATION AND ITS LIMITS

The degree of centralized decision-making within denominations varied according to the denomination and the issue. I have already touched on some of the information pertinent to this theme, but the

overall pattern needs to be sketched. The Adventist tradition of giving all tithes and a substantial proportion of all other donations to
the sixteen regional associations insured that their well-funded regional offices had the resources to direct a variety of special programs to their local congregations. The regional association also
appointed and paid pastors, as well as funding and directing the
Adventist network of schools, hospitals, and clinics. This centralized control was best exemplified by the standardized and very
professional Sabbath school curriculum set by the American head
offices for Adventists all over the world. Yet even here this pervasive central control was muted by the extreme shortage of pastors,
which left the actual running of the congregations in the hands of
locally appointed lay people who often jealously guarded their own
autonomy, selecting and rejecting programs according to local
needs. Presbyterians and Baptists had their regional and national
bodies that regularly met to discuss common goals and problems.
Both had an extensive network from local congregation to national
church. Yet these centralized structures were poorly and reluctantly
funded by local churches, which meant that their ability to implement common goals and programs was severely curtailed. Thus,
about 40 per cent of all member churches in the National Baptist
Convention made no financial donation whatsoever to the Convention and its related programs.[35] Contributions to local associations
and presbyteries were said to be equally sparse. Local congregational autonomy was then compounded by the shortage of Presbyterian pastors and by Baptist insistence on the ultimate sovereignty
of each congregation.

Pentecostals, of course, were highly fragmented by the presence
of so many independent churches and small, loosely affiliated groupings. Denominations like the Assemblies of God had a clear hierarchy – from congregation to district to region to national assembly –
that was dominated by the pastors, a written constitution, and a de-
claration of faith. MIEPI's major decisions were made by a small
group linked to its first church at Carretones in Mexico City, which
produced a monthly magazine that dictated doctrinal and biblical
study for all constituent churches. However, both of these denominations, which were some of the most centralized in the Pentecostal
world, suffered from chronic underfunding (the tithes of their pastors' tithes) and low regard for the paperwork and established procedure that are the prerequisites for effective central control. In
both cases it would be better to describe their structure as a hierarchy of notables who occasionally intervened at local level in case of
crisis but who preferred to leave the running of congregations to

Table 6.4
Interdenominational co-operation: types and frequency in congregations over
last year

	Advt (3)	Hist. (14)	Pent. (26)	Total (43)
Co-operation b/w pastors	0%	21%	69%	49%
Exchange preachers	0%	0%	46%	28%
Joint campaign/activity	0%	0%	27%	16%

local pastors and laity. With one exception,[36] the twenty-six Pentecostal congregations in my sample gave less than 10 per cent of their
meagre takings to their denomination, if they had one, and none received any financial support in return. For all intents and purposes,
Pentecostal congregations ran their own affairs and rarely looked
beyond these narrow confines for aid or guidance.

Not surprisingly, interdenominational co-operation was not very
common in the Evangelical world, though fragile links of this sort
were being developed in some parts of the country. No pastor I met
was prepared to condemn calls for greater co-operation. In practice, in the forty-three congregations, Table 6.4 shows that 21 (49
per cent) had taken part in some sort of co-operative gesture in the
previous year, but almost half of these (9 of 21) involved contacts
among pastors that did not involve their respective congregations.
One Baptist, for instance buried the member of a neighbouring
Assemblies of God church whose female pastor did not have the
authority to perform this ceremony. In another case, an outgoing
pastor attended the anniversary service of a few neighbours,
though she was not invited to preach. In the remaining congregations the pastors attended, with varying degrees of diligence, a
local association of Evangelical pastors, though this was a practice
largely confined to Pentecostals, most notably the Assemblies of
God. Adventists had nothing to do with regional associations outside their own denomination. Only one Baptist and one Presbyterian congregation from my sample of thirteen had a pastor so
inclined, although it is my impression that Presbyterians elsewhere
were more outgoing in this regard than were Baptists.

In the more personal context of inviting someone outside one's
denomination to preach, the practice was confined exclusively to
Pentecostals, with 46 per cent in Table 6.4 claiming to have done so
over the previous year. Typically the visiting preacher was from
outside the immediate area, which minimized the dangers of
sheep-stealing. Only in seven Pentecostal congregations (i.e., 16 per
cent of the total forty-three) did co-operation extend beyond the

occasional visiting preacher. All seven involved joint evangelistic efforts. Five of the seven congregations attended large rallies for the entire city in which they were located, which undoubtedly strengthened their religious fervour but did not bring them any closer to the other Evangelical churches in their immediate neighbourhoods. (All five congregations also failed to gain any new converts or members as a result of their participation.) Only two Mexico City congregations out of the total of forty-three shared a tent with neighbouring churches in a joint evangelistic campaign. However, this brief period of local co-operation did not endure for more than two years, as the participating churches could not agree how to share their joint converts. Catholic opposition also grew to the point where violent crowds threatened to burn down their tent. Better, they agreed, to disperse and revert to the familiar pattern of separate evangelistic efforts in each congregation. The threat of violence clearly shaped this particular decision, but five of the ten local congregations, all Pentecostal, refused to participate from the beginning, when there was no hint of violence. Two others were never more than marginally involved. My sample makes it clear that co-operative efforts between Evangelical congregations in any given neighbourhood were extremely rare. The major cause was the reluctance of pastors to encourage situations where their small flocks, on whom they relied for subsistence, might be drawn to another congregation or pastor just round the corner or down the street.

Regional associations of pastors of different Evangelical denominations were a new presence in the Evangelical world. In four of the five major research sites where I worked they were established in the 1970s and 1980s. The one exception was a town in the south, which was made less open to this innovation by its rural roots, smaller size, and Pentecostal minority, though a growing city nearby was in the process of forming its own association. Pastors involved in the northern and colonial heartland associations, both located in cities, estimated very roughly that about half of all Evangelical churches were nominal members, with about a third or less attending their monthly meetings. Of the 80 Evangelical churches in the southern city where I spent my sabbatical, 40 were counted as members by the leaders of the pastoral fraternity, who said that between 25 and 30 were regular participants. In the rapidly growing outreaches of Mexico City, informed guesses suggested that a lower proportion of all pastors were participants, though precise enumerations were even more difficult here. These impressions confirm my findings in Table 6.4 that no Adventists, very few Baptists, a scattering of Presbyterians, and a preponderance of Pentecostals made up the membership of these regional alliances of pastors.

At the national level an Evangelical Council had been founded as early as 1929 in Mexico City, but the Presbyterians and Baptists as well as most Pentecostals would not join because of its links with the liberal World Council of Churches.[37] For a time the Evangelical Council spawned a more conservative alternative, the Evangelical Convention, but both were effectively dormant, I was told, by the 1960s. Then, in 1982, CONEMEX (La Confraternidad Evangelica de Mexico) was founded, one month after CONELA, its counterpart for all Latin America. Ideologically both organizations traced their roots back to the 1974 Lausanne conference of Evangelicals all over the world, which affirmed their commitment to the Bible, Jesus, and the centrality of evangelism in Christian life. CONELA was founded as a clear reaction to and rejection of liberal Protestantism, with its sympathies for the social gospel, liberation theology, and ecumenism.[38] Struggles with the "heresies" of liberal Protestantism had never really been an issue in CONEMEX , nor in CONELA either, I suspect, since liberationist and ecumenical tendencies were almost as rare among Presbyterians, Methodists, and Baptists in Mexico as they were among the Pentecostal majority of Evangelicals. In 1988 CONEMEX was headed by Alfonso de los Reyes, the national leader of the Assemblies of God, but one of his three vice-presidents was a Methodist bishop and another was a Presbyterian. By 1990 CONEMEX claimed to represent some ten thousand Evangelical churches,[39] though, as always, numerical claims of this sort must be treated with caution. Very few of the pastors I met outside Mexico City had ever heard of CONEMEX , including those involved in their regional associations. The name was equally unfamiliar to the local pastors and congregations I interviewed in Mexico City. In the early 1990s it had no national name or co-ordinating power, though such attributes may emerge in the future. It would be better to describe CONEMEX , which had its offices in Mexico City, as a newly created institutional mechanism that enabled the leaders of the major Evangelical denominations based in the capital to consult with one another should the need arise.

CONEMEX and the regional pastoral alliances served as a forum where ideas and information could be exchanged within the fragmented Evangelical world on such important but ambiguous matters as government regulations on ownership of church property, religious use of the mass media, or the impact of the new constitutional changes regarding relations between church and state. At times they were also the vehicle for co-ordinating the large-scale evangelistic campaigns that occasionally took place in the major urban centres. Their most distinctive practice was the holding of an annual march of Evangelicals through the city centre in honour of

Benito Juarez on his birthday. First initiated by CONEMEX in Mexico City, the custom was spreading to more and more regional centres. The ostensible purpose was to honour Juarez's Reform Laws, which allowed religious liberty and made possible the subsequent founding of the Evangelical movement. The march also provided the opportunity to make fresh calls for religious liberty, the continuing separation of church and state, and freedom from religious persecution. In some parts of the country, pastors were also drawn to the ministerial alliance because it could provide information and human resources to seek redress against persecution of Evangelical churches and their members, which typically occurred in rural areas. A full analysis of the political orientations of Evangelicals and their relations with Mexican society is pursued in chapter 8. For reasons that will become apparent there, neither CONEMEX nor the pastoral alliances had become an organized pressure group in party politics, capable of negotiating privilege for votes. In the 1990s, as always, Evangelical leaders were still primarily concerned with more immediate issues of self-defence, in the face of what they regarded as a hostile world. When a specific need or crisis arose, pastors were grateful and happy to be able to turn to a pastors' association, if it existed. However, the primary goal of the pastors remained that of saving souls, and thus nurturing and expanding their small congregations. In this central enterprise they were inclined to regard their fellow pastors as potential competitors. There were clear limits on the type and degree of co-operation involved in such alliances. They remained loose coalitions of like-minded souls, fearful of sheep-stealing and of invidious comparisons with their own preaching and leadership talents.

This chapter, it may be recalled, started by analysing the various psychological, social, and material benefits of congregational membership that reinforced commitment. The Evangelical world, we saw, produced an abundant supply of potential leaders and future pastors who, in an entrepreneurial fashion, were obliged to transform small missions into churches or found their own. They were constantly seeking to add to their flock, driven by the twin motivations of their conversionist convictions and economic need. These were the organizational dynamics that produced the high baptismal rates and remarkable growth potential of Mexican Evangelicals charted in chapter 3.

The remainder of the chapter focused on the decentralized, denominationally fragmented, and schismatic character of Evangelical churches, which engendered much competition between local congregations and pastors. These forces have also weakened, though they have not eliminated, co-operative efforts at local, regional, and national levels. Observers of Pentecostalism elsewhere in the world have stressed the same organizational traits of being "decentralized ... schismatic," and "headless," but they have described this as a unqualified source of strength, allowing the movement to spread "across class and cultural boundaries" so that this "organizational smorgasbord" is able "to meet a variety of psychological as well as sociological needs."[40] There is certainly truth to such notions, but they are rather one-sided. The diversity of styles within the Evangelical world, from the humble, intimate, and spirit-filled ethos of the traditional Pentecostal church to the more upscale and cosmopolitan style of neo-Pentecostalism and the controlled and intellectualized emphasis of Adventists and the historical denominations – all these have increased the breadth of its appeal. However, decentralization, fragmentation, and schism have also produced a substantial measure of organizational precariousness. The many small congregations I surveyed had difficulty growing enough to retain a pastor and thereby survive in the face of so much unrestricted competition, while schisms, for a host of reasons, disrupted viable congregations. The resilience of the Evangelical world should not be ignored, but neither should we lose sight of the many who dropped out when schism, conflict, collapse, or the flight of the pastor caused new converts to be neglected or disillusioned. One can only infer that these were the real causes of some apostasy, since I did not explicitly study drop-outs, but they were commonly advanced by Evangelicals endeavouring to explain their organizational difficulties. The small size of congregations and the lack of co-operation between them may also have contributed to high mixed-married rates in the second generation. The marriage pool within most congregations was very limited, and there were relatively few situations where young unmarrieds from different congregations might meet socially. In short, tendencies to apostasy and short-term commitment were the other notable consequences of Evangelical organizational life, which must be set against their equally marked proclivity for evangelism and outreach.

7 The Missionaries

The previous chapter's treatment of Evangelical organization and leadership raised the contentious issue of the degree to which foreign missionaries, above all Americans, control the Evangelical world. Controversy stems from the common Catholic charge that the leadership, energy, and financial support for Evangelical churches comes from abroad. The clear implication is that Evangelical growth would slow and probably reverse if it had to rely exclusively on the energy, leadership, and commitment of Mexican Evangelicals. A recent Catholic denunciation, reported in a prominent national newspaper, claimed that Evangelicals were directly run by the American government, "from which they receive monthly money to cover the salaries of the evangelists and compensation for those who are co-opted."[1] Not all charges are so crude, but all the Catholic clergy I interviewed were agreed that material inducements and financial aid from Americans were at least partially responsible for Evangelical growth.

Behind such claims was the corollary charge that the Evangelical faith was an instrument of foreign cultural domination designed to divide and thereby conquer Mexico. According to Flaviano Amatulli Valente, executive secretary of the Vatican department on sectarianism, who has been working in Mexico for a number of years, the guerrilla war in Central America caused the Americans to shift their attention from the north to the south of Mexico. From the United States were "arriving Bibles and Protestant pastors, who wish to oppress and confuse the Latin American world, in order to control it economically and politically through religion."[2] So enraged were Evangelicals by such charges that they went to the considerable cost of taking out full-page notices in the major Mexico City newspapers in 1987 affirming their patriotism and categorically rejecting all charges that they were "a foreign invasion, with political and economic aims."[3] Then in 1990 the Methodists, Presbyterians, and Baptists combined to publish another open letter, this time addressed to the president and distributed in all their churches, again affirming their long history of patriotic service and protesting "the calumnies and defamations" of "our essential nature" in the mass media.[4] The political ramifications of the Evangelical faith will be explored in the next chapter, but some useful preliminary work can be done by exploring the actual influence of American missionaries in the founding and continued direction of Evangelical churches over the last twenty years. This is the theme of this chapter.

The growing doubts of liberal Protestantism over the propriety of evangelism in a pluralistic world made few inroads among Mexican Evangelicals, who gave their support to the call of the aforementioned Lausanne Conference in 1974 for renewed evangelistic effort. Nevertheless, by the 1960s there was a growing feeling that Mexicans should take more responsibility for their own affairs and that the day of foreign missionary control ought come to an end. In 1972, after one hundred years of Presbyterian missionary influence, it was agreed by both the national church and the various Presbyterian mission boards that their some sixty missionaries and their economic subvention of approximately $500,000 ought to be withdrawn.[5] In a similar spirit, the approximately fifty-member Mexico Mission of the American Southern Baptist Convention decided in the 1970s to subordinate itself to the Mexican National Convention.[6] In the mid-1980s it was agreed to eliminate over a five-year period the Mission's subvention to the National Convention, then running at approximately fifty per cent. The last subsidy was paid in 1993, though there were still about eighty missionaries in Mexico with no plans of leaving. The American Assemblies of God also had about 50 missionaries attached to their Mexican board, which gave no general subsidy to the Mexico national council, though it did respond to special requests. Both these missionary bodies were also agreed, and had been for some time, that they should not pay or in any way subsidize pastoral salaries. With over nine hundred churches affiliated to the Mexican Baptist Convention and about three thousand to the Assemblies of God, missionaries in the 1990s were not a major force in the lives of either church. There were also other major

Pentecostal groupings, like MIEPI, Iglesia Cristiana Interdenominational, Iglesia Cristiana Independiente, and the Iglesia Apostolica,
which have not had any missionary ties for many years.

One could, however, easily cite a host of specialized Evangelical
agencies, typically led and directed by foreign missionaries, with
offices in Mexico City, that provided specialized ministries in drug
and alcohol abuse, medical extension programs, family rehabilita-
tion, Christian education, Christian media, church building, evangelism, and church planting. Impressive as such a list might be to
the uninitiated, it would be misleading, for it gives no sense of how
many missionaries were to be found in these specialized ministries,
of how frequently their services were used, or of how decisive their
influence was.

WORKING WITH MESTIZOS

To get some sense of what missionaries typically did in Mestizo
areas (the situation in Indigenous regions is treated subsequently),
I surveyed missionary activities in two cities, one in the colonial
heartland and the other in the south, where I resided for a sabbati-
cal.7 Pretty and with temperate climates, they attracted a dispro-
portionate number of missionaries – and at least one sociologist. In
the colonial heartland city, with a population of about one million
and about forty-five Evangelical churches, I was able to locate nine
missionary couples. Two independent Baptists and a Pentecostal
each pastored small to medium-sized churches of fewer than one
hundred, which they had founded. Another couple directed a neo-
Pentecostal church with some 650 members, which also had two
full-time Mexican pastors. Two missionaries taught in Bible institutes; one ran youth activities in the neo-Pentecostal church; and a
Southern Baptist missionary preached, organized youth activities,
and gave short seminars on leadership training for local Baptist
churches. The remaining couple arranged about three work teams
a year from American churches to come down for approximately a
week at a time to help in local church construction. The husband's
remaining time was devoted to evangelism on public basketball
courts, though he spoke very little Spanish.

In the southern city, with a population of about 500,000 and
nearly eighty Evangelical churches, there were thirteen missionaries working with Mestizos. Two independent Baptists pastored
churches, though one was actively looking for a Mexican pastor
and the other was also involved in work with Indigenous peoples.
Two others were linked to Youth with a Mission (YWAM), which was
known for bringing in groups of young American Evangelicals for

short periods to give them practical experience of evangelism and mission work in the hope that it might stimulate their appetite for future missionary work. Here the two recently arrived YWAM couples had set up a six-month training program for middle-class, fee-paying Mexican Evangelicals that provided them with courses on Christian approaches to prayer, family life, and sexuality while teaching them some of the rudiments of street evangelism, public witnessing, and the like. The aim was to prepare evangelists for foreign fields and for work with Indigenous peoples, though the existing program, it was recognized, was not in itself sufficient to achieve these final goals.[8] Three couples were involved with orphaned or abandoned children, including one who ran a small orphanage for crippled children and another with nine adopted children of their own, who were building an orphanage for 150 with government approval and funding from a television evangelist. Of the remaining six, two ran separate Bible institutes; three preached and provided leadership training when asked in local congregations; and one newly arrived couple gave a few music classes at a Bible institute and ran a Sunday school program for children on weekends.

With the exception of those missionaries directly running churches in the above two cities, their direct impact on the growth and evolution of the Evangelical churches was marginal, although teaching in Bible institutes or the like clearly played an indirect role. Those involved in preaching and leadership training had not founded any of the congregations they visited. They may well have provided valued guidance and teaching, but their contacts with congregations, by their own accounts, were usually intermittent and short term as they moved from one congregation to another. Only one missionary, through her American church, provided a subsidy for a Mexican pastor, though most had made a few small donations to sick or needy pastors. Foreign funds had built two Bible institutes in the southern city, but the one missionary I contacted at a Bible institute had removed the subsidy of his predecessor because he believed that the local denomination would be better served if Mexicans were more involved in and responsible for their own leadership training. All were regularly asked for financial aid in church construction. The majority had made a partial contribution of this sort in recent years, but all were now adamant that they would only do so for projects that were already initiated, funded locally, and well under way. In theory if not always in practice, missionaries had come to accept that indigenous leadership and local responsibility were the secrets to sustained Evangelical growth.

The constitutional prohibition banning foreign ministers was rarely enforced by the authorities, although rumours of its very oc-casional implementation may have caused a few missionaries to take a less active role than they might otherwise have done. The more pervasive and immediate consequence of the ban was that al-most all missionaries resided in Mexico on tourist visas for a maxi-mum of six months, which obliged them to make twice yearly trips to the border to renew their residency papers. On Mexico's slow roads, with a few more days while in the u.s. for shopping, car re-pairs, some American food and a little English-language television, these regular trips could consume considerable amounts of time. Missionaries affiliated to boards not infrequently found themselves caught up in administration, board meetings, and conferences, which could further reduce their time at their mission base. For their part, independent missionaries, who depended financially on the giving of a network of individuals and local churches, often de-voted considerable lengths of time to the cultivation of their sup-port base in the u.s. All these pressures distracted the missionaries from their essential role, as did the mechanics of daily living in a situation where there was rarely a supervisor to check on how hard they worked. As missionaries came to accept that pastoring and the administration of denominations should be in the hands of nation-als, they saw themselves fulfilling a support role. Evangelism and church planting were their undisputed goals, but it was often not clear how support without control or dependence might be best achieved. The result was that not a few missionaries found them-selves helping out in a variety of small ways without significantly affecting the churches in which they worked, though there were some exceptions to this general rule. The impact of the many short-term missionaries was especially diminished because their Spanish was often very limited.

INDIGENOUS PEOPLES AND THE
SUMMER INSTITUTE OF LINGUISTICS

Charges of American control most commonly arose with reference to Evangelical growth among Mexico's Indigenous peoples. The pri-mary perpetrator was invariably identified as the now-everywhere-reviled Summer Institute of Linguistics (SIL). Its early history and its role in the Evangelical movement in Oxchuc, Chiapas, are outlined in chapter 2. The SIL's bogeyman status was of quite recent origin. In the middle of the 1960s SIL was in Mexico under official govern-ment auspices. Its 240 staff were given official letters of recommen-dation by the Department of Education (SEP) when working in the field. Its sponsoring committee contained a host of the politically powerful, including the president of Mexico.[9] Echeverria and even Portillo carried on this tradition, but a combination of forces quickly overturned SIL's insider status. The acculturationist policy of Saenz, Cardenas, and the Instituto Nacional Indigenista (INI) – that Indians be brought into the mainstream by cultural transformation – was superseded in the 1970s by a new rhetoric emphasizing the defence of Indian culture and rights against oppression. In theory, SIL could have adjusted to the change, since it was developing the written versions of Indigenous languages needed for bilingual education and cultural survival. However, the deteriorating national economy, the spread of Marxist forms of thought, and ever-present nationalism caused INI officials, anthropologists, and intellectuals as a whole to embrace a reductionist conspiracy theory. From this perspective, SIL's main goal was the control, cultural genocide, and pacification of Mexico's Indigenous peoples so as to insure security of access for the U.S. to the vast oilfields of the south, where Indigenous concentrations were greatest.[10] Though no hard evidence for conspiracy or any other charge was produced,[11] the ready fit of such theories with old animosities and current ideological fashion caused hardly any to question them. As Mexico's anthropology departments and universities grew, it was perhaps inevitable that resentment should grow towards a foreign agency defining itself as a defender of Indigenous culture. Nor should it be forgotten that the Mexican constitution prohibits foreigners from ministering in the churches, whose foundation was the avowed final object of Wycliffe Bible Translators, to which SIL and all its members were attached.

In late 1979 the government threw a sop to the increasingly vociferous complaints of INI officials, the National Indian Congress, the College of Ethnologists and Social Anthropologists, and the Communist Party of Mexico. Though not meeting the demand for outright expulsion, the government did end its sponsorship of SIL, which was more a symbolic gesture than anything else, since no financial contracts were involved. None of SIL's bases were required to be closed by the decision, and no SIL personnel were asked to leave, although SIL had recently closed its jungle training camp in Chiapas in the face of the mounting campaign against its presence. As a publicity measure in the face of the same press campaign, SIL formally declared the Chiapas field closed, since its translation work was essentially completed there. What remained to be done could easily be conducted from outside Chiapas. Elsewhere nothing changed directly on the ground, although SIL was now without the formal blessing of the federal government. More significantly,

SIL's presence was soon rapidly reduced when the government re-voked its former policy of issuing student visas to SIL's personnel.[12] As their student visas expired over 1981, most trickled back to their headquarters in Arizona, in the hope that they could continue their translation activities with visits by Indigenous language assistants and the occasional very brief foray back into Mexico.

Unlike other missionaries, SIL was not prepared to live in Mexico on six-month tourist visas, returning twice yearly to the border for renewals. When I visited its southern Mitla base in 1986, its once-thriving compound, now windswept, run-down and empty, was in-habited by a handful of aging missionaries who had received permanent residency papers many years before. In 1986 a bomb was set off at SIL's headquarters in Mexico City.[13] Anti-SIL propa-ganda continued in 1987 with charges by a senior INI official that SIL members were stealing valuable pre-Hispanic objects from ar-chaeological sites.[14] In 1989 SIL returned its headquarters in Tlalpan, Mexico City, to the government, though the original terms of the lease did not require this to be done for a few more years.[15] After the earthquake, government was in dire need of public buildings, while SIL saw the return of its Tlalpan headquarters as a chance to mend fences and to demonstrate its pro-Mexico policy.

In fact the tide against SIL, at least at the official government level, was already turning. In the later 1980s SIL applicants again began to receive residence visas (FM3s) without difficulty. Their number in 1993 rebounded to about a quarter of their peak in the late 1960s. Fewer translators were now needed, I was told, because translation of the Bible into Mexico's many Indigenous languages was so well advanced and should be completed by the year 2000.[16] Government opposition had dissipated. A serene twilight for the SIL in Mexico now seemed likely, though political forecasts of this sort can never be certain. More open to debate is SIL's legacy as a major force causing or shaping Evangelical growth.

From chapter 2, it will be recalled that Marianna Slocum and Florence Gerdel, both SIL members, played a part in Evangelical growth in Oxchuc. As I pointed out there, they were but one element, though an important one, in a constellation of forces that led to Evangelical growth. Slocum was actually sought out and invited to Coralito, where the Evangelical movement took off, by an Oxchucero who had been led to the gospel by another Oxchucero. By 1957, seven years after Slocum's arrival in Coralito, both Marianna and Florence were gone. By 1961 all missionaries were out of the munici-pio, though three couples in the Reformed Church mission contin-ued to provide leadership training at a nearby Bible institute. Neither in Oxchuc nor anywhere else in this part of the highlands did missionaries pastor any churches or fund any pastors.[17] This is precisely why they grew.

Similarly, in the nearby Tzotzil municipio of Chamula, whose story of religious persecution will be addressed in the next chapter, Ken Jacobs, the first SIL member to work extensively on translating the Bible into the Chamulan dialect, played a limited part in the Chamulans' subsequent mass conversion. Arriving in the late 1950s, Jacobs initially tried to live in Chamula, but the local authorities would not allow him to do so. Forced to live in the nearby Mestizo city of Las Casas, he encountered Domingo, a bilingual Chamulan seeking work, who was taken on as a gardener. Domingo, it was said, had already heard the gospel while working on a lowland plantation, but it was not until he began to serve as Jacobs' language assistant that he converted. Domingo then propagated the gospel in his home village or *paraje*, where he converted his brother-in-law, Miguel Gomez, a shaman, who later became the primary leader of Chamula's Evangelicals. Jacobs made two brief visits to house services held by Domingo at the very beginning, but he barely missed an angry mob on the second occasion and never returned.

In 1965 there were about thirty-five "believers" in Chamula.[18] Thereafter a small and then growing group of Chamulan Evangelicals gathered at Jacobs' house in Las Casas on a Saturday. While he tested the translation of the New Testament he had done over the previous week, they acquired the teaching they were to disseminate the next day in a growing body of clandestine house services in Chamula itself. In this indirect manner Jacobs played a crucial role in the spread of the new faith, but he did not himself evangelize or recruit any of the growing number of Evangelical Chamulans. At around the same time, another Chamulan and later Evangelical leader, Domingo Lopez Angel, converted in a Mestizo Adventist church on the coast, though he did not return to build up a following in Chamula until the early 1970s. By the mid-1970s there were reckoned to be some four thousand to five thousand Chamulan Evangelicals.[19] Jacobs was gone by 1978. By the early 1990s Evangelical numbers had grown to at least twelve thousand. During all this time no missionary ever set foot in Chamula.[20] To explain such transformations solely by reference to the intervention of missionaries is simply inadequate. Behind such conspiratorial notions, as Stoll rightly emphasizes,[21] lies a naïve contempt for Indigenous peoples that assumes they were and are unthinking pawns, duped into betrayal of their traditional culture by a few "gringos" after four hundred years of resistance to Mestizo culture and oppression. Their lengthy resistance gives an obvious lie to such facile explanations.

Slocum was part of the very first wave of SIL, when evangelism was still pursued with much the same vigour as translation. As SIL matured, translation of Scripture came to be seen as the essential task. Evangelism and church growth were thus defined as the responsibilities of others following in the footpaths of SIL. The first generation may not have been so thoroughly imbued with the founder Townsend's vision of SIL's distinctive mission as were later members. More important to the transformation, I think, was the WBT/SIL distinction, referred to in chapter 2, whereby Wycliffe, the international body, had explicitly religious and evangelistic aims, while SIL, working in the target countries, had primarily linguistic and translation goals. The distinction was politically convenient, especially in Mexico, where important sectors of public opinion were deeply opposed to Evangelical missionaries. The distinction may at first have been an essentially tactical method of gaining access to otherwise difficult countries, but SIL's public downplaying of its religious aims soon became a central principle in SIL life, especially when it was being attacked by outsiders. Ironically, though SIL's denial of evangelistic intent persuaded few outsiders, it had a substantial impact on SIL. The result was that SIL's role in shaping and stimulating Evangelical growth was curbed. This generalization, with predictable variations, is borne out by the three case studies I was able to accumulate of the long-term impact of SIL missionary work.

In the first case, a future head of SIL for all of Mexico entered a municipio in the southern portion of the Mixteca in 1957. His was the first foreign missionary presence, although a Mestizo Presbyterian had made three or four trips to the area three years before that had resulted in some four families in an outlying hamlet identifying themselves as believers. Only a rough logging trail gave access to the municipio, which was visited by an outside priest several times a year. Two years after the arrival of the missionary, his major language aide converted, though the precipitating factor was a visit to his sister in Mexico, where he converted in his sister's Pentecostal church, which was part of the MIEPI denomination. On his return he evangelized among relatives building up a small church, which was guided by visiting students from the MIEPI's Bible institute in the capital. They introduced the Spanish Bible and preached in Spanish. The missionary did not actively evangelize, as he believed that "this was not the way to go about it. It should be the people themselves evangelizing themselves." As a form of community service, the missionary and his wife ran a medical clinic during the several years they were in residence, which kept them very busy, as no other medical aid was available. Their efforts did not win them any converts, though they did secure the continued toleration of the authorities and improved relations with their neighbours. By the time the missionary officially left, twenty years later, a year before his translation of the New Testament was published, there were two Pentecostal and one Methodist congregations in the dispersed central town of the municipio. None had been founded by the missionary.[22]

On the missionary's most recent return in 1992, all four congregations were Pentecostal, though there were also one fair-sized Methodist church and several missions in outlying hamlets. Mestizos or returning Indigenous folk, converted while working elsewhere, were the principal instigators in every case. In the central town, only the smallest of the Pentecostal churches used a Bible in their own tongue, though services were conducted in Spanish in only one of the four. They preferred the Spanish Bible because they saw it as the language of progress and because their Mestizo mentors from outside were inclined to regard it as the only true word of God. Most of the Methodist congregations used the missionary's translation, but their founder was dying of cancer and they appeared ripe for Pentecostal takeover. A politically active member of the oldest Pentecostal church claimed that about a sixth (17 per cent) of the six hundred households in the central town were Evangelical in the early 1990s, though the 1990 census put Evangelicals at 7 per cent of the total municipio. This represents substantial growth, but the missionary could not be regarded as its major cause.

In the second case, the missionary entered the high Mixteca in 1969, leaving eleven years later when his student visa could not be renewed. On his arrival there were two families identified as "believers" in the central market town. They were the remnant of some ten family heads who had been converted many years before during the Second World War, by Mestizos, while working in a mine. The converts had held services for a number of years, but commitment had eroded, leaving the two families of "believers" at the time the missionary arrived. Apart from personal evangelism, most notably with his language helper, the missionary's only public effort was to sell, weekly at the Sunday market, copies of the Gospel of Mark and some Bible stories in the Mixtec dialect he was translating. When the missionary left, the families of two brothers of the translator were holding irregular services in the home of the translator. In 1986 the missionary's translation of the New Testament was presented to the community. On his last return in 1990 to dedicate the roof of a new Presbyterian church there were about two hundred adult communicants. The congregation is reported to have grown substantially since then.

This growth, which began some two years after the missionary

left, occurred when a group of Mestizo Pentecostals from outside
showed Christian films for several days, using the home of the language assistant, Isadoro, at the invitation of his wife. When Isadoro
returned from working in Baja, California, he was confronted by a
group of neighbours stimulated by the films who wanted him to tell
them about this new faith, which he had read and translated alongside the missionary. Their inquiries led to a strengthening of
Isadoro's faith. For some years the slowly growing congregation
was attended sporadically by the Mestizos from the district seat. As
the demands on Isadoro's time grew and the guidance of the Mestizos became more sporadic, he sought guidance from the now-de-
parted missionary. The latter put Isadoro in touch with a Bible
institute for lay people run by a dynamic Mixe Presbyterian.[23]
Under the direction of the Presbyterian, who introduced a system of
elders and leadership training, the congregation was weaned of its
Pentecostal ways. The Mestizo Pentecostals complained of sheep-
stealing, but to no avail. They lost against a strong leader who could
claim a common Indigenous heritage with the disputed congregation and who was revered for once having been left for dead by
Catholic persecutors. At last report, only a few Pentecostals remained in the municipio. In this case the missionary provided key
advice at a crucial point in the development of the congregation,
but he was neither instrumental in its foundation nor the major
force leading to its Presbyterian affiliation.

In the third and last case, a missionary couple entered Chatino
country in the fall of 1979, just as the government was revoking its
agreement with SIL. Another SIL member, who had previously lived
for three years in another hamlet of the municipio they had chosen,
introduced them to the town president, who welcomed then and offered to help them find accommodation. Their SIL mentors had advised them to deny their SIL affiliation for about two years, or until
they could explain their purpose in Chatino, though the municipal
president was certainly aware of their SIL membership. Their goal,
they were repeatedly told, was exclusively that of translation.

SIL's presence in the nine municipios where the Chatino are based
was of almost forty years' standing when the couple entered. Two
other SIL teams had resided for several years between them in the
1970s in the particular municipio where the couple settled. In 1979,
the evangelistic fruit of the total of seven SIL teams, that had already worked throughout Chatino country since 1942 was one
small Pentecostal mission church centred around a former transla-
tor-assistant, though the missionaries were Baptists.[24] In 1981 in the
nine municipios were approximately 18,000 Chatino speakers over
the age of five.[25]

In the principle town of the municipio, where Chatinos were a minority of the population, there was a Spanish-speaking Pentecostal church. It had been founded some ten years earlier by Mestizos from a municipio closer to the coast. No Chatinos were members. In the particular "agencia" or village where the missionaries came to reside, there were two related families of Evangelicals already holding house services. They had been converted by a Mestizo travelling preacher from the same Pentecostal church that had earlier founded the Mestizo church in the principle town. The missionaries knew nothing of these two families when they chose the village. The first convert was a bilingual male Mestizo married to a local Chatino. The second convert and the first Chatino convert (regarded by the Chatinos as the first convert) was the brother-in-law of the first convert. He had learnt Spanish from his Mestizo wife. He was also a prominent member of his village, having formerly served as village president. Their house services, to which the missionary couple were invited, were held in Spanish, though a goodly number of the two households could not understand it. The male missionary, who spoke flawless Spanish, urged them to use Chatino and confessed his SIL membership, in violation of his instructions. However, their burgeoning relationship was broken within two months of their arrival by the sudden demand of the village council that the missionaries leave. The pretext given was that their rented house was needed by a relative of the owner. The real reason, they discovered, was that the Catholic priest in the principle town had refused to baptize any babies from the village until the missionaries left. They did so a few days later, settling in Mitla, SIL's major base in southern Mexico, which was and is several hours away from Chatino country on unpaved roads. The missionaries stayed in Mitla about six months, working with a language helper recruited from the village on a subsequent brief visit.

When their student visas expired, the missionary couple, like all other SIL teams, moved to Catalina in Arizona to continue their work, but they felt unhappy and out of touch there because their knowledge of Chatino was so little advanced. They decided to leave SIL and join another faith mission, the United Indian Mission, which had at that time only four couples working in Mexico, all located in the north. In the interim period of 1980 to 1985 they made a few brief visits to the village, including an early stay for two months in the house of the municipal president in the principal town, but their contact with the village was necessarily limited.[26] On settling back in the state capital, but not the village from which they were still barred, they discovered in 1985 that the two family groups of Evangelicals had expanded to include between sixty and seventy members. After a schism in the Mestizo church nearer the coast had caused it to neglect the fledgling village church, the latter was left on its own for a while. It came to be pastored for about a year by a travelling Mestizo evangelist, this time from Mexico City, who was eventually expelled by the local authorities for interfering in village life. The first Chatino pastor, who has since guided the church, was appointed in 1984. He was the son of the first Chatino member. Like his father, he was bilingual, an able leader, and a former village president who had to flee after holding office because of unexplained deficiencies in his administration's budget, which his father subsequently paid off. During his years away, working in a city, the future Chatino pastor became a Pentecostal. The husband of the missionary couple tried to recruit him as a language assistant because of his intelligence and fluency in both languages, but the missionary failed. Then on a return visit the first member's son decided to stay and take over the leadership of the church. In short, here as before, the founding and early evolution of the village church was not significantly shaped by the missionary.

After the missionary couple's return to Mexico in 1985 the husband usually made two or three brief visits to the village a year, from a city six hours distant by road. Normally he stayed one or two nights. Freed of the restrictions of SIL, he became much more active in the life of the village church, though the actual amount of time he spent there was extremely small. He devoted the remainder of his energies to translation work and to the running of a small church in his home base in the state capital. In this city he also set up and ran a leadership training program for four days a month for the pastor and eight other Chatinos, who were instrumental in founding two missions. When the church was expanded, he purchased the materials for the roof. He was also the source of a few bags of second-hand clothing and twenty-five latrine kits distributed here, but in no other of the forty-three sample congregations. In the latter part of the 1980s he channelled a donation from a Hispanic church in California when the pastor was considering seeking secular work to supplement the meagre sums he was receiving from his congregation. Thereafter local contributions stopped growing and failed to keep up with ever-rising inflation. By 1993 the foreign subsidy of one hundred dollars monthly amounted to 60 per cent of the pastor's income. Since the congregation had grown to approximately one hundred families, it should have been able to support its own pastor, but the members were unwilling to give more, as the missionary himself admitted, because they regarded him as an endless source of funds. This organizational precariousness was accentuated in 1993, when a long-standing rump of disaffected Pentecostals in the congregation created a schism, leading thirty-five of the one hundred families out to form a new congregation linked to the Mestizo church in the principal town of the municipio. The Mestizo church was in turn affiliated to a Mexican Pentecostal denomination based in Mexico City, with no foreign ties.[27] At about 25 per cent of the village's population just prior to the schism, Evangelical growth was considerable, but it had not been initiated by the Baptist missionary and its future course seemed to be slipping from his control.

Outside of SIL, which would not have allowed the varied influences outlined above, there appeared to be few other missionaries working among Indigenous people. Only in Chiapas did six Presbyterian couples stay on in Indian areas, under a special agreement with the Chiapas presbytery. However, it was their firm policy not to provide funding for pastoral salaries and church buildings, on the grounds that such aid fostered passive dependency and hindered autonomous growth. Their major emphasis was on teaching and leadership training, though three of the six couples in 1993 were devoting most of their time to translation work. Among the some forty Southern Baptist Convention missionary couples, not one in 1993 worked primarily among Indigenous peoples, lived in their areas, or was trying to learn one of their many languages. On the Pentecostal side, not one of the official list of sixty-six Assemblies of God missionaries worked with Indigenous peoples in 1993, while MIEPI and other large Pentecostal denominations had no tradition of foreign missionaries.

There were, of course, an indeterminate number of independent missionaries resident in Mexico, but they typically lacked the support network, long-term commitment, and language skills needed to work in remote Indigenous areas. The striking exception was the missionary couple among the Chatinos cited above, who were joined in the 1980s by two other couples to whom they were related by marriage or blood.[28] In the city of Oaxaca, which is the capital of the state with more Indians than any other, I was able to find only one Pentecostal couple who had been working with a specific Indigenous group for a number of years and could speak their language. The wife had been born and raised in a Zapotec village with SIL parents.[29] She knew the state intimately. Yet she could think of only one other Pentecostal throughout the entire state, a former member of SIL, who was still working among Indigenous people and could speak their language. She could identify several younger Pentecostal missionaries elsewhere in the state working in Spanish. At their bases in regional towns they endeavoured to provide leadership training for Indigenous people, but they made no more than brief forays into the Indigenous villages they hoped to reach. Similarly, in Las Casas, the gateway to the highlands of Chiapas, only one Pentecostal missionary in 1992 was working among Indians in rural areas. None could be recalled ever having worked in Oxchuc.

THEIR IMPACT ON CONGREGATIONAL LIFE

The examples above tell us something of the number and activities of missionaries in a given region or area, but they do not really reveal how frequently and in what ways missionaries affected the Mexican Evangelical world as a whole. Some sense of the overall impact of missionaries on Evangelical churches may be derived from my sample of forty-three Evangelical churches. Missionaries played a part in the founding of nine, or 21 per cent, of the local congregations. Four of the eight missionary-planted churches were right on the northern border. The leadership in one case came from a Hispanic-speaking Baptist church in Texas. Another was evangelized by a Mexican-American from California who happened to have relatives in this particular neighbourhood and worked with the first Assemblies of God church in this Mexican city. Of the five mission-planted churches in the heartland and south, three were older churches established in the era when missionaries still dominated the Evangelical world, though the driving force in at least one case (details were sketchy in the others) was a Mexican lay evangelist. The fourth, a small rural Pentecostal church in the south, was also founded in the late 1970s by a Mexican evangelist with American links. In his case, it would be more accurate to describe him as reviving a defunct mission that had been initially founded solely by Mexicans. Not long after, the founder embraced Pentecostalism, severed his connection with the missionary denomination, and left his son in charge of what was an independent church in 1993. The one remaining congregation was the large neo-Pentecostal church, to which reference has already been made, which was founded in the early 1980s by a second-generation, fluently bilingual missionary. The founding of the other thirty-four Evangelical churches was entirely the product of Mexican evangelistic efforts.

Identical figures emerge on the related issue of missionary aid in the acquisition of land for churches. Three Baptist churches on the northern border and two older Presbyterian churches in the centre both had their property fully purchased by American churches or missionaries. Four others received partial funding from missionary sources, while 79 per cent acquired their land through Mexican initiative and funding. In fact, only ten, or 23 per cent, obtained land through the co-operative efforts of their members. In the other twenty-four churches, which represent by far the largest category, the church's land was donated as a gift by a founding member.

The subsequent construction of the church was also done exclusively by the co-operative efforts of their members in 63 per cent of the churches. Typically it was a slow, laborious process as members acquired the needed materials, with donations over and beyond their regular tithe. A skilled builder would sometimes be hired for some of the more difficult stages, but much of the labour was commonly provided by the pastor and the members. Building as they did in a piecemeal manner, not a few churches were in a permanent state of construction, Here, however, American aid was more extensive, with 37 per cent receiving some degree of outside support, though only three (7 per cent) were fully funded by outside sources. Typical were the three Pentecostal congregations that received partial support from Wayne Myers's missionary organization, which has helped many Evangelical churches by paying for the cost of the roof, provided the congregation completed the remainder. Far less common was the recent effort by a Kentucky Assemblies of God church, which paid for all the materials and then subsequently built a church for a sister Mexican congregation through the labour of work teams sent down for the purpose. The experience may have been spiritually and culturally uplifting for the Kentucky Pentecostals, but the Mexican church was built in an area where there were already many other Evangelical churches and for a pastor who has since been unable to expand his inadequate congregation of some thirty-five baptized members. Had they not intervened, the pastor might well have moved on, but he was reluctant to desert his large though rather empty edifice. This is why missionaries soon learned to contribute to church building only when the local congregation had shown the commitment to build a substantial portion of it themselves.[30] The fact remains that 37 per cent of my sample of congregations received some degree of financial aid in the building of their churches; the majority did not.

The foregoing figures largely refer to past events, but the congregational sample also explored the current degree of missionary contact in the immediately preceding year. In the forty-three churches, only the large neo-Pentecostal church had an American missionary pastor, though it should be recalled that it also had two Mexican pastors who did most of the daily pastoral work. Only fifteen (36 per cent) of forty-two[31] congregations had no contacts whatsoever with foreign missionaries over the previous year, but the figure is misleading because it is largely owing to the over half of all churches (62 per cent) with one or more foreign preachers who had no sustained contact with the congregation. Moreover, almost half of these visiting preachers were Hispanics, mainly from the United States but also from Nicaragua and Puerto Rico. Eleven congregations, 24 per cent of the total, were visited by a group of foreigners with the aim of doing something in the congregation. These too were all short-lived visits. Thus two Baptist churches on the border were visited for a few days by a small medical team that offered free treatment for anyone in the neighbourhood. Both these border churches, with their easy access to the u.s., were also visited by a group of American young people holding their week-long vocational Bible school for neighbourhood children during the summer holidays. Similar help with the summer Bible school occurred in one congregation in Mexico City and in another in the colonial heartland, though the latter group were Mexican teens funded by American sources. One rural Baptist church was visited for a week by a Hispanic Baptist group from Detroit who toured the countryside and showed Christian films in the evenings. Three Pentecostal congregations were also visited by groups from American churches who sang nicely and communicated as best they could, though few had any Spanish. One other rural church was visited weekly for a few months by a young missionary couple who ran a Saturday afternoon program for children. Only the neo-Pentecostal church, in the throes of building a seminary, was visited by several American church groups, there to help in the construction. These visits were motivated on the American side by the desire to share their faith and to do something for those less fortunate than themselves, while having a vacation. Apart from the concrete effects of aid in the building of churches, the visits left an ephemeral sense of mutual good will, but they had little impact on the long-term vitality of the Mexican Evangelical world.

In the same sample, nine, or 21 per cent, of the congregations had received some sort of financial aid from foreign sources in the preceding year. Three were on the border, where links of this sort are most predictable. One new, independent Baptist church received a gift of a school bus and a loan for the purchase of their church's property, which had to be repaid. Another Baptist church was given a partial donation for the repair of its second floor. In the third case, the founding Hispanic church in Texas had subsidized the pastor's salary when it was a small mission. Ten years later the American church continued to give the same subsidy, though its value had diminished over the years and now amounted to a fraction of the pastor's salary. Only in the Chatino Indian church and in the neo-Pentecostal congregation, both referred to earlier, did a pastor receive a significant amount of foreign financial support, though the two Mexican pastors in the latter church were entirely funded by local giving. In the other cases, the visiting Detroit group contributed one hundred dollars to mission work; another Mexican congregation received some funds for the purchase of building materials for a mission, and a third was grateful for an offering that enabled them to repair a leaky roof. In the last church to receive any aid, the pastor's original religious mentor, a Mexican, who now pastored a Hispanic church in New York, contributed to some medical expenses and the purchase of a truck. With the partial exception of the Chatino church, the survival of none of these recipient churches was reliant to any significant degree on foreign giving. Among the remaining thirty-three churches in the sample, amounting to 79 per cent of the total, none had received any financial support in the preceding year.

Given Mexico's long land border with the United States and the incalculable number of affluent Evangelical churches in the American southern Bible belt, with a rich tradition of tithing and giving to missions, it is scarcely surprising that an American missionary presence could be found. Yet according to all the various avenues by which I tried to assess the actual degree of American influence among both Mestizos and Indigenous peoples, the Mexican Evangelical world in the 1980s and 1990s was largely self-directed and self-sustaining. Catholic convictions to the contrary are to be expected. Far more palatable is the reassuring, if erroneous explanation that Mexican Evangelicals were the bribed dupes of an alien superpower. The less appealing alternative is that they were neglected or disaffected Catholics seeking a new faith.

More problematic, I think, is the question why the missionary presence had so little influence. In SIL's case its failure was partly an unintended consequence of the institute's political manoeuvring. It also stemmed from the difficulty modern missionaries have encountered in forsaking direct control and support of Indigenous churches in the name of autonomous, self-sustaining growth, and yet finding some way to have a real influence. They have moved a long way in the former direction, but they have been less successful in solving the latter. Whatever strategy they ultimately choose, there must always be severe limits on their power to transform. In part this is because they are alien to the culture in which they work and are always transient. It is also because they cannot coerce their constituency of potential believers, no matter how much or how little control they may exercise in churches and institutional structures. In the end, conversion, commitment, apostasy, growth, and decline – all depend on the response of Mexicans to the new faith, and not on what missionaries may or may not do.

8 Societal Links: El Mundo

Just as the flesh or worldly pleasures have been seen as sinful and the Spirit or relations with the supernatural as holy, so in the Evangelical world have the confines of church and Christian community been regarded as the right and proper place for believers. The outside world, by contrast, has been seen as Satan's terrain, tempting, corrupting, and dangerous. From this stems the exclusivist, world-rejecting propensity of Evangelicals. It in turn engenders the charge that they have been politically passive and therefore the unwitting supporters of corrupt, worldly regimes. Yet this is far from the whole story. Evangelicals have also felt a deep call, both individually and collectively, to reach out, to evangelize, to save lost souls. In Bromley and Shupe's phrase, they are a "redemptive social movement"[1] in that they have given priority to individual and spiritual transformation rather than the collective and material changes typically stressed by secular political movements and by liberal Protestantism. Evangelicals, and conversionist sects in general, have long believed that "the world is corrupt because men are corrupt."[2] By this logic the salvation of the world will only come when we are all evangelized, converted, and saved. Fuelled by the "Great Commission," Evangelical outreach stands in stark contrast to its exclusivist, world-rejecting tendencies. This contradiction or dialectic of contrasting principles is the central theme of this chapter, as Evangelicals have been obliged to confront and resolve it in their dealings with the wider Mexican society they inhabit. The same general theme will also lead us to examine the degree of persecution of

Evangelicals by other Mexicans and the treatment accorded them
by the state.

LOCAL COMMUNITY RELATIONS

Catholic relatives were the most intimate layer of the wider
Mexican society with which Evangelicals interacted. Family loyalties in general, with their attendant bonds of mutual support and
recreational network, continued to be highly prized in Mexico in
the 1980s.[3] Conversion to an Evangelical church necessarily implied
a break with Catholic family. Among the 225[4] converts I interviewed, 61 per cent said that their initial decision caused a real rift
with the remainder of the family, which ranged from beatings and
ejections from home to the more prevalent response of argument,
ridicule, and social ostracism. One convert was told by his still un-
reconciled father: "Choose. Do you prefer the one to whom you
owe respect or your own beliefs?" Far more typical was the experience of a twenty-five-year-old Pentecostal convert who, just prior
to his conversion, had dabbled heavily in drugs and been dishon-
ourably discharged from the army for a knife fight. "When I converted, I was filled with joy. I wanted to tell everyone, to let them
know what I felt and knew, that Christ is coming, but they laughed
at me." Such responses were by no means universal. Fully 35 per
cent said their Catholic relatives were tolerant of or indifferent to
their conversion decision, while a tiny 4 per cent voiced their clear
approval, typically because it freed the convert from a former life of
alcoholism, family neglect, or wife abuse. A goodly number of the
converts also claimed that the opposition of their parents and other
kin to their conversion subsequently grew less bitter and intense.
Nevertheless, a division was typically established, which often
grew and rarely eroded as the years passed.

Table 8.1 summarizes the magnitude of the gulf. Among the 339
in the interview sample who had "some" or "many" Catholic relatives in the village, town, or city where they lived, 60 per cent said
they never or very rarely visited their Catholic relatives. Pentecostals, second-generation Evangelicals, and city dwellers had less
contact of this sort with Catholic relatives than did members of the
historical denominations, converts, and rural folk, though none of
the differences enumerated in Table 8.1 is large. All are surely
predictable. Many (40 per cent) said they maintained regular or
frequent contact with at least some Catholic relatives, but they
were usually referring to brief visits during the week. The short
weekend of Saturday night and Sunday was still the major time for

Table 8.1
Evangelicals who visit their Catholic kin,* interview sample

	Hist. %	Pent. %	Male %	Female %	City %	Rural %	Conv. %	2nd gen. %	Total
Never	17	25	24	23	24	16	20	29	23%
Rare	32	41	35	38	37	40	37	37	37%
Reg./often	51	34	40	40	39	44	43	34	40%
Total	100%	100%	100%	100%	100%	100%	100%	100%	100%
	(110)	(209)	(127)	(212)	(148)	(138)	(179)	(131)	(339)

* Excludes Evangelicals with "none" or "few" Catholic relatives in the area where they reside.

Table 8.2
Evangelicals who attend celebrations of Catholic relatives,* interview sample

	Hist. %	Pent. %	Male %	Female %	City %	Rural %	Conv. %	2nd gen. %	Total %
Never	48	74	67	65	70	57	70	59	66
Rare/brief	34	24	32	25	25	33	28	27	27
Yes	18	2	2	10	5	10	2	15	7
Total	100%	100%	100%	100%	100%	100%	100%	100%	100%
	(110)	(209)	(127)	(211)	(147)	(138)	(179)	(131)	(338)

* Excludes respondents with "none" or "few" Catholic relatives in the area where they reside.

socializing for most Catholics. The specific event bringing people together in any number was typically a birthday (often held on the person's saint's day), first communion, *quinze anos*,[5] or a wedding. Table 8.2 shows that far fewer Evangelicals attended such events. Two-thirds said they never did. Another 27 per cent admitted to doing so very infrequently, or said that they attended for a short time to show their respect, leaving before the dancing and partying really began. Most of the renegade 7 per cent who did attend such events denied they drank or danced. They were a disparate group composed of wives with Catholic spouses and a scattering of better-educated, often second-generation Evangelicals who believed they had the maturity to set an example to the non-Evangelical world without surrendering to its temptations.[6] Few other Evangelicals believed this was right or possible. At the key social gatherings of Catholic kin, Evangelicals were conspicuous by their absence or by their aberrant behaviour while there.

The reluctance of Evangelicals to involve themselves in the social life of their Catholic kin should not cause surprise. The Catholic ritual linked to first communions, *quinze anos*, and weddings all disinclined Evangelicals to attend and thereby give credence to a faith they so vehemently rejected. The drinking, smoking, and dancing at such events were all taboo for Evangelicals. When the fiesta took place on a Sunday, the challenge of contending allegiances was all the more clear-cut. These value differences also extended into the quieter kinds of family visits charted in Table 8.1, which makes me suspect that Evangelicals overstated the degree of their intimacy here. When the zeal of new converts was rebuffed or ignored, as it usually was, it was predictably discouraging. Catholic relatives too must have tired of evangelistic efforts, which implied, however politely, that their Catholic tradition was wanting. Evangelicals tried to maintain some sort of contact with their Catholic relatives, especially their parents, when they were not overtly hostile. Most were conscious of the call to evangelize should the opportunity arise, but the gap between the two groups typically grew. These various factors were neatly expressed in the following description from a now fifty-six-year-old Pentecostal convert and night watchman, married to a lapsed Catholic, of his relations with his in-laws: "We do not share anything in common. Visits with them include drinking and smoking. Their conversation is completely different from what one expects. This is why we do not visit them. A long time ago, we used to talk to them of the gospel, but they rejected it. They were always arguing. There is no point. They know but they do not want to accept. I consider them as relatives but nothing more. There is no rejection but there is no communication."

The anti-Catholic and puritanical values of Evangelicals also insulated them from the most popular communal festivals at all levels of society, from local neighbourhood to village, town, city, and nation. Evangelicals could and sometimes did participate in celebrations of Independence Day or Benito Juarez's birthday, but the really big events of the year, publicly celebrated everywhere, all had such a visibly Catholic tenor to them that Evangelicals regarded public participation as unthinkable. This was most obvious in the week-long series of processions, outdoor fairs, torch-carrying relays, and public displays of penitence building up to the annual celebration of the Virgin of Guadalupe on 12 December. Evangelical participation here was no more thinkable than it was at the earlier festival of the "Day of the Dead," or Feast of All Saints, when elaborate altars, adorned with food and skeletons, were everywhere constructed. A goodly portion of the population also flocked to the nation's cemeteries to commune with their "dead ones." Evangelicals celebrated Christmas and Easter, but they did so separately and indoors, having nothing to do with the outdoor Catholic processions and celebrations, which Evangelicals regarded as superstitious and heretical.

Similar sentiments also infused Evangelical perceptions of the many celebrations of Catholic saints and virgins, each with its fair, procession, and dance. Permeated by Catholic symbolism, this recreational cycle was the product of an agricultural economy, though fewer and fewer Mexicans each year were so employed.

In the anonymity of larger urban areas, less notice was taken of the Evangelical unwillingness to participate in these communal traditions. School vacations, the two-day weekend, and holidays defined by the commercial or industrial cycle were all starting to mark the secularization of urban society, which offered alternatives to the traditional Catholic recreational calendar, undermining its importance and obligatory nature. A host of secular recreational forms were emerging, from television to football to discos and movies, which further diminished the link between Catholicism and public life, though the puritanical values of Evangelicals still left most wary of these new alternatives. This emerging secular version of Mexican society and identity, which was far from complete, was beginning to undermine the traditional intertwining of folk Catholicism with Mexican identity described in chapter 5, and symbolized by the Virgin Of Guadalupe. As secularization made its slow inroads, Evangelicals might more comfortably proclaim their Mexicanness while remaining separate from the mainstream.

Such developments were much less advanced in rural areas. In some communities and for some fiestas, all were expected to contribute financially and to participate. Elsewhere, fiestas were organized and funded by groups of men and women called *mayordomias* or *cofradias*. These groups included several ranked *mayordomos*, with ever higher levels of prestige, authority, and financial responsibility. Neighbourhood fiestas were smaller than those for the village, but those who hosted the latter accumulated more prestige and spent more money. The acquisition of prestige within the community typically depended upon the successful fufilment of these socially prescribed roles in the fiestas, known as *cargos*. The importance of the *cargo* system was most marked in Indigenous communities, where the hierarchy of religious posts was sometimes integrated with the civic political structure, so that a person was expected to alternate back and forth between the two, acquiring more prestige the further up the ladder one went.[7]

After 1945 the intertwining of civil and religious hierarchies began to erode as the principal locus of power shifted to an autonomous political hierarchy, increasingly dependent on external funding and on skill in dealing with the outside world. By the 1980s the prevailing pattern was a separate religious *cargo* system.[8]

Nevertheless, the Evangelical refusal to participate was undeniable rebellion against a key element of traditional village life. Initially and perhaps inevitably this decision was the source of considerable tensions, sometimes resulting in fines, jailings, and worse, as we shall see shortly when the issue of persecution is addressed. In Oxchuc, where the secular political system split away from the traditional tribal structure and religious *cargo* system many years ago, tensions of this sort no longer existed in the early 1990s. Among the Chatino, where an independent and secular political system emerged more recently,[9] an accommodation had also been reached in the particular village I studied. Here, when collections were made for the costs of fiestas, Evangelicals were exempted, provided their names had been submitted to the village authorities by the pastor. If anyone on the list was seen by village officials to be participating in the fiesta, he or she could be fined. Similarly, in Mixe country, where every municipio once fought against Evangelical withdrawal from the traditional fiesta system, all, I was told in 1993, were now resigned to this state of affairs. Some exceptions to this general trend will be outlined shortly, but such arrangements signified a new, institutionalized, though less than eager acceptance of religious pluralism and secular separation of church and state.

Socializing with Catholics may have been largely taboo, but Evangelicals were far more willing to join ranks with others for the good of their shared local communities. Table 8.3 shows that 63 per cent of Evangelicals participated in activities to improve their local neighbourhoods, while another 11 per cent said no such opportunity existed. Only just over a quarter said they were not involved, of whom about three-quarters were either young unmarrieds not yet of an age to do so or married women who left such matters to their husbands. Communal involvement was much less marked in the cities, where anonymous municipal governments tended to be in charge and there were fewer opportunities. In rural areas, where the practice of *tejio* (obligatory contributions of labour by household as a substitute for monetary taxes) was far more prevalent, 85 per cent of Evangelicals claimed they were so involved. As a matter of principle, 90 per cent (see Table 8.4) said that it was a Christian duty to be so; only 2 per cent expressed any doubts at all. Their pastors were even more emphatic: 88 per cent of the forty-nine I queried (93 per cent in the historical denominations and 84 per cent of Pentecostals) concurred that community involvement was a Christian obligation, while the remainder defined it as primarily a duty of citizenship. None of the pastors expressed any doubts

Table 8.3
Evangelical involvement in activities to improve local community, interview sample

	Hist. %	Pent. %	Male %	Female %	City %	Rural %	Conv. %	2nd gen. %	Total
Yes	62	63	67	61	51	85	64	66	63%
No	18	30	20	29	35	15	25	24	26%
n/a*	20	7	12	10	15	0	11	11	11%
Total	100%	100%	100%	100%	100%	100%	100%	100%	100%
	(136)	(279)	(163)	(288)	(210)	(168)	(232)	(186)	(451)

* Respondents claimed that no organized efforts to improve their local community existed in their particular neighbourhood.

Table 8.4
Evangelical views on participation in local community improvement, interview sample

	Hist. %	Pent. %	Male %	Female %	City %	Rural %	Conv. %	2nd gen. %	Total
Ought	91	88	93	88	85	96	90	90	90%
Can	7	9	6	9	12	3	8	9	8%
Doubt	1	2	1	2	2	1	0	1	1%
No	1	1	1	1	2	0	1	0	1%
Total	100%	100%	100%	100%	100%	100%	100%	100%	100%
	(136)	(275)	(161)	(286)	(206)	(168)	(230)	(187)	(447)

about the propriety of such activities. To quote but one pastor, a Pentecostal, "According to the Bible, we have the obligation to respect the authorities and collaborate in all that is demanded of us as citizens." Evangelical attitudes and behaviours of this sort bear little correspondence to the popular stereotype of them as insular, anti-national folk, hostile to the responsibilities of citizenship.

Evangelical notions of how they ought to relate to the outside world are more fully revealed by another question, which asked whether they ought to serve as leaders or committee members in organizations and activities seeking the material welfare of their local communities. Tables 8.5 and 8.6 summarize the views of the laity and pastors respectively. When it came to an active role of leadership to secure material betterment, there was less consensus, though Evangelicals were much more activist in orientation than is commonly thought. A little over half the laity (55 per cent) and 49 per cent of pastors defined it as a Christian obligation, while a quarter or less questioned its propriety. Those in between stressed that leadership here was not a specifically Christian calling, though

Table 8.5
Evangelical views on leadership in improving local communities, interview sample

	Hist. %	Pent. %	Male %	Female %	City %	Rural %	Conv. %	2nd gen. %	Total
Ought	66	51	63	51	50	64	55	56	55
Can	19	20	20	21	24	17	20	23	21
Doubt	14	19	11	21	18	16	16	18	18
No	1	10	6	7	9	3	9	3	7
Total	100%	100%	100%	100%	100%	100%	100%	100%	100%
	(106)	(237)	(128)	(231)	(191)	(150)	(193)	(142)	(359)

Table 8.6
Pastors on Evangelical leadership in improving local communities, pastor sample

	Advt %	Hist. %	Pent. %	Total
Ought	67	67	39	49%
Can	33	20	42	35%
Doubt	0	13	16	14%
No	0	0	3	2%
Total	100% (3)	100% (15)	100% (31)	100% (49)

they were equally emphatic that Christians were free to participate. Pentecostals, women, and city dwellers were more likely than Baptists, Presbyterians, males, and rural folk to question the wisdom of social activism, though none of the differences is large. Pastors were also slightly less likely than the laity to question outreach of this sort. Apart from religious motivations, Evangelical diffidence was undoubtedly shaped by the pervasive Mexican distrust of all but family and the widespread reluctance among all Mexicans to participate in associational activities.[10]

Doubts among Evangelicals stemmed from the belief that "it would be better to devote oneself to spiritual things" because "there are temptations" and because "it often interferes with commitment to the church." Most commonly, I was told that committee work often entailed "deals and arguments over money" and it was therefore "better to avoid problems" by not taking on leadership responsibilities. Others objected on the grounds that school committees and the like often raised funds through raffles and public dances, which caused predictable difficulties for Evangelicals. In spite of all these problems, only a minority were prepared to advise against Evangelicals' taking leadership positions. The great majority felt that it was either a Christian responsibility to serve in this way or, at a minimum, that there were no religious obstacles to doing so. Though I had no effective way of making a statistical assessment, it seemed to me that the Evangelical presence on local committees was at least equal to their proportion of the population. In the thirteen rural congregations, all had one or more members on either the school committee or the local *commisario ejidal*, which was the local committee of the communal lands occupied by many Mexican peasants. Evangelicals were sought out, it was said, because they were sober and thought to be trustworthy handling money.

This outreach should not be viewed as some sort of hidden social-gospel orientation among Evangelicals. Three-quarters (76 per cent) of the pastors denied that they had any special responsibility in their ministry to address problems of poverty, lack of employment, social services, and the like. As one pastor explained, "we lose our spiritual mission by dealing with the material world." The remaining quarter who did bring up such issues in church services did so infrequently, in order to illustrate "how it brings one to spiritual salvation." The great majority of laity and pastors, who believed that Evangelicals should or could be leaders in communal activities, often talked in a general way of working for "the good of the community" and of the responsibility to be good citizens. More important for them was the possibility that their occupancy of leadership positions might provide "an opportunity to witness," "to speak to the people of Christ," and "to set an example to Catholics of how we act, of how we are." If Evangelicals also gained "the help of someone who has links with the authorities," then the blessing was all the greater. The final goal for Evangelicals was the reform and transformation of individuals through a personal relationship with Christ rather than the reform of social institutions and practices. This was the primary justification for Evangelical involvement in local communal leadership.

Evangelistic fervour was one of the major sources of tensions between Catholics and Evangelicals at local community level. Apart from those communities where the Evangelical right to withdraw from Catholic festivals was not yet institutionalized, no other issue was so potent a source of friction. The constant evangelistic campaigns of most churches and the many small groups of women and teens who evangelized from door to door insured that most households in most neighbourhoods had been canvassed several times. The resentment this could engender was evident in the posted signs, seen everywhere throughout Mexico, on the fronts of homes, saying, "We are Catholic and Mexican. We are followers of the

Virgin of Guadalupe. We do not want to have anything to do with foreign Protestant propaganda."

Local Catholic ire was most powerfully provoked by outbreaks of religious enthusiasm, usually among Pentecostals, which could sometimes make for very noisy neighbourhoods. Two examples of their effect will suffice. One is the previously mentioned incident in a Mexico City congregation, when a loud outdoor campaign, in conjunction with four other churches, caused an angry Catholic crowd to surround the campaign tent, threatening to burn it down. The police intervened and the crowd dispersed, but the tent came down. In the other case, an old, small, and conservative Pentecostal mission experienced some miraculous healings, which in turn led to many conversions. During an intense revival over several months there were nightly services of two to three hours' duration that not infrequently lasted till midnight. To disseminate the already loud message and music further, additional loudspeakers were placed outside the church, facing the street. The neighbours complained and issued threats, prompting the village authorities to demand that the noise level be reduced and cut off at an early hour. The congregation in turn saw the complaints as religious persecution, inspired by a jealous Catholic priest. Hence they ignored all complaints and requests. The situation came to a head when a member of the congregation was shot and killed, returning home from a late service. The outside speakers were withdrawn, though the services continued. These are extreme examples. Few Catholic responses were so vehement; rather, low-key versions of similar incidents abounded in the multitude of small house-churches, which brought together recent converts in worship. Next door to where I lived for a year in southern Mexico, for instance, a small Pentecostal prayer group frequently played loud and lengthy recordings of a hectoring revivalist preacher, accompanied by much weeping and wailing, which did little to improve local community relations.

Underlying tensions between Evangelicals and Catholics were widespread, but it was rare for them to erupt into overt aggression. Among those in the labour-force, enumerated in Table 8.7, 82 per cent said that they had never been treated badly in their place of work because of their religion. A goodly number in this category said that they had been helped by the Evangelical reputation for honesty, sobriety, and hard work. Another 13 per cent said that negative or rude comments had been made about their faith. Only a very small 5 per cent said that they had ever been discriminated against because of their religion. Four of the thirteen who made this claim were Adventists who felt they had been badly treated at work

Table 8.7
Evangelicals reporting discrimination in labour force, interview sample

	Advt %	Hist. %	Pent. %	Male %	Female %	Rural %	City %	Total
No	74	88	80	79	87	85	79	82%
No/but*	5	9	16	16	8	14	14	13%
Yes	21	4	4	5	5	1	7	5%
Total	100%	100%	100%	100%	100%	100%	100%	100%
	(19)	(81)	(156)	(157)	(99)	(81)	(132)	(256)

* Rude or negative comments about respondents' Evangelical allegiance from Catholic co-workers, which did not extend to discriminatory treatment.

because of their refusal to work on Saturday, though only one claimed actually to have lost a job for this reason. In a similar vein, a young Pentecostal nurse said she was forced to resign because her hospital would not arrange her shift-work schedule around the five services a week she attended. Persistent efforts to proselytize led the bosses of two others to forbid them from doing so any more at work, which they defined as discrimination, though others might disagree. Among the remaining varied cases, a Baptist working at a gas plant filling tanks felt he was fired for his honesty when he admitted to inspectors that none of the tanks was ever filled to its legal weight. A poor former alcoholic and recent convert, working in a supermarket, did not lose his job but said he was viciously mocked by a hostile boss for accepting a promotion to run the wine and beer department – and then never paid for the new responsibilities. Individual cases of discrimination certainly occurred, but my survey suggests that they were not on a significant scale.

Local relations between Catholics and Evangelicals were usually quite good, though this conclusion depends on how the frequency of tensions is measured. In the last two years, six (14 per cent) of the forty-three sample congregations had experienced some degree of manifest hostility on the part of Catholics. Two were part of the just-mentioned joint campaign in a Mexico City neighbourhood that brought out an angry Catholic mob. Evangelistic efforts also provoked threats and stonings by Catholics against a small Baptist group from a big-city congregation endeavouring to set up a house-church and mission in a rural hamlet where an Evangelical presence had yet to be established. Loud and noisy services were the cause of hostility in two other cases. In one, angered Catholic neighbours complained vociferously, threw a few rocks, and tore down a banner outside the church. In the other a well-connected neighbour adjacent to the Pentecostal church was able to persuade municipal authorities to close the church for noise violations, though the Evangelicals had the ban lifted six days later on the grounds of religious persecution and religious freedom.

In the last congregation, located in an Oaxacan village, rather different pressures were at work. Founded some thirteen years earlier by a Mexican evangelist around an older, defunct mission, the newly revived mission so offended village authorities that they jailed a few of the men who attended services. These men were released a few days later when the outside evangelist, who knew a sympathetic official, was able to obtain an official letter from the justice department in the capital, which informed the village officials that they could not violate the constitutional right of freedom of worship. Official pressure stopped, though Evangelicals from the village felt obliged for a further few years to provide an escort for the pastor in and out of the village on his weekly visits. They also continued to be obliged to pay the quota, or mandatory contribution required of all working men between the ages of eighteen and sixty, for a variety of Catholic village festivals held throughout the year. Over the last several years three of the Evangelicals I interviewed had been jailed briefly for refusing to pay their quotas. Another official government letter secured the release of one of those jailed, while the other two had their quotas paid by Catholic relatives.

By the time I arrived in 1993, mandatory contributions were no longer being imposed for three minor Catholic festivals, but the village authorities still insisted that all contribute to the annual eight-day festival devoted to the patron saint of the village. The expected quota, amounting to approximately a week's wages for a working man, was by no means inconsiderable. The village authorities argued that this was a cultural, not a religious event, to which all must contribute. The Evangelical reply was that the festival was centred on a Catholic saint, involving payments for candles, dances, and alcohol, which offended their religious convictions. Their sense of injustice was further fuelled by their conviction, which I could not verify, that some Catholics did not pay the full quota, while all Evangelicals were required to do so. Whether all this constitutes persecution is open to debate. Their struggle, Evangelicals insisted, was with the village authorities not their Catholic neighbours, with whom they claimed to have cordial relations. The pressures to pay were clearly weakening and had no legal or official sanction outside local village authorities. Incidents of this sort should also not obscure the fact that thirty-six, or 88 per cent of the forty-three sample congregations, according to their own pastors, experienced no maltreatment or discrimination over the preceding two years.

Table 8.8
Evangelicals reporting hostile treatment in local neighbourhood in last two years,
interview sample

	Advt %	Hist, %	Pent. %	Male %	Female %	Rural %	City %	Total
No	77	86	79	79	82	75	85	81%
Words*	21	10	12	13	11	14	10	12%
Social rejection**	3	3	4	2	4	2	5	3%
Hostility***	0	1	2	4	1	3	1	2%
Institutional****	0	0	3	2	2	6	0	2%
Total	100%	100%	100%	100%	100%	100%	100%	100%
	(34)	(136)	(296)	(170)	(296)	(161)	(240)	(466)

* Rude or negative comments about the respondent's Evangelical faith from neighbours.
** Social exclusion, refusals to chat, or displays of coldness from neighbours.
*** Violence or threats of violence from neighbours against respondents or their property.
**** Discriminatory or abusive treatment from local authorities.

A similar picture emerges from the data in Table 8.8, which summarizes how many Evangelicals had been badly treated because of their religion in their local neighbourhoods over the last two years. A full 81 per cent said nothing of this sort had happened to them, though another 12 per cent added that they had run into the occasional epithet of "Hallelujah" or the like on the street. Only 3 per cent spoke of their neighbours as "cold," not wanting to have anything to do with them, though the degree of polite social separation was obviously much greater. It is perhaps noteworthy that five of the thirteen in this last category admitted that their persistent efforts at proselytism were the reason their neighbours "don't want to talk to us." The 2 per cent listed in the "institutional" category in Table 8.8 were all residents in the Oaxacan village discussed immediately above. There remained only eight, or 2 per cent, who said they had encountered overt hostility for religious reasons over the last two years. Two in a rural hamlet claimed that religious prejudice drove a neighbour to treat their animals badly whenever the opportunity arose. A recent convert from the same area said that drunken former friends threatened to beat him for becoming an Evangelical. The remaining five cases were all related to evangelistic efforts. Two respondents recalled stones being thrown at their house while holding a prayer service. Two others said threats of violence late at night were made by neighbours angered at late services in the local church. The one remaining person was an urban Baptist trying to evangelize in a rural hamlet with no prior experience of Evangelicals. Revealing as these few examples may be, the overwhelming majority of the Evangelicals in my sample from all

Table 8.9
Evangelicals reporting hostile treatment in local neighbourhood before 1980s,
interview sample

	Advt %	Hist. %	Pent. %	Male %	Female %	Rural %	Urban %	Total
No	62	59	54	55	57	55	61	57%
Words*	35	17	21	24	20	25	13	21%
Social rejection**	0	11	15	10	14	6	18	13%
Hostility***	3	12	10	11	9	15	7	10%
Total	100%	100%	100%	100%	100%	100%	100%	100%
	(29)	(106)	(169)	(100)	(204)	(126)	(127)	(304)

* Rude or negative comments about the respondent's Evangelical faith by neighbours.
** Social exclusion, refusals to chat, or displays of coldness by neighbours.
*** Violence or threats of violence by neighbours against respondents or their property.

over Mexico said that their relations with their Catholic neighbours
were harmonious though rather distant.

Evangelicals everywhere told me that their relations with Catholics had eased in recent years. Table 8.9 gives some credence to
their impressions, though the contrast is not as great as some have
thought. Before the 1980s, 57 per cent of Evangelicals said they had
never been mistreated by their Catholic neighbours. A full 81 per
cent made the same claim of their experiences in the previous two
years. Relations before the 1980s with Catholics were certainly
frostier, with 34 per cent claiming that they had been subject to
taunts or overt exclusion by their neighbours. A small 10 per cent
said they had personally encountered what they would describe as
hostility or aggression. Of the thirty who made this latter claim, by
far the largest number (twenty-one) recalled threatening incidents
related to the founding of their church, to which I will return mo-
mentarily. Another six talked of rock-throwing and the like at
school, while one vividly recalled returning as a teenager with her
church's choir from a visit to a rural church and being threatened
with guns by drunken men on horseback. In the other case a young
married couple in the 1960s lived for a while in a highly conservative Catholic village in the colonial heartland, where they were
obliged to go to mass after threats were made on their lives.

The frequency of persecution seems much higher if one looks at
the proportion of churches, rather than individuals, that experienced overt hostility before the 1980s, though the same causes were
at work. In the thirty-four churches founded before the 1980s, Table
8.10 shows that no persecution or aggression was recalled in fewer
than half (44 per cent), while the precise details of the early years

Table 8.10
Churches reporting hostile treatment before 1980s, congregational sample

	Advt %	Hist. %	Pent. %	City %	Rural %	Total
No	100	50	32	47	20	44%
Yes	0	25	58	29	80	41%
d.k.*	0	25	11	24	0	15%
Total	100%	100%	100%	100%	100%	100%
	(3)	(12)	(19)	(17)	(10)	(34)

* Information not available.

could not be remembered in 15 per cent of the churches, which were all founded many years ago. Nevertheless, 41 per cent did experience persecution at one time. This figure rises to 48 per cent if the churches for which I have no information are excluded. Table 8.10 reveals that rural areas were especially prone to persecution.

The reasons varied. In one case, a customs official living very close to a lively and noisy Pentecostal church in the north entered a service near the end of an evangelistic campaign waving a pistol and threatening to kill the pastor if he did not stop. A group of old ladies surrounded him, praying loudly, which caused him to flee. He is said to have shouted threats from outside on other occasions and to have burnt smelly refuse when the prevailing winds were church-directed, but he never again entered the church. In another case, in a village in the colonial heartland in the early 1950s, the pastor called out a greeting to someone he recognized in a Catholic religious procession carrying the statue of a saint. Some in the crowd thought they heard the pastor defame their saint. There followed a brief period of acute persecution, including the jailing of the pastor. Angry crowds gathered around the homes of Evangelicals, which led to the closing of their small chapel for about four years, though some continued with house services. Relations must already have been quite tense for such an incident to provoke such a strong response.

In the Chatino Indian village church whose founding is outlined in the previous chapter, threats had been made and rocks thrown during house services almost from the beginning. Tensions came to a head a few years later when several Evangelicals refused to contribute to the major Catholic festival in the village. They were jailed for a short time. Extravagant charges were also made in the court of the regional town that Evangelicals were refusing to pay any taxes, were not contributing the voluntary labour (*tejio*) required of them, and were plotting to destroy the Catholic church and its saint. Led by the ranking Chatino member of the church, who had long been active in community affairs, an Evangelical deputation persuaded the court that all the charges were fallacious. Not long after it was the turn of the Mestizo pastor to be jailed when he intervened on behalf of two more members being pressured to pay the festival quota. The situation was then resolved when the head office of the pastor's denomination in Mexico City was able to arrange for an official government letter to be sent to the village, informing the local authorities that religious freedom was guaranteed by the constitution and that no one could be obliged to contribute to a religious event. Peace has since reigned.

In all the other cases of persecution, the clear reason was initial Catholic resistance to the founding or introduction of an organized Evangelical presence in a community. Two brief examples will suffice. In one case in the colonial heartland a small Pentecostal mission was established in the 1940s by two local residents who had been converted while working in the Unites States. After they constructed a mission church of cardboard and wood on land donated by one of the founders, an irate crowd of Catholics arrived in trucks during a service, throwing rocks and threatening to kill the Evangelicals. The congregation hid in the cellar until a platoon of soldiers from a nearby barracks dispersed the crowd. The crowd took no further action, apparently because of the army's intervention, though the numbers attending the mission fell dramatically for a time. In the other example, in a nearby rural area, whose founding by a Presbyterian medical missionary I have already recounted, a crowd eventually descended on the small mission "with rocks and clubs to close the church." The small congregation was terrified. Its menfolk either fled or refused to leave their homes. Not long after, Presbyterians from the nearby city, hearing of the event, held a meeting in the mission, where they offered their assistance and convinced the mission to continue. At the next Sunday service, another Catholic crowd descended on the mission. This time it was met by a Presbyterian army captain who showed them his papers and berated them for their illegal behaviour.[11] Open opposition never occurred again. In these two dramatic cases, as in all others, overt Catholic opposition and attendant persecution were short-lived, though animosities and resentment lingered far longer. However grudgingly granted and frailly maintained, the principle of religious liberty and pluralism were eventually established in these communities.

There were some exceptions to or variations on the general pattern outlined above. Dennis gives a brief account of the growth of an Adventist church in Tlacochahuaya, Oaxaca, for instance, in the

1920s. People were drawn to the new faith, he says, because they wanted to escape the burdens of public service in the intertwined religious and political cargo system. Following the 1917 constitution, landless peasants in the area were for land redistribution, which was predictably opposed by the larger landowners, including some of the local Catholic clergy, who themselves owned land. As the Adventist pastor favoured land reform, his church was identified with the land movement, which may have strengthened, though it cannot fully account for the appeal of the Adventist faith. Tensions culminated in 1935, when a crowd attacked the Adventist church during a service, destroying the building and killing the pastor and several other members of his congregation. The Adventist movement died.[12] Such intense persecution seems to have been due to the overlapping of religious and economic tensions. My sample would suggest that persecution of this sort was rare, but when it did occur it did not allow for religious diversity.

The most enduring and largest-scale case of persecution in Mexico is undoubtedly that of San Juan Chamula, the large Tzotzil municipio in the highlands of Chiapas. The previous chapter discussed how limited the role of missionaries was in bringing about Evangelical growth in Chamula. Persecution, in this case in the form of expulsion of all Evangelicals from their homes and lands, took place within a year after the first Evangelical group of one hundred was formed in the second half of the 1960s. After federal and state government officials condemned the action as contrary to the constitution, the Chamulan authorities allowed many of the refugees to return. Their leaders, Domingo Hernandez and Miguel Gomez Hernandez, never again settled permanently in Chamula, for fear of retribution, though Miguel often returned to visit and evangelize. Then, after 1973, further convulsions shook Chamula, which led to the jailing and expulsion of some two thousand Evangelical Chamulans, many of whom were forced to sign papers giving up all claim to their homes and land. Thereafter, when the state and federal governments did nothing more than reiterate their disapproval, the Chamulan authorities embarked on a policy of expelling all who refused to participate in an elaborate cycle of religious festivals, built on a complex cosmology that was as Mayan as it was Catholic.

In the second half of the 1970s the first of the Evangelical refugee settlements, Nueva Esperanza (New Hope), was formed on the outskirts of the nearby city of Las Casas. The four-acre site was purchased by Miguel Gomez Hernandez and divided up into house lots, with a loan from the National Presbyterian church, which was subsequently repaid by the occupants. The pattern was then repeated in 1981 with the creation of a second Evangelical community, Betania, this time with loans from Presbyterian missionaries on land provided by the mayor of Las Casas. Here too all loans were repaid, though the missionaries did not charge any interest. This pattern has since been repeated several times over, creating a total refugee community in the environs of Las Casas thought to number about fifteen thousand in the early 1990s. About three thousand were modern Catholics who had also been expelled for not participating in the traditional fiesta system. The remainder were all Evangelicals. As government condemnations of the expulsions grew in the 1980s, the number of new refugees fell, though they did not stop. In 1993 there were signs that the expulsions might again start to grow.[13] Then in 1994, after my fieldwork was completed, small groups of the expelled Evangelicals were said to be returning to Chamula,[14] but this was soon followed by reports that three Evangelicals had been killed in Chamula and the homes of another two families had been torched.[15] Evangelical Chamulan leaders all spoke of their desire and right to return, but they admitted that the prospects were slim. Having also made new lives for themselves with social amenities and living standards no worse and often better than what they left behind, it is less than clear that many would want to return.[16]

There are three broad reasons for the determined and enduring policy of expulsion of Evangelicals from Chamula. The first is cultural or religious. The traditionalists felt they could not countenance the rejection of the deities of their ancestors, above all San Juan, who nourished and sustained them for as long as can be remembered. If the Evangelicals were not punished and banished, all might suffer disease, poor crops, and bad fortune, because the traditional deities would surely be angered. Behind this was the more general perception that their traditional culture, enshrined in the fiesta system, was threatened by Evangelicals and modern Catholics, and needed to be defended at all costs. More material considerations certainly motivated the political bosses, or *caciques*, who often propagated such views, but there must have been a pervasive acceptance of religious and cultural threats for the expulsions to have been so devoutly pursued.

The second reason had to do with a set of more material or pragmatic interests accruing from the expulsions. Hunger for land in this most densely populated municipio in the highlands[17] probably played a part, though such motivations were blunted by the government's insistence in the early 1980s that the expelled still owned their land. Since that date the lands of the refugees have been left unoccupied. This does not apply to earlier refugees, whose lands had already been absorbed by other Chamulans. The refusal of Evangelicals to drink alcohol and to buy the candles and incense for their many fiestas also threatened the pocketbooks of the powerful *caciques*, who monopolized the sale and distribution of all these commodities. If all had become Evangelicals, their losses would have been considerable.

The third and more basic reason for the expulsions is rooted in the continued intertwining of the civil and religious cargo systems in Chamula. Unlike Oxchuc and the general trend in most other Indigenous communities, the new generation of political bosses, schoolteachers, and entrepreneurs actively participated in the religious cargo system and the attendant fiestas as well as the political hierarchy. By the 1950s "they had displaced village elders both as political leaders and as guardians of religious orthodoxy."[18] In Chamula the religious cargo and fiesta system continued to be far more elaborate and vibrant than anywhere else in Chiapas.[19] In Chamula, unlike Oxchuc, the refusal to participate in traditional fiesta was a direct rejection of political leaders and their authority. As long as the political authority and economic interests of Chamulan leaders were intertwined with the fiesta system, the Evangelical refusal to participate implied political dissidence and was likely to engender strong opposition and continuing persecution. Put differently, Evangelical refusal to participate in fiestas in Chamula had political ramifications that existed in few other Indigenous communities by the 1980s.[20] If Oxchuc and the Chatino experience were any indication, a measure of secularization, or differentiation of religious and political hierarchies, would be needed before religious tolerance could be established in Chamula. This did not seem likely in the early 1990s. Federal and state authorities had often condemned the Chamulan authorities for their refusal to respect the constitutional principle of religious liberty, but they had never intervened in any decisive way to insure implementation. Given the large size of Chamula, the defiance of its leaders, and the large block of votes they delivered to PRI, the perpetual victor on election day, governmental timidity was hardly surprising. Government inaction was also surely linked to the widespread public tendency to doubt the depth and authenticity of Evangelical nationalism.

POLITICAL LEANINGS

Outside local community structures, in the secular power structures of Mexican society, persecution was least marked. Evangelical

Table 8.11
Laity and pastors* opposed to Evangelical leadership in unions and political parties, interview and pastor samples

	Unions		Political parties	
	Laity*	Pastors*	Laity	Pastors
Advt	41% (22)	100% (3)	74% (35)	100% (3)
Hist.	49% (66)	31% (13)	61% (124)	53% (15)
Pent.	54% (148)	46% (22)	71% (241)	65% (31)
Female	53% (145)		68% (250)	
Male	48% (91)		67% (150)	
City	48% (173)		63% (171)	
Rural	63% (19)		71% (159)	
Secondary ed. or more	28% (58)		36% (64)	
Primary ed. or less	63% (118)		75% (253)	
Convert	50% (137)		71% (207)	
2nd gen.	51% (82)		64% (165)	
Total	51% (236)	45% (38)	68% (400)	63% (49)

* Excludes laity and pastors in rural areas with no union experience.

outreach here was also more reticent. Whereas about a quarter had doubts about Evangelical leadership at local community level, 51 per cent of the laity and 45 per cent of pastors were opposed to Evangelical participation in the leadership of unions. When it came to involvement in the leadership of political parties, Evangelical opposition rose to around two-thirds of both pastors and their members. In this sphere of real secular power, only 17 per cent of the laity and 18 per cent of pastors viewed Evangelical participation as a Christian duty. Table 8.11, which summarizes these findings, shows that Pentecostals, women, rural folk, and the little educated were less open to such activities. Only the minority of Evangelicals with a completed secondary education or more (16 per cent of the total congregational sample) differed radically from the general pattern.

Here and there Evangelicals could point to individuals active in unions or politics who remained active members of their churches, but most agreed that it was an extremely difficult combination of allegiances to maintain. In the south-east many Evangelicals gave me the example of a second-generation Presbyterian elder who was elected president of the local branch of the cocoa producers' association. He did so well, transforming the deficit he inherited into a substantial surplus, that he was re-elected for another two-year term. While in office he sold his truck to the association and then used it as president. With the profit he paid the down payment on a twenty-five-hectare farm, which was large by local standards. His political opponents in the association then accused him of corruption. After damaging newspaper articles appeared, he felt obliged to resign, though he was subsequently cleared of all wrongdoing. Many of his fellow church members were appalled at the bad reputation he had given them all. They were also quick to point out that his church attendance had fallen off while he had been president. Despite a subsequent audit, some still wondered how he could have acquired so much so quickly for himself. His supporters said he had always been good with money. Chastened and back in the fold of the church, he told me that other Evangelicals should not do what he had done because "there are too many pressures to do corrupt things. At a certain moment one has to decide."

A similar decision was also reached by a Pentecostal neighbour who has been active in his *ejido*, cocoa producers' association, and *campesino* organizations for over twenty years. Though he said that Evangelicals "could" be leaders if they wished, he stepped down from the executive of the cocoa producers' association when he reported the graft of some colleagues and was threatened with violence by others after he refused to take part himself. Even those who felt Evangelicals "ought" to be political and union leaders often acknowledged the problem of dealing with corrupt institutions. In the colonial heartland a Presbyterian achieved a very high level of prominence as mayor of the state capital, president of the state university, and as a PRI senator, but his fellow Evangelicals admitted that he had not attended church in twenty years and had "not helped Evangelicals." Some bluntly concluded that "we cannot serve two masters," while others anguished over leaving "everything to non-believers" who "are so badly handling things." In either case, the majority decision, especially in the political realm, was that Evangelicals should not be involved. The benefits of witnessing in a corrupt world were usually seen to be outweighed by the danger of apostasy.

All the pastors I talked to stressed that voting was a civic responsibility incumbent on all Christians. In the presidential elections of 1988, 60 per cent voted among the 389 in my congregational sample of Evangelicals who were of voting age at that time. Table 8.12 shows that abstentions were particularly marked among women (45 per cent, vs 31 per cent for men), on the northern border (45 per cent), and in my colonial heartland base (48 per cent), which was the home state of the principal opposition candidate, Cardenas. There were three major reasons given for Evangelical abstentions, the relative importance of which I can only estimate roughly. First, the

Table 8.12
Voting trends of Evangelicals and all Mexicans for president in 1988, interview sample and national results*

	PRI %	Frente/Card %	PAN %	Others %	Not vote %	All Mexicans
All Voters	25	16	9	1	50	100% (38,074,926)
All Evang.	39	19	1	0	40	100% (389)
North	38	16	2	0	45	100% (96)
Centre	19	33	0	0	48	100% (128)
Capital	46	29	2	0	24	100% (55)
South	62	2	2	0	35	100% (110)
Advt	37	3	9	0	51	100% (35)
Hist.	47	22	1	0	30	100% (115)
Pent.	36	21	0	0	43	100% (239)
City	37	20	2	0	42	100% (172)
Rural	34	24	0	0	43	100% (152)
Female	34	20	1	0	45	100% (252)
Male	50	18	2	0	31	100% (137)
Prim. ed. or less	43	19	0	0	38	100% (263)
Sec. ed. or more	30	21	6	0	43	100% (53)
Convert	39	19	0	0	42	100% (204)
2nd gen.	40	21	3	0	36	100% (156)

* Gonzalez Graf, *Las elecciones de 1988*, 339.

smallest sub-category consisted of people, most notably women, who said they had never had an interest in elections or politics. Second were the substantial minority who claimed that they could not get voting credentials, though it is always difficult to say how many here might better be put in the first or next category. The third and largest group were those whose abstention represented a protest against what they regarded as a rigged election among corrupt politicians. "There was no point" was the common refrain. Such a high abstention rate reflects the disillusionment felt by so many Evangelicals with the political process, but abstentions were certainly higher among Catholics, since the official rate for Mexico was 50 per cent. Most experts agree that the real rate was probably higher.[21] Despite the economic ravages of the 1980s, very large numbers of all religions in Mexico appeared to agree that salvation was not to be found in the political system.

The party preferences of voting Evangelicals, outlined in Table 8.12, differ in predictable ways from Mexicans as a whole. It might appear that Evangelicals gave greater support to Cardenas (19 per cent) than did the remainder of the country (16 per cent), but this should be set against the widespread belief that the official results understated the Cardenas vote and hence the degree of Catholic support for him. Whether Cardenas did or did not win a real plurality of the votes cast on that particular day is something we will never know. It does seem clear that a substantial minority of Evangelicals supported the leading opponent of the PRI establishment. In Cardenas's home state of Michoacan almost twice as many Evangelicals gave support to Cardenas as they did to Salinas de Gortari, the PRI victor.[22] Cardenas would undoubtedly have garnered more Evangelical votes, and their abstention rates would surely have been lower, had it not been for their fear that certain elements in Cardenas's leftist coalition were hostile to religion in general and to Evangelicals in particular because of their presumed American connections. In the north, not only was there a markedly high abstention rate among Evangelicals, but a third (11 of 35) of those who voted for PRI at the presidential level were firm supporters at the municipal level of PARM, a minor opposition party. PARM had endorsed Cardenas,[23] but many Evangelical supporters could not follow their party here, causing them either to abstain or to vote reluctantly for PRI. The other major opposition candidate, Clouthier, stood for PAN, the conservative Catholic party. Only 2 per cent in my Evangelical sample voted for PAN; the great majority simply could not countenance such an option.

Evangelicals gave more of their votes to PRI than to any other party. The 39 per cent of Evangelicals voting for Salinas was also substantially more than the 25 per cent of all Mexicans who supported the PRI candidate for president. The fact remains that only a minority of all Evangelical voters supported Salinas in 1988. Any notion that Evangelicals voted as a bloc for PRI is obviated by such statistics, though the exceptional circumstances of generalized discontent in the free-falling economy of the day cannot be ignored.

Among Evangelical voters for PRI, it was my strong impression in interviews, though I can put no precise numbers to it, that most gave their support very guardedly. They did so because they felt they should vote and because they were even more opposed to the alternatives. Their support for PRI was tepid, tinged with distaste for its undemocratic and corrupt practices, and yet paradoxically secure for the future, if not for this particular day. Their thinking was succinctly conveyed by the following comment, a month before the 1988 election, by Alfonso de los Reyes, then general superintendent of the Assemblies of God and later president of CONEMEX: "Better the old for being known say many of our faithful. This is why we are going to vote for PRI; in spite of everything the system has guaranteed religious liberty. Let us hope the next government brings about a moral renovation."[24]

There were five principal reasons given by Evangelicals for their support of PRI. First, some government employees and contractors reliant on government largesse bowed to the pressure of their unions to vote PRI. Others, though they were a small minority, said that the Bible required them to obey legally constituted authority and therefore they were obliged to abide by PRI's request to vote for it one more time. Shorn of religious justification, rather more proffered much the same explanation when they said that they voted for PRI because "it gives us schools, roads, and hospitals." The underlying assumption of both these explanations was the equivalence of PRI with government, which prevailed most commonly among the less educated. Such an assumption is perhaps understandable in a state where one-party rule has persisted for as long as anyone can remember. For such people the democratic notion of choosing among competing parties for government office was simply alien. A minority also felt that PRI was best able to handle the current crisis. Lastly and by far most commonly, Evangelicals said they voted for PRI, in spite of all their reservations, because it was the only party that had a proven record of guaranteeing them religious liberty. The other two opposition groups, for reasons already mentioned, were regarded as suspect on this most crucial of all considerations.

The reluctance of Evangelicals to become involved in political opposition and struggles for political change is most clearly evident in their response to the question of whether Evangelicals should or could participate in demonstrations or political protests against the authorities in pursuit of justice or material improvements. Overall, Table 8.13 shows that 77 per cent of Evangelicals and 85 per cent of the preponderant body of Pentecostals felt they "should not" do so, or that they "could, but it would be better not." At the other end of the scale, only 5 per cent said Evangelicals had a Christian duty to do so. The remaining 18 per cent felt Evangelicals might participate if they wished, while denying any religious injunction in the area. Pastors were in full agreement, with 92 per cent (36 of 39) advising that demonstrations and political protests were not suitable activities for Evangelicals. Table 8.12 reveals a broad-ranging consensus, with only the better-educated and historical denominations showing a little liberality, though even here the majority disapproved.

Evangelical objections to political protest and demonstrations ranged from opposition to violence to doubts over their efficacy and to suspicion that leaders were often motivated more by self-interest than by a genuine concern for the common good. Behind such practical, worldly considerations lay the religious premise that "God has set the authorities over us" and that therefore "as Christians we have the obligation to respect the authorities," even if "the

Table 8.13
Participation in demonstrations or political protest for justice or material
improvements, interview sample

	Ought %	Can %	No %	Total
Hist.	10	27	63	100% (95)
Pent.	3	12	85	100% (209)
Male	7	19	74	100% (113)
Female	4	18	78	100% (204)
City	5	17	77	100% (172)
Rural	5	20	75	100% (134)
Convert	2	19	78	100% (169)
2nd gen.	8	17	75	100% (125)
Prim. ed. or less	5	16	80	100% (200)
Sec. ed. or more	9	28	63	100% (46)
Total	5%	18%	77%	100% (317)

authority is corrupt." "It is far more biblical," Evangelicals said, "to
pray for our leaders" and "to put our faith in God." Believing fervently in the efficacy of prayer, they denied that they passively condoned injustice. They insisted, "we have the right to demand our
rights," but they were equally insistent that this be done in an "orderly, quiet" manner, usually through elections or the sending of
delegations to persuade recalcitrant authorities. Yet no Evangelicals
I met were prepared to condemn the parades or demonstrations
held by Evangelicals themselves on Juarez's birthday, because they
were organized in an orderly manner, they made a point of demon-
strating their respect for the authorities, and they were demanding
religious liberty. Secular political demonstrations, by contrast, were
not appropriate places for Evangelicals, they claimed, because here
there was typically much "shouting," "aggression," and "blas-
phemy." Evangelical participation in demonstrations, they believed,
might "compromise greatly our witness," by which they meant
their effort to demonstrate to others how their conversion had completely changed their formerly sinful selves. Here, as everywhere
else, the guiding principle for Evangelicals was individual redemption through personal conversion rather than the transformation of society as a whole. Demonstrations were taboo because they
typically did not further this ultimate goal.

   Evangelicals had a general aversion to political protest, but there
were situations, typically involving local interests, where they were
prepared to become political actors in opposition to the status quo.
The three best-known examples of this tendency are presented here,
two of which were part of my own inquiries. One is the emergence

of the Pacto Ribereno (PR) in the mid-1970s in the Chontalpa region of Tabasco, where Evangelicals were estimated to be some 17 per cent of the population in 1984 and where Evangelical temples outnumbered Catholic by a margin roughly of two to one.[25] The several pastors and many laity I talked to in the area denied that the Pacto leader, Eulogio Mendez, was a Presbyterian pastor, as has been suggested in the press and elsewhere,[26] though they acknowledged that a good number of the rank and file were Evangelicals, since they were so numerous in the area. The PR emerged as a coalition of *campesinos* or small landholders in 1976, seeking compensation for the damage done to their lands by PEMEX, the national oil company. The rapidly expanding operations of PEMEX at this time were centred on Tabasco and on the Chontalpa in particular. When PEMEX and government proved largely unresponsive to their genuine grievances, the PR embarked on an extended campaign of road blockages, seizure of wells, and kidnapping of high officials. On occasion PR succeeded in shutting down more than half the operating wells in this the major production field for PEMEX in all Mexico. Their central demand for compensation of 4,123 million pesos was never met, though the air was rife with charges of lawyers absconding with lesser sums. In the end, in late 1983, state forces intervened massively, removing the demonstrators, jailing their leaders, and effectively crushing the PR. Mendez was said to have escaped.[27] There was no sign of the PR's having revived when I was in the region during the summer of 1989.

This was undeniable activism of the most militant sort against rampant abuse of rich agricultural lands by a huge state company seeking to maximize profits in the shortest period of time. Any landholder in the Chontalpa, regardless of his or her religion, would have been angered by these depredations. Even assuming that the Evangelical proportion of PR's rank and file was commensurate with their 17 per cent of the local population, there was no evidence that they were especially active in the militant cadres of the PR, which led the seizures and blockades. The PR's principal leader was not an Evangelical. Evangelical churches took no public stance in the struggle. Nor did they give any support to the PR, though certain factions in the Catholic Church did so most volubly in the latter stages.[28] The Evangelical tradition was not in this case much of a deterrent to joining a protest movement, but neither did it foster it in any particular way.

In the second case study, a Pentecostal church of Totonac Indigenous peoples was led by a young Totonac pastor to join forces with Totonac Catholics to form a joint political pressure group, UNIPAC.

They then established a union of local coffee producers, separate from the other local association of coffee producers, which was dominated by Mestizos. The new Totonac union of coffee producers founded a successful co-operative store that enhanced its reputation as well as that of UNIPAC. In 1983 UNIPAC's Pentecostal-Catholic coalition of Totonacs decided to contest the municipal election. It first approached PRI for support but was rebuffed, because PRI had ties with the Mestizo group already in power in the municipio. It then allied itself with a leftist party, PSUM, through contacts the Pentecostal leader had made while working in a factory in the state capital. In the closely fought municipal elections, UNIPAC, led by the now former Pentecostal pastor (he had left the running of the church, it was said, to others), lost by a close margin. In the aftermath the UNIPAC leaders occupied the municipal building in protest, gathering considerable support from the surrounding Indigenous hamlets. Six months later the army intervened, ejecting the UNIPAC group from the municipal offices and staying on to keep the peace. Garma, the author of this account, stresses how Pentecostal churches provided a forum and training ground for the emergence of Indigenous leaders in their struggles with Mestizo domination. He is undoubtedly right, though he does not make clear how much support, if any, the former Pentecostal pastor received from the other local Evangelical churches, or indeed from his own church, after he gave up pastoring it.[29]

The third case involves the Chamulans, whose story of religious persecution and missionary involvement has already been charted. In the later 1960s and early 1970s, at precisely the time when Evangelical growth began, there emerged a coalition of forces opposed to oppressive *cacique* rule. It was led by a younger generation of bilingual teachers excluded from the networks of power and privilege controlled by the *caciques*. The opposition was said to be supported by Evangelicals, by residents in outlying hamlets, and by a group of "modern" Catholics who were moving away from the syncretic folk religion controlled by the *caciques*. Under the direction of a new bishop, Samuel Ruiz, the old priest tolerant of the traditional folk Catholicism was replaced in 1965 by a new mission committed to principles of liberation theology. Health, educational, and agricultural projects were initiated, at the same time that catechists began to be trained in the outlying hamlets, inevitably appearing as a parallel authority structure to the traditional *cargo* system. Father Polo, who headed the mission, soon found himself in confrontation with *cacique* rule. He was prohibited by the authorities from visiting the outlying villages; his catechists were

intimidated and threatened; and he was charged, as so often happened to Evangelicals, with violating cultural tradition and communal solidarity. So tense were relations that Bishop Ruiz moved
Father Polo into the city of Las Casas, though Father Polo continued to work in Chamula.

At the same time, general discontent was fuelled by new taxes
and by rumours that the *caciques* behind the authorities were pock-
eting the new monies raised. There followed four years (1970–74) of
intense political struggle in which the *cacique* candidate eventually
emerged the victor, with the backing of the army and the PRI,
though it was widely believed that he had lost the election to the
dissidents. The latter, with the reputed backing of Father Polo and
Miguel Gomez Hernandez, the Evangelical leader, occupied the
municipal buildings in Chamula in protest before being bloodily removed by the authorities. The dissidents allied themselves for a
time with the PAN, the conservative Catholic party, which must
have been as uncomfortable an alliance for the liberationist-minded
Catholics as it surely was for the Evangelicals. It was in this context
that the victorious *caciques* instituted their policy of expelling all
Evangelicals and modern Catholics.[30]

Such a general state of discontent with an elite so closely tied to
the traditional fiesta system helps us to understand why so many
were inclined to become Evangelicals, but it cannot fully explain it.
If political discontent had been the principal cause, then surely the
dissidents would have attached themselves to Father Polo and liberation theology, which offered a clearer agenda of material improvement and greater continuity with Chamulan traditions. Citing
Father Polo as her source, Robledo claims most dissidents had initially been modern Catholics who became Evangelical only when
the Catholic Church deserted them after 1974.[31] The Evangelical
leaders I talked to disputed this, saying some two thousand Evangelicals were in the first large wave of expulsions. No independent
evidence exists to refute these contrary claims, though there is general agreement that most of today's Chamulan Evangelicals converted and were expelled after 1974. After 1976 the Catholic Church
did withdraw all services from Chamula, but it continued to offer
these services to the refugees in a church set aside for this purpose
in Las Casas.[32] Evangelicals, of course, had never been able to function openly in Chamula. It is also worth recalling that Samuel Ruiz,
the resident bishop in Las Casas, where the refugees settled, was
noted throughout Mexico for his devotion to liberation theology
and the cause of Indigenous peoples. Despite his support, the great
majority of religious dissidents from Chamula embraced Evangelicalism, not Catholicism.

After 1974 Miguel Gomez Hernandez continued to struggle for the right of the expelled Evangelicals to return. He and his followers wrote denunciations to the federal and state authorities; they sent deputations, and they sometimes sent demonstrations to back up their demands for the right to return and for freedom of religion.[33] When Miguel was killed in 1981, skinned, scalped, and then crucified by Chamulan traditionalists, opposition flickered for a while. In the early 1980s the voice of protest passed to CRIACH, which included Catholics as well as Evangelicals in its efforts to defend the interests of Chamulans and all other Indigenous people expelled from their communities. The major leader to emerge out of CRIACH was Domingo Lopez Angel, a Chamulan convert to Adventism, who broke away from the Adventists to found his own Evangelical church and neighbourhood on the hills just outside Chamula and Las Casas. Under his leadership CRIACH made its big push in the latter part of the 1980s, kidnapping, shaving, and putting to public work a number of federal officials in Jerusalem, a mainly Pentecostal community of Evangelical refugees located some distance outside of La Casas. By any standard this was a direct challenge to the existing powers. The aim was to call attention to their plight, though specific calls ranged from demands for no further expulsions to the right to return to Chamula, and to wood-cutting rights for their refugee settlements in this chilly mountainous region. When Presbyterian Chamulan elders questioned publicly the wisdom of Domingo's action, some were jailed alongside the federal officials by Domingo's people, while others were driven underground. In the aftermath, Evangelical support for Domingo Angel and CRIACH rapidly withered. The Presbyterians, now organized into their own Tzotzil presbytery, withdrew and founded their own organization, CEDECH, dedicated to pursuing the same goals by more pacific means.[34] At around the same time a Presbyterian Chamulan pastor led a three-thousand-strong demonstration to the state capital, Tuxtla Gutierrez, where he denounced the governor for his lack of action on their just complaints but stressed that CEDECH supporters did not condone "occupied highways or buildings" or "kidnapped officials."[35]

Domingo's more militant style was still not without its supporters. In April of 1992, after another small wave of Chamulan Evangelicals had been expelled, enraged Chamulan Evangelicals from the refugee settlements kidnapped a judge from Chamula. This provoked an ugly confrontation between Evangelical and traditionalist Chamulans on the ring road around Las Casas, with about five hundred men on each side armed with guns, staves, and machetes. How many were killed or injured on this day is uncertain, but the mutual hostility continued. One could argue that all this tells us rather more about Chamulans than it does about Evangelicals, but it would be well to recall that other Evangelicals encountering persecution have been willing to suffer for their faith and have shown vigour in defending it. Evangelicals may have been generally reluctant to involve themselves in politics, but they suffered far fewer inhibitions when their religious and personal rights were involved.

CHURCH–STATE RELATIONS

Evangelical dealings with state and federal governments in the 1990s were still tinged with fear and circumscribed with caution. In part this is simply because the typically poor and/or modest social background of Evangelical church leaders gave them little confidence or experience in dealing with officialdom, especially at higher levels. They may also have been daunted by the typical press portrayal of them as unpatriotic American pawns.[36] What most shaped their thinking was the practical experience that their treatment varied enormously from official to official and from administration to administration. State and federal governments were not responsible for the persecution documented earlier, but they differed greatly in the alacrity with which they tried to suppress it. The constitutionally granted power to state governments to set the number of pastors and churches for every denomination did not worry Evangelicals, since it had not been exercised for many years. More worrying was the constitutional requirement that all church property and building be nationalized, or formally handed over so as to become state property. A full 88 per cent of the forty-three churches in the congregation sample were nationalized or were in the process of being so, but few pastors welcomed the lengthy bureaucratic process involved, which consumed much time and sometimes a few bribes. Pastors of independent churches were especially reluctant to hand over to the state the land and buildings, typically accumulated over a lengthy period of time, that were usually their major source of capital or security. All churches felt restricted by the rules, regardless of how pleasant or unpleasant their own bureaucratic dealings had been, because nationalized lands and buildings could not then be sold, which served as a real constraint on growing churches.

So much seemed to depend on the personal predilections of people in power at the time. In the colonial heartland state Evangelicals found relations with the state government quite good, since the wife of the most recent governor sometimes attended an Evangelical church, but they had no idea what to expect with their new governor. In another state in the south-east the former governor had banned missionaries, disallowed most public campaigns, and pressured churches to have their lands and buildings nationalized. The governor had been doing no more than applying the constitution, but some Evangelicals complained of discrimination and darker motives, saying Catholics were not subject to the same pressures, though not all Evangelicals agreed. Yet with the arrival of a new governor, all pressure disappeared. Even a large, out-of-doors, and state-wide campaign by Alberto Mottesi was allowed, which included using a main plaza in the capital.[37] A month before, informed Evangelicals were disturbed by a statement of an official from the state of Hidalgo that all churches not nationalized in the next three months would be closed throughout Mexico.[38] Some saw this as a calculated Catholic attack on their innumerable house-churches and small missions, which were rarely nationalized. In fact, I was told, the threat was never implemented in Hidalgo or anywhere else. It is also likely that many Evangelicals outside Hidalgo have never heard this particular rumour. The fact remains that such rumours abounded, giving an extra edge to church-state relations for Evangelicals.

Evangelical anxieties in the early 1990s were centred on the growing rapprochement between the Catholic Church and the administration of Salinas de Gortari. Recall that Evangelicals had long relied on the anti-clerical tradition within the Mexican state to serve as the protector of their rights and as a counterweight against Catholic aggression. Evangelical anxieties were predictably fanned when the apostolic delegate, a cardinal, and a clutch of bishops were invited to the investiture of President Salinas for the first time since the revolution.[39] No Evangelicals were invited. Two years later Salinas apparently rectified the balance by receiving a group of Evangelical notables at his official residence, Los Pinos, though the event seems to have been sparked by the brutal beating of a group of Evangelicals on the outskirts of Mexico City.[40] At the historic meeting he claimed that "the doors of the President have not been closed to Protestants and remain open." He reassured them that "you, in contrast to other religious expressions, do not cause problems for the state." He also committed himself to "liberty of conscience and liberty of belief," and he promised that "cases of religious intolerance will be looked into directly by my government so that they do not occur any more."[41] To both this meeting and another historic, first invitation in 1991 to the president's annual state-of-the-union address, only representatives of the historical Evangelical denominations were invited. This may have caused some initial concern on the part of Pentecostal leaders. However, no slight seems to have been intended, since five of the ten Evangelical leaders invited to the next presidential address were Pentecostals.[42]

Apart from such symbolic gestures, to which might be added the resumption of formal relations between Mexico and the Vatican in 1992,[43] the major event was the passing in December 1991 of sweeping changes in the constitutional provisions affecting religion. This time, Salinas consulted with twenty Evangelical leaders before sending his constitutional package to Congress.[44] The laws implementing the constitutional changes were then passed and made public in July 1992. A year later, when I left Mexico, there was still massive confusion about how the new laws and provisions would effect Evangelicals. It will probably take many more years before an accurate assessment can be made. What follows is a very preliminary effort.

The separation between church and state was reaffirmed, as were the basic liberties of religious expression, religious association, and freedom from obligation to contribute to any religious group or activity. Greater freedom for religions to involve themselves in education was granted. The former right of states to restrict the numbers of clergy and services was removed. Clergy were granted the right to vote, though the former restriction on their right to involve themselves or comment on political matters was retained. Access to radio and television also continued to be curtailed. The most significant change was that religions were granted legal standing in Mexican law, which they had lacked before. They now had the right to own property, necessary to fulfil their task. To achieve such rights, however, religions were obliged to register as legally constituted religious associations. Registered religious associations had to have been active in Mexico for at least five years. They also had to provide descriptions of their internal government, goals, articles of faith, board of directors, pastors, property holdings, capital goods, and other administrative matters. The major Evangelical denominations were all proceeding apace with these lengthy and often costly requirements for registration, though there was massive ignorance at local congregational level and little information forthcoming. Those especially at sea were the unknown but certainly very large number of independent churches and small, loosely affiliated associations. They typically lacked the knowledge, the financial resources, and the legal contacts to be registered. Many independents, including four I visited in 1993, were completely unaware of the new laws. Churches not attached to registered associations would be severely restricted in their rights. Already nationalized churches that failed to register by July 1993 would no longer have a legal right to use their property or building.[45] For those churches not affiliated to a registered association, the future was uncertain.

The further and more disturbing concern was that the constitutional changes and restoration of official relations with the Vatican signified a historic shift by the state to a more pro-Catholic stance, leaving Evangelicals more vulnerable to Catholic aggression and exclusivism. Particularly worrisome was the demand by various representatives of the Catholic hierarchy that their church be granted preferential treatment under the new law because of the greater size of their constituency.[46] Evangelicals were also reported to be "very concerned" over rumours that a new Catholic political party might be formed that could shatter the separation of church and state, weaken PRI, and cause repression of all non-Catholic religions.[47] By the end of 1993, none of these fears had been realized, but Evangelicals remained as wary and defensive as ever in their dealings with government.

This chapter began by asking how the Evangelical principles of evangelism and exclusivism worked themselves out in Evangelical relations with the wider society. With all the usual qualifications, Evangelicals largely confined their outreach to the conversion of individuals and the fufilment of the duties of citizenship at local level. Beyond this familiar terrain Evangelicals became increasingly wary of active participation as they moved from leadership of local communal associations to that of unions and political parties. The call of evangelism prevented them from prohibiting political activism, but fears of corruption, temptations, and divided loyalties were their predominant concerns in these wider fields. What Evangelicals did not share was the common secular notion that society might be saved by good works and institutional reform. For Evangelicals, personal transformation through religious conversion was the only way society could be reformed. From this perspective, the value of public service lay primarily in the degree to which it fostered personal conversion by setting an example to others of right Evangelical conduct. When this endeavour was threatened or made difficult by corrupt power structures, as Evangelicals believed it often was, their whole rationale for public service was undermined. To Evangelicals, public leadership was no more important and rather more dangerous than any other forum for leading people to salvation.

The Evangelical tradition in Mexico was not fundamentally concerned with political protest, as some would have it. In Chamula and throughout Mexico the Evangelical faith and conversion to it was a protest against the problems and sufferings of the world, but the solution that was embraced was spiritual, not material in form. Yet neither was the Evangelical tradition a propagator of political passivity. Evangelicals were wary of political demonstrations, but only a minority of Evangelicals voted for PRI at the last presidential election. The lack of a united political front among Evangelicals, given the large amount of time they spent together, is surely re-markable. It stems from the lack of attention that local congrega-tions paid to politics. Rather than fostering some generalized level of political passivity, that inattention allowed people to vote ac-cording to non-religious considerations. The political thinking of Evangelicals showed few signs of political activism or ideological sophistication, but it should be recalled that most Evangelicals were simple, uneducated folk with limited life-experiences beyond their own immediate world. Their thinking also needs to be set against the deeply rooted cynicism of the Mexican electorate in general, which saw half of its fellow-citizens fail to vote at a time of un-precedented economic difficulties and with an attractive opposition candidate. Evangelicals had little faith in the political process, but this was equally true of other Mexicans. Neither the stereotype of political passivity nor the dream of political activism applies to Evangelicals, for theirs was a call to personal transformation.

9 Conclusion

Driven by the "Great Commission," the themes of evangelism, outreach, and growth have long been the central preoccupation of Mexican Evangelicals. By their own lights, the degree to which they succeed in growing is the essential criterion by which they should be judged. My review in the Introduction of sectarian theorizing and of Evangelicals elsewhere in Latin America touches on a variety of issues, but there too I argue that the long-term significance of Evangelicals hinges on their capacity for sustained growth. Questions about American domination or the political ramifications of Evangelical allegiance deserve our attention, but their implications for Mexican society surely depend on how many Mexicans become Evangelical. Are Evangelicals destined to remain a small but vibrant minority, or are they capable of embracing sufficient numbers of Mexicans for Mexican society as a whole to be transformed? This is the central issue that underlies my concluding comments.

Faced with a country where Catholic imagery has been so intimately a part of national identity, the very fact that Evangelicals were able to thrive is itself an achievement. The peripheral regions of the country, both geographically and culturally, continued in 1990 to be most open to Evangelical advance, but Evangelical growth over the last twenty years has been substantial even in the colonial heartland, superseding growth rates in the north and in the capital. Only in the south has Evangelical growth been greater. As the general rate of population growth slowed in the 1980s, Evangelical growth also fell, but Evangelicals continued to increase in number at a rate almost five times faster than Catholics in this most recent period. According to the congregations I surveyed, they had the potential to grow by an impressive 255 per cent in the 1980s.[1] Had they kept all their converts, Evangelicals would have numbered almost 8 million and been 9.6 per cent of the Mexican population in 1990. As it was, when drop-outs were counted, the net growth in the same congregations fell to 104 per cent over the same period, which would have produced an Evangelical community of 4,495,686 in 1990, amounting to 5.5 per cent of all Mexicans. These far more modest numbers, which probably underestimate the number of drop-outs, are much closer to the 3,969,858 estimate of the census for 1990. The net growth figures, based on information provided by pastors, clearly call into question the claims of some Evangelicals that their community was two or three times greater than the official census estimate. In sum, Evangelicals have not yet broken through to the status of a sizeable minority except in a few remote and rural communities in the south of Mexico.

Nevertheless, the census shows that 1,767,949 Mexicans were added to the ranks of the Evangelical world in the 1980s alone. If the annual baptismal rate of 13.5 per cent from the sample congregations is our standard, then the Evangelical world succeeded in recruiting, but not retaining, 5,609,700 souls in the 1980s. Extrapolated into the future, the baptismal rate suggests that half of all Mexicans would become Evangelical as early as the year 2006.[2] All projections are, of course, suspect, because they assume that current conditions will continue into the future. In fact, birth and death rates affecting all Mexicans are likely to vary in the future. Nor can we be certain that the Evangelical outreach and Catholic receptivity of the 1980s will continue unabated into the next century. Even more problematic is the assumption that all those evangelized and converted will remain Evangelicals. In fact, almost half (43 per cent) of those raised in the Evangelical world dropped out in their adult years. Pervasive apostasy among converts is also the only feasible explanation for the fact that net growth in the congregations was only 40 per cent of their baptismal rate. If the 80 per cent net growth of Evangelicals recorded by the census is our guide, then only 32 per cent of those baptized in the 1980s continued to be Evangelicals in 1990. This estimate is given further support by the previously cited figures of the Mexican National Baptist Convention showing that their net growth in the 1980s was only 31 per cent of the baptisms they recorded. So overwhelming is this evidence that no credence should be put in a projection based on the baptismal rate. Its value lies in its demonstration that Evangelicals had a very substantial measure of appeal and outreach, not just in terms of individuals attending a few services or evangelistic campaigns but of people who made the much longer-term decision to be baptized.

Deprivation and disorganization have been the two principal theories used by sociologists to explain the emergence of sects, or new religious movements. Both provide some insight into modern-day Mexican Evangelicals, in that local congregations have offered a variety of social, psychological, and material supports or compensations that particularly appealed to the poor and the uprooted. However, we also saw that the majority of converts had not suffered the disorganization caused by migration. In relative terms, neither were Evangelical converts especially deprived, in that they resided in the vast underclass of peasants and urban workers to which the great majority of Mexicans belong. Of course, a strong case can be made for saying that all members of this popular class have long been deprived by any objective standard. There is also much to support the view that deprivation, insecurity, and suffering all grew during the economic crisis of the 1980s, when unemployment and inflation soared as living standards and government services were eroded. The general failure of Evangelicals to make any significant inroads among the rich and powerful would seem to add further weight to the notion that Evangelicalism's appeal was rooted in deprivation. Comparatively, too, the larger Evangelical communities in Nicaragua, Guatemala, and El Salvador might be explained, at least in part, by the greater degree of deprivation and uprootedness that they have experienced as a result of their respective wars. Nevertheless, the causal importance of deprivation should not be overstated. The proportions of Evangelicals in Brazil and Chile have also been reported to be far higher than those in Mexico, but it would be difficult to argue that levels of deprivation and discontent have been significantly greater there than in Mexico. Moreover and more pointedly, deprivation and its attendant disorganization have affected a huge swath of Mexican society, but only a minority of the deprived have embraced an Evangelical faith.

Others have explained Evangelicalism's appeal as a vehicle of protest against oppression and injustice. The pattern has been most evident in Indigenous communities, where civil and religious obligations are most strongly interlinked. Elsewhere too, and in a more generalized way, the embrace of Evangelicalism has implied a rejection of tradition and the seeking of new alternatives. The Evangelical traditions of sobriety, asceticism, and literacy have also awakened a desire for discipline, rectitude, and reform. By definition, the embrace of a new faith is a protest against the status quo, but beyond this general truth lies the now familiar qualification that only a minority of Mexicans suffering oppression and injustice have become Evangelicals.

Disorganization, deprivation, and protest have all played a part in Evangelicalism's appeal, but they cannot explain why the discontented, or at least some of them, were drawn to a religious and, specifically, an Evangelical solution to their problems. Part of the answer lies in the recentness of urbanization for so many Mexicans and the prevalence of rural, traditional ways of thinking, where doubts about the presence and power of the supernatural were little developed. Evangelicalism's appeal has also lain in the failure of the Catholic Church to respond to the discontents of its constituency. These difficulties in Mexico are rooted in its limited manpower and the time-consuming responsibilities of its priests in overseeing the rituals of baptism, first communion, marriage, death, and mass. Historically, Latin American Catholic churches have been further constrained by a tradition of serving the elites and establishment while neglecting the poor, from whose ranks Evangelicals have been drawn. Savage disestablishment and subsequent struggles with the post-revolutionary state left the Catholic church in Mexico particularly debilitated. Its links with the democratic right and recent moves to resolve the old church-state conflict then combined to insure that liberation theology and its "option for the poor" were rarely embraced in Mexico. The charismatic movement has been the other major innovation within the Catholic church in recent years, but its capacity to halt Evangelical advance has been curbed by clerical suspicions and by its predominant appeal to the middle class. This combination of institutional Catholic neglect of the popular classes and their openness to supernatural solutions to their problems thus created a receptive vacuum for Evangelical advance.

Liberation theology is little developed in Mexico, but this does not explain why Evangelicals have been increasing in strength and numbers. The liberationist format of Christian base communities is particularly well developed in Brazil, but it is worth recalling that far more Brazilians are Evangelicals[3] than even the most optimistic of my estimates for Mexico. In Mexico, Bishop Samuel Ruiz, the leader of Mexico's small liberationist faction, has some of the highest Evangelical concentrations in the country in his diocese of Las Casas. Martin is undoubtedly correct when he attributes liberation theology's competitive disadvantage to the intellectual and middle-class style of its leaders. They stand in sharp contrast to the abundant supply of Evangelical pastors who have been raised in and speak the language of the popular classes they serve.[4] Stoll, looking at Central America, would add that liberation theology's call to struggle and resistance has usually produced very little liberation but much oppression and violence, which has been borne by the people, not their leaders.[5] These extreme conditions have not prevailed in Mexico. But here too, among the Chamulans, the great majority of the expelled dissidents have embraced Evangelicalism, not the modern and progressive Catholicism that is so actively championed by Bishop Ruiz from his nearby base in Las Casas.

What has distinguished the Evangelical tradition is their offering of an all-powerful source of solace and support in the face of life's difficulties. The supernatural source of this bounty is presented as being personally and intimately concerned with the well-being of all. In return are asked faith and obedience, which even the humblest of folk can offer. For Stoll this is a message of "escapism" and "fatalistic acceptance," though Evangelicals could surely claim that their prescriptions are no less escapist or less likely to succeed than are movements of secular protest in Mexico. Profiles of passive resignation are equally questionable, as was made clear by the active involvement of Chamulan, Totonac, and Chontalpan Evangelicals in political protest. No less acceptable are the formula portraits of Evangelicals as tranquillized millennialists, indifferent to the world around them as they passively await Christ's imminent return. The problem with this notion is that millennialist doctrines have not seemed to be heavily emphasized by pastors. Even among Pentecostals, half said they were uncertain whether Christ would return in their own lifetime. Their emphasis was always on the need to convert and to lead a Christian life rather than on passive waiting for future events. Thus Evangelicals have been willing and active participants in the local communities in which they reside, because they believe that individual change is always possible.[6]

As Stoll admits, Evangelicalism calls for a life of discipline, asceticism, and personal transformation, which is within the grasp of the poor and oppressed and avoids betrayal by corrupt leaders. It has also often led, as we saw in chapter 5, to a modest level of material improvement. Such a world-view, as we then saw in chapter 8, has no fixed or permanent political orientation, since it rejects political solutions of all stripes as suspect at the same time as it calls for an agenda of personal transformation. In its own way, such a redemptive social movement, to recall Bromley and Shupe's evocative phrase, is as utopian and as all-encompassing as any vision propounded by secular revolutionaries. Personal redemption through the unconditional power and love of God is offered by

Evangelicals to all prepared to make a leap of faith. This is the core of their message and appeal.

As we saw in chapter 1, both Lalive D'Epinay and Bastian attribute the success of Evangelicalism, particularly Pentecostalism, to its ability to recreate the familiar if oppressive ways of the past. At the most general level, Evangelicalism's affirmation of the power and presence of the supernatural is at one with the traditional culture of Latin America. The tradition of lay leadership in ritual and organization is also to be found in both Evangelicalism and folk Catholicism, as is the common stress on the very specific and concrete rewards that accrue from right relationship with the supernatural. Stark is surely correct when he suggests that the success of any new religion depends on its having a measure of continuity with prior religious traditions, so that potential converts are predisposed to embrace that which is presented as new.[7]

This suggestion should not blind us to the equally striking discontinuities of Evangelicalism with traditional cultural practices. Paternalism and authoritarianism were to be found in Evangelical pastors and churches, but everywhere they were held in check by the freedom of disgruntled members to drop out or to switch allegiance to another church. What D'Epinay and Bastian miss is the principle of voluntarism in Evangelical affiliation that so sets it apart from the traditional obligations to the hacienda, the patron, and the saints of folk Catholicism. In the latter, the notion of choice is largely absent. Bastian is equally erroneous in portraying Pentecostalism as an "unlettered," "oral religion."[8] Services in all denominations required that all bring a Bible, which was regularly consulted by all in response to a constant stream of biblical proofs, cited by all speakers and preachers. From my lay sample it may be recalled that 64 per cent of Pentecostals said they read the Bible three or more times a week; 88 per cent did so weekly. This is hardly the characteristic of an unlettered people. Their puritanical values regarding alcohol, gambling, and sexual relations outside marriage also led them to repudiate the traditional values of *machismo*, though the continued dominance of men in their churches is a reminder that female equality is not a central value in the Evangelical world. Even in their emphasis on miracles and faith healing, which Evangelicalism so closely shared with folk Catholicism, they explicitly rejected any magical notions that they could control the supernatural, or that proper performance of the ritual was a guarantee of a successful outcome. In sum, elements of tradition and modernity were both so prevalent in the Evangelical world that there is little value in portraying it as essentially one or the other. Behind the critical and perceptive observations of both Lalive D'Epinay and Bastian lies their acute concern that Pentecostalism has not brought about the social and political reforms that they would like to see unfold. I too have doubts about Evangelicalism's long-term impact, but for rather different reasons to be summarized shortly. Their analysis, it seems to me, undervalues Evangelicalism's dynamism and its central call for individual transformation as the essential prerequisite for social change.

Questions about Evangelicalism's social agenda lead us to the issue of American influence. As we saw on so many occasions, Catholics, nationalists, and leftists have been inclined to portray Evangelicalism as the product of an American imperialist conspiracy designed to divide, subvert, pacify, and ultimately control Mexico. From this perspective, all leadership and funding of the Evangelical world is assumed to have come from the United States, in turn the presumed source of Evangelicalism's appeal.

In assessing the charge, we must recognize that an American connection did and does exist. As we saw in chapter 2, the religious dissidence generated in Mexico during the reform era of the last century fell under American missionary control during the Porfiriato. After the revolution, as the Evangelical community grew and the constitutional restrictions on foreign clergy were implemented, the number of American missionaries and their day-to-day leadership steadily diminished in the historical Protestant denominations, although their influence at national assemblies and their subsidies did not cease until after 1970. Particularly noteworthy is Bennett's analysis, showing that the first major burst in Evangelical growth in Mexico, by Presbyterians in Tabasco, did not occur until after the missionaries were forced to withdraw.[9] As for the more recent and now dominant Pentecostals, the movement was overwhelmingly under Mexican direction from the very beginning. In the 1980s only one of the forty-three sample congregations was co-pastored by a missionary. (In contrast, in the 1970s about 75 per cent of all Catholic priests in the Mexico City diocese and 13 per cent of all males in religious orders were foreigners.)[10] Apart from a few small and occasional gifts, no congregation received a subsidy on which it depended. With the exception of the provision of a few latrines in one Indigenous congregation, no other congregation or missionary I queried was involved in distributing directly to church members anything more than the very occasional bag of second-hand clothing. Only in the area of church construction had a significant 37 per cent of congregations received outside aid, though the gift was partial in all but a few cases, and 63 per cent were fully funded locally.

Equally, and perhaps more surprisingly, the influence of SIL missionaries in directing and nurturing Evangelical growth in Indigenous areas was far less than commonly thought. Even in Oxchuc, where the dynamic Marianna Slocum worked, it was primarily Indigenous needs, energies, and leadership that led to Evangelical growth. Despite the presence of missionaries in many parts of Mexico, all my various lines of inquiry led to the common conclusion that they have not played a significant role in the growth and sustenance of the Evangelical community in recent years.

The dilemma with conspiracy theories is that they assume that converts are either the bribed and/or the stupid dupes of the missionaries. These characterizations are as offensive as they are unfounded. There is also the danger of ignoring all the other agencies of change. These range from schools to television to progressive priests and to returning migrants who have worked elsewhere in Mexico or in the United States. Living culture is never static. Mexicans of various persuasions may not like the values they think are enshrined in the Evangelical world, but these antipathies should not obscure the fact that the Evangelical movement has been peopled, led, funded, and driven by predominantly poor Mexicans, be they Mestizo or Indigenous.

In assessing the future trajectory of Mexican Evangelicalism, I suggested in the introductory chapter that sociological theorizing offers two possible scenarios. One is that of continued growth and expansion, which is typically accompanied by the process of denominationalization. With growth, so this line of reasoning goes, comes entropy, or an erosion of the high commitment and tensions with the world that once characterized the original sects. However, Mexican Evangelicals show few signs of denominationalization. Between first and second generation there has been no significant decline in the average number of services attended weekly (3.6 vs 3.5). The percentage who tithe (54 per cent vs 52 per cent) and the proportion of frequent tongue-speakers among Pentecostals (33 vs 33 per cent) further confirm the lack of any appreciable decline in commitment over generations. Doubts about the propriety of dancing (98 vs 96 per cent) and attending movies (90 vs 89 per cent) remain equally widespread in the first and generations, though the second generation have been a little less inclined to condemn such activities as invariably sinful. Objections to the use of makeup (78 vs 66 per cent) or to participation in sports clubs outside the Evangelical world (51 vs 42 per cent) show a small decline in sectarian zeal over the generations, but the difference is probably attributable to the lower percentage of Pentecostals in the second generation. And again, attitudes to participation in the wider structures of Mexican society, summarized in the tables of chapter 8, reveal no significant change in the second generation.

Had I been able to survey the 43 per cent of the second generation who dropped out in their adult years, it is very likely that generational differences would have been much greater. However, this is precisely the major point. So strong is and was their tradition of sectarian zeal that Mexican Evangelicals have been presented with the option of either conformity or complete apostasy. Denominationalization has been curbed by a revolving door that winnows out the less committed and those who might be inclined to take a more tolerant, less tension-ridden view of Mexican society and culture. Sectarian zeal has thereby been retained by a high rate of apostasy or of drop-outs. According to the calculations at the beginning of this chapter, as many as two thirds (68 per cent) of those baptized in Evangelical churches in the 1980s had dropped out by the end of the decade. The cost was a dramatically reduced rate of growth.

There are three major reasons for apostasy. The first is rooted in the heavy emphasis that Evangelicals, especially Pentecostals, place on faith as the essential prerequisite for salvation. Accessible to all, this simple formulation gives Pentecostalism much of its appeal, but in various ways it also causes some to question the depth and the authenticity of their salvation. Uncertainty arises because Mexican Evangelicals have not been given any clear benchmark or objective criteria by which they can be assured that their faith is sufficient and their salvation certain. These doubts have then been fuelled by their common conviction that unanswered prayers for healing or recourse to a doctor might signify a lack of faith. Since most Evangelicals in my study did resort to doctors and not all their prayers were answered, the potential grounds for doubting the depth of their faith were widespread. Doubt was especially common among Pentecostals, since a full half were unable to speak in tongues, which they defined as the distinctive mark of their tradition and the treasured means of close communication with God. Anxiety might impel some to ever greater levels of commitment, but there is every reason to believe that others are driven to apathy and despair by these recurring grounds for questioning whether their salvation was ever sufficient or secure.

Secondly, Evangelicals' high levels of commitment and their repudiation of so much Mexican tradition have inevitably generated a measure of burn-out. Tithing, several hours weekly of attendance at services, and a host of other demands to contribute to the life of the local congregation must surely have frayed the long-term commitment of some. Equally burdensome are their puritanical values and their intense opposition to folk Catholicism, which require them to eschew all the major festivities and most of the worldly pleasures of other Mexicans. These interdictions weigh most heavily on men, tempted and derided by the *machismo* tradition of drinking and womanizing. This is surely why men are a minority among both converts and Evangelicals in the second generation. So much change is called for and so absolute is the rejection of all worldly pleasure that one might question whether the majority of any society would ever permanently embrace so demanding a faith.

Lastly, a degree of apostasy would seem to be an inevitable by-product of the distinctive organizational features of the Evangelical world. The small size of so many congregations and their intense competition for members made difficult and uncertain their capacity to support a pastor, to survive, and hence to nurture the new members they recruit. This organizational precariousness was then compounded by schisms and nasty internal conflicts, which had, in the immediately preceding ten years, occurred in 38 per cent of the congregations I surveyed. It is scarcely surprising that, faced with the acrimony and swirling rumours of moral, financial, and doctrinal impropriety among the contenders for power, some members, especially those recently converted, might grow disillusioned and fall away.

Apostasy is thus an integral feature of the Mexican Evangelical world. It is the critical counterbalancing force to the sectarian zeal, constant evangelism, and substantial appeal that is the other, equally important face of Evangelicalism. Taken together, these two components suggest that the most likely future scenario for Evangelicals is that they will remain a small but vibrant minority in Mexico, always recruiting new members but never growing as much as they would like, because of the constant drain of apostasy.

It is now thirty years since Bryan Wilson called us to look beyond the sect-to-denomination theorizing of Niebuhr, because not all sects are transformed into denominations. My analysis suggests that this stricture also applies to conversionist sects, which Wilson identifies as the type most likely to denominationalize.[11] The failure of Mexican Evangelicals either to denominationalize or to grow stems from the most basic and essential of their characteristics. These include their tendency to be in high tension with their surrounding society, the very high standards of commitment required of their members, their propensity to schism, and their chronic anxieties over whether their salvation is secure. Some of these traits are confined to conversionist sects, while others apply to all sects. In either case, sectarian studies might profit from a more sustained focus on the forces that hinder growth and sustain sectarian vigour rather than on pressures to grow and denominationalize. If any general axiom can be derived from my investigations, it would be that widespread change in the religious affiliation of a society is as difficult as it is rare.

My forecast may be too conservative by giving too much weight to the limiting effects of apostasy. Based on the census, which measures net growth after apostasy has made its inroads, Evangelical growth rates in the 1980s would lead to a majority of Mexicans being Evangelicals by about the middle of the next century. This projection, like all others, should not be taken seriously or literally, since it makes the untenable assumption that all the conditions of the 1980s will prevail unchanged for almost sixty years. However, it does have the merit of reminding us that Evangelicals in the 1980s were growing, despite drop-outs, and may be expected to do so in the future.

The many reports of much higher Evangelical proportions in Brazil, Chile, Guatemala, Nicaragua, and El Salvador, usually put at between 20 to 25 per cent,[12] add further weight to the notion that Mexican Evangelicals may be able to grow beyond their current status of a 5–7 per cent minority. Table 9.1 lists the most recent estimates for the early 1990s. Why Mexico should be less receptive than elsewhere to Evangelicalism is not clear to me. I have already alluded to how differences in levels of deprivation might possibly explain higher Evangelical percentages in Guatemala and El Salvador but not in Brazil and Chile. It is also possible that the Catholic church has been stronger in Mexico than elsewhere and thereby more effective in inhibiting Evangelical advance. Figures from the 1994 *Catholic Almanac*, summarized in Table 9.1, suggest that the ratio of people to priests was greater in Guatemala (12,007), El Salvador (10,821), and Brazil (10,484) than in Mexico (7,575). Yet the apparently weaker state of the Catholic church in these three countries vis-à-vis Mexico is hardly of sufficient magnitude to account for the far greater size of their Evangelical communities. Nor do the ratios for Chile (6,107), Panama (6,811), and Costa Rica (4,983) fit with the notion that Evangelical advance and a weak Catholic church are always and strongly correlated. Compared to other Latin American countries, the size and scope of foreign missionary endeavour in Mexico was uniquely constrained by the constitutional prohibition on foreign clergy. According to Table 9.1, Mexico had one of the highest ratios of general population to

Table 9.1
Latin American comparisons

	% Protestant		Population per Missionary		Population per Priest	
	Rank		Rank	No.	Rank	No.
Chile	1	27.9%	10	23,315	5	6,107
Guatemala	2	24.1%	6	13,157	16	12,007
Brazil	3	21.6%	15	44,474	13	10,484
El Salvador	4	20.6%	17	51,491	14	10,829
Nicaragua	5	17.3%	14	35,843	15	11,911
Panama	6	16.7%	5	10,605	6	6,811
Honduras	7	11.0%	7	13,380	17	16,574
Costa Rica	8	10.7%	1	6,670	1	4,983
Bolivia	9	9.3%	2	7,234	10	7,916
Argentina	10	8.0%	13	35,402	3	5,581
Peru	11	7.1%	9	21,494	11	9,232
Paraguay	12	6.0%	3	8,193	8	7,490
Venezuela	13	5.3%	11	30,982	12	9,632
Mexico	14	5.2%	16	46,852	9	7,575
Ecuador	15	3.8%	4	9,661	7	7,052
Colombia	16	3.8%	12	33,635	2	5,067
Uruguay	17	3.6%	8	14,347	4	5,825

Data on the total population, the number of Protestants, and the number of Protestant
missionaries were obtained from Johnstone, *Operation World*. Johnstone uses the United
Nations estimate of Mexico's population, which was 88,598,000. The number of priests was
obtained from the 1994 *Catholic Almanac*. The numbered rank order in each column starts with
the country with the highest percentage of Protestants, greatest concentration of missionaries,
and lowest ratio of people to Catholic priest.

Protestant missionaries in Latin America.[13] Yet the same table also
shows that the missionary presence was similarly thin in Brazil
(44,474), El Salvador (51,491), and Nicaragua (35,843), which all
had much higher concentrations of Evangelicals than did Mexico.
Missionaries were more prevalent in Chile (23,315) and Guatemala
(13,157), where the Evangelical community was much larger than
in Mexico, but missionaries were equally or even more widely
spread in Uruguay (14,347) and Ecuador (9,661), which had smaller
Evangelical communities than Mexico. There is, it seems, no clear
and unambiguous relationship between missionary ratios and the
size of the Evangelical community. It also needs to be remembered
that my inquiries in Mexico found that missionaries played a marginal role in the growth and sustenance of the Evangelical community. In short, no one factor or set of differences unambiguously
accounts for the comparatively small size of the Evangelical community in Mexico. Further inquiry is clearly needed.

One other possibility needs to be considered, namely that the estimates of the Evangelical populations in some Latin American countries may be inflated. Might it be that Mexico is more typical of Latin America than Table 9.1 suggests? The possibility exists because these estimates, including those in Table 9.1, are often based on denominational figures of varying degrees of accuracy and completeness, which rely on figures provided by local congregations. Table 9.1 lists Chile as having proportionately more Evangelicals than any other country in Latin America, but *Operation World*, the source for this figure, admits that "Estimates vary from 16 per cent to 30 per cent ... Nearly all Pentecostal figures are estimates: few keep records."[14] In Guatemala's case, earlier widely touted estimates that 30 per cent of the nation had become Evangelical by the 1980s were based on the assumption that church membership figures should be multiplied by a factor of 4 or 3.5 to calculate the total Evangelical population. No doubt it is questioning of such a generous and unsubstantiated assumption that caused *Operation World* to put Evangelicals as a more modest 24 per cent of all Guatemalans. Then in 1991 a new very careful study by SEPAL, a missionary agency in Guatemala, calculated that it would be better to reduce the Evangelical proportion to 19 per cent. This most recent of studies was based on an enumeration of Sunday attendance of all Evangelical churches in a selected set of regions throughout Guatemala. SEPAL's methodology is better than its predecessors because it focuses on actual attenders rather than the more restrictive category of formal members, who are sometimes defined in different ways by their respective denominations. However, SEPAL still based its 19 per cent estimate on the questionable assumption that the total Evangelical community was 2.3 times larger than the Sunday attenders enumerated in their survey. Others might be inclined to confine the Evangelical community to all who attend on Sunday. By this standard, only 8.3 per cent of Guatemalans were Evangelicals in 1991.[15] In fact, of the figures for the four countries in Table 9.1 with more than 20 per cent of their population recorded as Evangelical, only the estimate for Brazil is based on a national census, though this figure is based on a projection from the most recent census of 1980.[16]

Denominational estimates also fail to take account of drop-outs, as I have done for Mexico. Perceptive investigators like Stoll and Gerrard-Burnett acknowledge this possibility,[17] but they continue to use denominational estimates because no others exist. A noteworthy exception is a recent survey in Costa Rica, which found that the 8.7 per cent who claimed to be Evangelicals were almost equally matched by another 8 per cent who said that they had been Evangelicals at an earlier point in their lives. This amounts to a 47 per cent rate of apostasy.[18] Similarly in Guatemala, there is every reason to believe that a substantial measure of apostasy lies behind SEPAL's estimate that 19 per cent of Guatemalans were Evangelicals, since the estimate implies that 57 per cent of Evangelicals had not attended a church service in the previous week. Systematic research on the causes and extent of apostasy elsewhere in Latin America is largely absent and clearly needed. We also need to clarify – in Mexico as well as elsewhere – whether the drop-outs revert back to Catholicism, fall into secular indifference, or retain a residual attachment to the Evangelical tradition.[19] Until this is done, we will never really know if a religious revolution in Latin America is now in process and what form it is taking. If the experience of Mexican Evangelicals is our guide, then the prospects of Latin America's turning Protestant are slim and remote.

Let me reiterate one last time that speculation about the total size of the Evangelical community and its future trajectory is inevitably fraught with much uncertainty. What is clear is that the vibrant community of Mexican Evangelicals has had its capacity to transform Mexican society severely curtailed by its inability to retain the many new members it has attracted.

Notes

CHAPTER ONE

1 Martin, *Tongues of Fire*, 50–2; Stoll, *Is Latin America Turning Protestant?* 3–10, 333–8.
2 Johnstone, *Operation World*. Both Martin and Stoll draw upon the earlier, fourth edition of Johnstone for their figures on Protestant numbers. It cannot be emphasized too much that these figures are estimates based on data provided by Protestant denominations and are of varying degrees of accuracy and completeness.
3 Benjamin, "Iglesias evangelicas y conflicto politico en El Salvador," 109. For lower figures but none the less remarkable rates of growth, see Aguilar, Sandoval, and Coleman, "Protestantism in El Salvador," 120.
4 Green, "Shifting Affiliations," 161. On Rios Montt and Serrano, see Trudeau, *Guatemalan Politics*, 61–3, 142–51.
5 The 17.5 per cent figure was put out by the National Forum of Evangelical Christian Churches in Mexico. It was the most widely touted figure when I was resident in Mexico in 1992–93. Dawn Ministries estimated that Mexico was an Evangelical "hot spot" in 1990, when it put the Evangelical proportion at 10 per cent. Other estimates have gone as high as 25 per cent. For a listing of these "estimates," see Metz, "Protestantism in Mexico," 57–78.
6 Beckford, *Religion and Advanced Industrial Society*, 18–41.
7 See Berger, *The Sacred Canopy*; Martin, *A General Theory of Secularization*.
8 Caplow, "Contrasting Trends in European and American Religion," 101–8; Warner, "Work in Progress toward a New Paradigm," 1044–58.

9 Stark and Bainbridge, *The Future of Religion*, 429–56. I am especially wary of the weight that Stark and Bainbridge attach to recent interest in cults, which they see as evidence of continuing religious interest and as a sign that secularization's limits have been reached. More persuasive, I think, is Wilson's view that the largely transitory cult movement has no long-term religious significance. Wilson, *Contemporary Transformations of Religion*, 108–12.

10 See Berger, *The Sacred Canopy*, and Bellah, "Religious Evolution."

11 Barrett, "Statistics, Global," 812.

12 Bibby, *Fragmented Gods*, 12–16, 25–30; Roof and McKinney, *American Mainline Religion*, 82–5.

13 My use of the Evangelical and fundamentalist terms comes out of Hunter, "Operationalizing Evangelism," and Ammerman, "Operationalizing Evangelicalism: An Amendment."

14 A good overview of this literature is to be found in Roberts, *Religion in Sociological Perspective*, 180–202.

15 Stark and Bainbridge, *The Future of Religion*, 21–6.

16 Because Mexican Catholicism has been openly derogatory of Evangelical faiths, using the term "sect" in a dismissive, negative, and pejorative manner, one major writer on Mexican Evangelicals has recently opted to drop the term in favour of the more neutral characterization of them as a "society of ideas." See Bastian, *Los dissidentes*, 2–3.

17 See Wilson, *Magic and the Millennium*, 9–19.

18 I confined the north to those states immediately adjacent to the border and Baja California Sur. The others are Baja California, Coahuila, Chihuahua, Nuevo Leon, Sonora, and Tamaulipas.

19 This includes all states not specifically enumerated in the other three regions.

20 This includes the states of Campeche, Chiapas, Oaxaca, Quintana Roo, Tabasco, and the Yucatan. Though parts of the state of Oaxaca have roots in the old colonial patrimony, I have included it in the south because of its high Indigenous population today and because it has been a depressed and marginal state throughout much of this century. See Murphy and Stepick, *Social Inequality in Oaxaca*.

21 Singleton, Straits, et al., *Approaches to Social Research*, 153.

22 Snow and Machalek, "The Sociology of Conversion," 168–70.

23 Thus members of the historical denominations, who have shifted to Pentecostalism in recent years, typically would regard themselves as being involved in more than switching, as would those Evangelicals who were former Jehovah's Witnesses.

24 Kilbourne and Richardson, "Paradigm Conflict, Types of Conversion, and Conversion Theories," 1–8.

25 Nelson and Bromley, "Another Look at Conversion and Defection in Conservative Churches," 55.

26 See, for instance, the reporting of rumour without documentation in Willems, *Followers of the New Faith*, 123; and Dirksen, "Pentecostal Healing," 140.

27 Kanter, "Commitment and Social Organization," 499–517.

28 Kelley, "Why Conservative Churches are Still Growing."

29 Bruce, *A House Divided*, 140.

30 Quoted in Hine, "The Deprivation and Disorganization Theories of Social Movements," 647.

31 Lalive D'Epinay, *Haven of the Masses,,* 33.

32 Ibid., 38.

33 Willems, *Followers of the New Faith*, 125.

34 Ibid., 251.

35 Martin, *Tongues of Fire*, 271.

36 Ibid., 274.

37 Ibid., 280.

38 Ibid., 278.

39 Ibid., 280.

40 Ibid., 284.

41 Glock and Stark, *Religion and Society in Tension*, 246.

42 Ibid., 249.

43 Ibid., 249.

44 See Wilson, *Religion in Sociological Perspective*, 113–18.

45 This was brought to my attention by Wilson, *The Social Dimensions of Sectarianism*, 195–6.

46 Wilson, *Religion in Sociological Perspective*, 27.

47 Stoll, *Is Latin America Turning Protestant?* 13–18.

48 Garma, "Los estudios antropologicos sobre el protestantismo en Mexico," 95.

49 See, for example, Dominguez and Huntington, "The Salvation Brokers," 2–36.

50 Stoll, *Is Latin America Turning Protestant?* 135–304.

51 Anderson, *Vision of the Disinherited*, 229, 239.

52 Bastian, *Breve historia del protestantismo en America Latina*, 154–78.

53 Lalive D'Epinay, *Haven of the Masses*, 108–33; and Rolim, "El pentecostalismo," 51–70.

54 Lalive D"Epinay, "Political Regimes and Millenarianism," 48–51.

55 Lalive D'Epinay, *Haven of the Masses*, 122–7.

56 Willems, *Followers of the New Faith*, 220–30. See also Chambliss, "Pentecostalism," 81–94.

57 See research by Cornelia Flora Butler, cited in Stoll, *Is Latin America Turning Protestant?* 116.

58 Cited in Martin, *Tongues of Fire*, 240.

59 Stoll, *Is Latin America Turning Protestant?* 218–65.

60 Aguilar, et al. "Protestantism in El Salvador," 130–5.

61 Stoll, *Is Latin America Turning Protestant?* 301.
62 A recent, very similar conclusion, based on a variety of case studies, is to be found in Garrard-Burnett, "Conclusion," 201.
63 Wallis, "Coping with Institutional Fragility," 25–43.
64 Martin, *Tongues of Fire*, 14–23.
65 Niebuhr, *The Social Sources of Denominationalism*, 19–20.
66 Yinger, *Religion, Society and the Individual*, 150.
67 Wilson, "An Analysis of Sect Development," 482–97.
68 Stark and Bainbridge, *The Future of Religion*, 167.
69 Wilson, "An Analysis of Sect Development," 496–7.
70 Wilson, *Magic and the Millenium*, 24–9, 107–23.
71 Willems, *Followers of the New Faith*, 31–54, 173–97, 258.
72 Bastian, "The Metamorphosis of Latin American Protestant Groups," 33–57.

CHAPTER TWO

1 On the colonial church, see Meyer and Sherman, *The Course of Mexican History*, 184–202, 285–98.
2 Bastian, *Los dissidentes*, 27.
3 Moseley, "The Religious Impact of the American Occupation," 39–52.
4 Goddard, "Iglesia y estadio en el porfiriato," 1–16.
5 Baldwin, *Protestants and the Mexican Revolution*, 13–18; Bastian, *Los dissidentes*, 32–48.
6 Bastian, *Los dissidentes*, 48–49.
7 Penton, "Mexico's Reformation," 68: Baldwin, *Protestants and the Mexican Revolution*, 17.
8 Baez Comargo and Grubb, *Religion in the Republic of Mexico*, 89.
9 Bastian, *Los dissidentes*, 56–62; Baldwin, *Protestants and the Mexican Revolution*, 16–18.
10 Wilson, *Religious Sects*, 57.
11 Penton, "Mexico's Reformation," 102–4.
12 For more details on this world-view, see Baldwin, *Protestants and the Mexican Revolution*, 18–22; Bastian, *Los dissidentes*, 51–4.
13 Butler, "Protestant Christianity in Mexico," 348. Missionaries usually put the number of their schools at about 500 (Baldwin, *Protestants and the Mexican Revolution*, 57), but Bastian (*Los dissidentes*, 147) puts it at 163. They are much closer in their estimates of total number of students.
14 Baldwin, *Protestants and the Mexican Revolution*, 101.
15 Ibid., 34.
16 Bastian, *Los dissidentes*, 109.
17 Butler, "Protestant Christianity in Mexico," 348.
18 Baldwin, *Protestants and the Mexican Revolution*, 102.

19 See ibid., 49–58; Butler, "Protestant Christianity in Mexico," 348; INEGI, *IV Censo General de Poblacion y Vivienda, Resumen General*, Cuadro LVIII.
20 Bastian, *Los dissidentes*, 62–9, 87–141; Baldwin, *Protestants and the Mexican Revolution*, 30–59.
21 Bennett, *Tinder in Tabasco*, 42–66; Bastian, *Los dissidentes*, 111–18.
22 Vazquez, *Los que sembraron*, 213–16; Bastian, *Los dissidentes*, 100–1.
23 Bastian, *Los dissidentes*, 80–5.
24 Baez Camargo and Grubb, *Religion in the Republic of Mexico*, 90; Penton, "Mexico's Reformation," 105–6.
25 Goddard, "Iglesia y estadio en el porfiriato," 1–16; Bastian, *Los dissidentes*, 174–9.
26 Schmitt, "American Protestant Missionaries and the Diaz Regime," 88–93.
27 Baldwin, *Protestants and the Mexican Revolution*, 105–6.
28 Bastian, *Los dissidentes*, 173–262.
29 Quoted in Baldwin, *Protestants and the Mexican Revolution*, 77.
30 Bastian, *Los dissidentes*, 263–301.
31 Ibid., p.294.
32 Quirk, *The Mexican Revolution and the Catholic Church*, 25.
33 Baldwin, *Protestants and the Mexican Revolution*, 110–18.
34 Penton, "Mexico's Reformation," 120–3; Baldwin, *Protestants and the Mexican Revolution*, 123–4.
35 The Catholic party did later withdraw its support for Huerta in the presidential elections, but this was a mater of internal wrangling within conservative ranks. Quirk, *The Mexican Revolution and the Catholic Church*, 38–9, 46–62.
36 Quirk, *The Mexican Revolution and the Catholic Church*, 54–61.
37 Baldwin, *Protestants and the Mexican Revolution*, 125–49; Bastian, *Protestantismo y sociedad en Mexico*, 116–45.
38 Quirk, *The Mexican Revolution and the Catholic Church*, 86.
39 A complete listing of all these articles and their subsequent regulatory interpretations is found in Baez Comargo and Grubb, *Religion in the Republic of Mexico*, app. 4.
40 Baldwin, *Protestants and the Mexican Revolution*, 166–9.
41 Quirk, *The Mexican Revolution and the Catholic Church*, 102.
42 Ibid., 112–44.
43 Ibid., 145–87.
44 Ibid., 244. A recent review of the literature on the Cristero rebellion suggests that it was driven by land shortages and class conflicts as well as religious protest, while not denying that the spark was the conflict between church and state. Jrade, "Inquiries into the Cristero Insurrection," 53–69.
45 Baez Camargo and Grubb, *Religion in the Republic of Mexico*, 81–6; Penton, "Mexico's Reformation," 137–41; Bennett, *Tinder in Tabasco*, 70–95.

46 Bastian, *Protestantismo y sociedad en Mexico*, 190.

47 Garma, "Los estudios antropologicos sobre el protestantismo en Mexico," 94; Baldwin, *Protestants and the Mexican Revolution*, p.137.

48 Penton, "Mexico's Reformation," 150.

49 Ibid., 135.

50 Aulie, "The Christian Movement among the Chols of Mexico," 97.

51 For Catholic and Evangelical numbers in 1935, see Baez Camargo and Grubb, *Religion in the Republic of Mexico*, 144–5. For 1911, see Butler, "Protestant Christianity in Mexico," 348.

52 Baez Camargo and Grubb, *Religion in the Republic of Mexico*, 111. Estimates for the pre-revolutionary number of students range from 15,893 to 11,682. See Bastian, *Los dissisentes*, 147; and Butler, "Protestant Christianity in Mexico," 348.

53 Penton, "Mexico's Reformation," 135.

54 Baez Camargo and Grubb (*Religion in the Republic of Mexico*, 112) derive this figure from a survey of eighteen Evangelical schools in 1929. The total number of schools and pupils was certainly higher.

55 Vazquez, *Los que sembraron*, 216.

56 These are the words of the constitutional amendment. Baez Camargo and Grubb, *Religion in the Republic of Mexico*, 150.

57 Based on interviews in June 1991 with Eufemia and Antonio Manjares, former pupils and teachers, in Zitacuaro. Eufemia Manjares was one of the teachers who refused to sign in 1934. She later became mayor (presidente municipal) of Zitacuaro.

58 Baez Comargo and Grubb, *Religion in the Republic of Mexico*, 111; Bastian, *Protestantismo y sociedad en Mexico*, 193.

59 This survey was confined to the major historical denominations. It does not include the growing body of Pentecostal churches, which were much less reliant on missionary direction and funding. Davis, *La base economica de la iglesia evangelica en Mexico*, 37–63.

60 Davis, *La base economica de la iglesia evangelica en Mexico*, 55.

61 Baez Camargo and Grubb, *Religion in the Republic of Mexico*, 121.

62 Bennett, *Tinder in Tabasco*, 61. Bastian (*Los dissidentes*, 117), citing a missionary report, talks of 2,000 active Presbyterian members in 1910, influencing up to 15,000 more, but the census for 1910 listed only 400 in Tabasco.

63 Bennett, *Tinder in Tabasco*, 96–119.

64 Anderson, *Vision of the Disinherited*; Hollenweger, *The Pentecostals*.

65 Gaxiola, *La serpienta y la paloma*.

66 Movimiento de la Iglesia Cristiana Independiente Pentecostes, *Bodas de oro*.

67 Barrett, *World Christian Encyclopedia*, 490–2.

68 Iglesia Cristiana Interdenominational, *50 aniversario*, 18.

69 Penton, "Mexico's Reformation," 241–5.
70 *Noticiero Milamex* 17, no. 204 (Nov. 1987).
71 De los Reyes, *Historia de las assambleas de Dios en Mexico*, 1:34–8; Dominguez, *Pioneros de pentecosteses*, 1:41–6.
72 Dominguez, *Pioneros de pentecosteses*, 1:23–46; De los Reyes, *Historia de las assambleas de Dios en Mexico*, 1:53–63.
73 Dominguez, *Pioneros de pentecosteses*, 1: 47–60; De los Reyes, *Historia de las assambleas de Dios en Mexico*, 1:45–53, 55–6.
74 Penton, "Mexico's Reformation," 246.
75 Loaeza-Lajous, "Continuity and Change in the Mexican Catholic Church," 284.
76 Sandoval Arriaga, "La poblacion en Mexico," 102.
77 See Gonzalez Casanova, *Democracy in Mexico*, 104–36; Meyer and Sherman, *The Course of Mexican History*, 627–709.
78 Bailey, "The Church since 1940," 237.
79 Bailey and Loaeza-Lajous portray Camacho and the politicians as the first to initiate the reconciliation, but Penton claims that the first move came from Archbishop Martinez, who gave public backing to Cardenas in his struggle with the foreign oil companies. See Bailey, "The Church since 1940," 237; Loaeza-Lajous, "Continuity and Change in the Mexican Catholic Church," 283–5; Penton, "Mexico's Reformation," 142.
80 Olivera de Bonfil, "La iglesia en Mexico," 307.
81 Loaeza, "Notas para el estudio de la iglesia," 54.
82 Gutierrez Casillas, *Historia de la iglesia en Mexico*, 567–9.
83 Thus Catholic pressure in the 1950s and 1960s obliged the state to revise unfavourable portraits of the church in the textbooks approved by the secretary of education. Bailey, "The Church since 1940," 237–8.
84 Eckstein, *The Poverty of Revolution*, 108–124. For a contrary view stressing how anti-clericalism continued to curb the political power of the Catholic church, causing it to work "circumspectly" and "indirectly," see Fagan and Tuohy, *Politics and Privilege in a Mexican City*, 61.
85 Loaeza, "Notas para el estudio de la iglesia," 54.
86 Simpson, *Many Mexicos*, 303–4.
87 Penton, "Mexico's Reformation," 143–56.
88 Interviews with various Evangelical leaders in the summer of 1988.
89 Penton, "Mexico's Reformation," 145–53.
90 McGavran, et al., *Church Growth in Mexico*, 33.
91 Penton, "Mexico's Reformation," 292.
92 Read, et al., *Latin American Church Growth*, 154.
93 For a general review of the problems associated with these estimates, see Penton, "Mexico's Reformation," 288–94.
94 Read, et al., *Latin American Church Growth*, 166.
95 Bennett, *Tinder in Tabasco*, 37.

96 This estimate is based on the census figure that 15.3 per cent of Mexicans over the age of five in 1900 and 15.1 per cent in 1940 were able to speak an Indigenous language. Half (49.7 per cent) in 1940 were monolingual, only speaking an Indigenous language, while the remainder were bilingual. Iturriaga, *La estructura social y cultural de Mexico*, 219.

97 Baldwin, *Protestants and the Mexican Revolution*, 54.

98 Baez Camargo and Grubb, *Religion in the Republic of Mexico*, 99.

99 See Penton, "Mexico's Reformation," 223–5; and Davis, *La base economica de la iglesia evangelica en Mexico*, 88–92.

100 Rus and Wasserstrom, "Evangelization and Political Control," 171.

101 This distinction was elaborated by the SIL missionaries I interviewed and by the many others I met when my children and theirs were attending the same English-speaking school in Mexico.

102 On Saenz's educational policy see Quirk, *The Mexican Revolution and the Catholic Church*, 115–19; and Bastian, *Protestantismo y sociedad en Mexico*, 156–67.

103 The most detailed account of SIL's founding is found in Stoll, *Fishers of Men or Founders of Empire*, 62–79.

104 In 1970 the Evangelical proportion of the population in Oxchuc was 25 per cent and in Tumbala 20 per cent. They ranked fourth and eighth of all municipios in Mexico in the proportion who were Evangelical. All figures are taken from the national census. Bridges, *Expansion evangelica en Mexico*, 33.

105 Aulie, "The Christian Movement among the Chols of Mexico."

106 Slocum and Walkins, *The Good Seed*, 30–93.

107 Slocum, "Cultural Change among the Oxchuc Tzeltals," 491.

108 See Siverts, "Social and Cultural Change in a Tzeltal (Mayan) Municipio," 177; Stoll, *Fishers of Men or Founders of Empire*, 51.

109 *VII Censo general de Poblacion y Vivienda*, 1960. Paul Mayerlink, a Presbyterian missionary in Coralito in the mid-1950s, suggested that Slocum's figure was accurate for the area around Coralito but that the census was probably a better approximation for the municipio as a whole.

110 Both missionaries I have interviewed who worked in the Oxchuc area dismissed suggestions made by some anthropologists that they encouraged Evangelical migration to the lowlands so as to deter them from fighting for land reform and in order to create a closed world in the lowland that they, the missionaries, could control. The missionaries claim that the migration was driven by a desire for more and better land. Government played an active part in encouraging it. See Rus and Wasserstrom, "Evangelization and Political Control," 168. See also Harmon, "Enclavememt, Fusion, and Adaption," 216; Harmon, "Medical and Social Changes in a Tzeltal Mayan Community," 120.

111 Siverts, "Social and Cultural Change in a Tzeltal (Mayan) Municipio," 185.

112 Harmon, "Medical and Social Changes in a Tzeltal Mayan Community," 132–4.
113 Siverts, "Social and Cultural Change in a Tzeltal (Mayan) Municipio," 184–5.
114 I have this from the missionaries and pastors I interviewed in Oxchuc.
115 On the impact of population growth in promoting social change in Yochib, see Harmon, "Medical and Social Changes in a Tzeltal Mayan Community," 119–21.
116 Ibid., 14.
117 The introduction of government health promoters and clinics in the 1950s calls into question the claim by Rus and Wasserstrom that it was "strategic use" by missionaries of "Antibiotics and the Word" that accounts for Evangelical growth. Marianna had translated Mark by 1947, when Florence Gerdel, a trained nurse, joined her, but they saw no appreciable growth in Yochib over the next two years. Some souls were undoubtedly won through antibiotics, but there is no evidence that this was the major cause. The Protestant clinic near Yochib was not constructed until 1956, by which time the government program was already under way. Protestants had no monopoly on antibiotics. See Rus and Waserstrom, "Evangelization and Political Control," 168; Harmon, "Medical and Social Changes in a Tzeltal Mayan Community," 14, 78; Slocum and Walkins, *The Good Seed*, 198–9.
118 Harmon, "Medical and Social Changes in a Tzeltal Mayan Community," 50.
119 Ensin listened to Martin Gourd's records at an early stage and his son converted, which may account for the less than decisive action of the tribal leaders. Slocum and Walkins, *The Good Seed*, 113–29.
120 Siverts, "Social and Cultural Change in a Tzeltal (Mayan) Municipio," 185–6.
121 McGavran, et al., *Church Growth in Mexico*, 166.

CHAPTER THREE

1 Ramirez, "The Social and Economic Consequences of the National Austerity Program in Mexico," 143–70.
2 *Proceso*, no. 831, 5 Nov. 1992.
3 INEGI, "XI Censo general de poblacion y vivienda," 1990.
4 Castaneda, "One Party Has Been Well-Engineered in Mexico"; Sandoval, "La poblacion en Mexico," 100–1.
5 Moreno, "The Linkage between Population and Economic Growth in Mexico," 162.
6 Manuel Urbina, secretary general of the National Advisory Board on Population, cited in *Uno Mas Uno*, 7 July 1991.

7 Ramirez, "The Social and Economic Consequences of the National Austerity Program in Mexico," 162.

8 The 1990 census puts the urban percentage at 71.3 per cent, using 2,500 or more inhabitants in an area as the cut-off line. I have raised this line to 10,000 to identify more accurately truly urban areas. Some would raise the cut off-point even higher. See Sandoval Arriaga, "La poblacion en Mexico," 102.

9 Hellman, *Mexico in Crisis*, 95–130; and Gonzales Casanova, *Democracy in Mexico*, 221.

10 Riding, *Distant Neighbours*, 145–62; and a variety of articles in Gentleman, *Mexican Politics in Transition*.

11 Gonzalez Graf, *Las elecciones de 1988*, 335–9.

12 Loaeza-Lajous, "Continuity and Change in the Mexican Catholic Church," 289.

13 De la Rosa, "Iglesia y sociedad en el Mexico de hoy," 274–6; Gonzalez Gary, "Poder y presiones de la iglesia," 262–3.

14 Gonzalez Gary, "Poder y presiones de la iglesia," 268; Grayson, *The Church in Contemporary Mexico*, 28–36.

15 Villafain and Pastor Escobar, *Jerarquia catolica y modernizacion politica en Mexico*, 21–3. For a recent statement along the same lines by the Secretary of the CEM, or Mexican episcopacy, see *El Universal*, 5 Feb. 1993.

16 Villafain and Pastor Escobar, *Jerarquia Catolica y modernizacion politica en Mexico*, 26; and Guttierez Casillas, *Historia de la iglesia en Mexico*, 14.

17 Loaeza-Lajous, "Continuity and Change in the Mexican Catholic Church," 292.

18 Villafain and Pastor Escobar, *Jerarquia catolica y modernizacion politica en Mexico*, 26.

19 All these figures are provided by the Catholic church and reported in Guttierez Casillas, *Historia de la iglesia en Mexico*, 566–9.

20 Grayson (*The Church in Contemporary Mexico*, 28) cites figures for 1990 suggesting that the laity-to-clergy ratio had stabilized at 7,179, but it is not clear whether Grayson's enumeration can be compared to earlier figures, which are all drawn from Guttierez Casillas, *Historia de la iglesia en Mexico*. Data from the 1994 *Catholic Almanac* put the laity/clergy ratio at 7,575. See Table 9.1 in the conclusion.

21 *El Imparcial*, 23 Mar. 1993.

22 Barrett, *World Christian Encyclopedia*, 487.

23 Garma Navarro, "Liderazgo, mensaje religioso y contexto social," 94.

24 *New York Times*, 12 May 1990.

25 *Uno Mas Uno*, 9 Nov. 1990.

26 The 1990 census listed the population five years and over by religion, not the total population. Prior to this, all censuses listed the total population of each religion. I have therefore estimated the total population

affiliated to each religious category in order to make more meaningful comparisons.

27 See Sandoval Arriaga, "La poblacion en Mexico," 101.

28 *El Imparcial*, 27 Mar. 93.

29 Bridges, *Expansion evangelica en Mexico*, 16.

30 If those giving no reply are added, non-Catholics were 10.3 per cent of all Mexicans in 1990.

31 Wilson, *Religious Sects*, 104; and *Watchtower*, 1 Jan. 1990.

32 See Penton, "Mexico's Reformation," 265; Barrett, *World Christian Encyclopedia*, 491.

33 According to a Witness spokesperson, "We believe that nationalism only divides peoples, as does politics ... When we refuse to salute the flag or sing a national anthem, it is from considering it an act of idolatry, but this does not signify that we do not respect the flag or authorities, since they are in charge of maintaining order." *Uno Mas Uno*, 25 Mar. 1990. See also Penton, *Apocalypse Delayed*, 149.

34 Penton, "Mexico's Reformation," 267. See also, more recently for Oaxaca, Parnell, *Escalating Disputes*.

35 Penton, *Mexico's Reformation*, 98–101, 258–60.

36 *New York Times*, 15 Sept. 1991.

37 Murphy and Stepick, *Social Inequality in Oaxaca*.

38 This is based on the common measure of the percentage of the population over age five who spoke an Indigenous language in 1990. Nationally, 7.5 per cent of the Mexican population did so. INEGI, "XI Censo general de poblacion y vivienda," 1990.

39 A similar pattern exists in municipios where Indigenous peoples were the overwhelming majority. In the twenty-four municipios where 80 per cent or more were Indigenous, 21.5 per cent were Evangelicals. Just under four-fifths (79.5 per cent) of all Evangelicals in Chiapas resided outside of these twenty-four municipios, where they were 15.3 per cent of the total population.

40 Convencion Nacional Bautista de Mexico, *Libro de Informes: LXXXIII Reunion Anual* (Morelia, Michoacan, 1992), 126.

41 In 1985 it stood at 5.6 per 10,000 of the population. Sandoval Arriaga, "La poblacion en Mexico," 61.

42 This new breed of Pentecostal church is distinguished by a larger middle-class sector in its membership than is typical of other Pentecostal churches. They also tend to be larger than other Pentecostal churches, which creates different dynamics in participation and commitment.

43 The methodological comments made for Tables 3.2 and 3.3 also apply here. Owing to the large size of the one neo-Pentecostal church in my sample, no one was sufficiently familiar with the newly baptized and general membership to permit me to conduct a general census,

although I was able to survey the members of one prayer group. Elsewhere, I have a complete accounting of the newly baptized, but a couple of pastors evaded my repeated requests to enumerate their general membership. In two other cases, at the beginning of my research, I failed to collect the latter data.

CHAPTER FOUR

1 The diminishing involvement of mission boards in the years before 1970 has already been traced in chapter 2. The current involvement of missionaries is assessed in chapter 7.
2 Barrett, *World Christian Encyclopedia*, 391.
3 *Noticiero Milamex* 20, no. 242 (Dec. 1990).
4 For methodological comments on this sample, see chap. 3, n 43.
5 Unlike the congregational sample, the census does not classify as migrants those who migrated within their own state. However, the congregational sample compares current residence with the major residence of childhood, rather than place of birth, which is employed by the census. The first difference suggests that the census underestimates migration, while the second may overstate it. The two measures are not strictly comparable. The smaller interview sample shows migration rates about 10 per cent higher than does the congregational sample. In the interview sample, for instance, 55 per cent of all converts and 68 per cent of all urban converts were migrants, though this is true of only 61 per cent of Mexico City's converts. Since this main interview sample leans towards adult respondents, it underestimates the teen and young adult Evangelicals who were less likely to be migrants. I have therefore used the more representative and larger congregational sample in Table 4.3.
6 Lofland and Skonovd, "Conversion Motifs," 862–74.
7 Camp, "The Cross in the Polling Booth," 80. Barrett (*World Christian Encyclopedia*, 487) cites survey data for the 1970s suggesting Catholic weekly attendance was about 20 per cent.
8 Camp, "The Cross in the Polling Booth," 81; and Hernandez Medina, "Religion de los mexicanos," 143–7.
9 Indirect confirmation for this conclusion may be derived from the congregational sample, which reveals that only 10 per cent of the 745 Evangelical converts had belonged to a sect or another Evangelical denomination immediately prior to joining their current one. Another 7 per cent had switched from another congregation within their current denomination. Among the latter it is reasonable to assume that some switched because of a job change, a move, or other pragmatic consideration. The remaining 83 per cent all converted directly from Catholicism.

10 Interview in December 1992 with Paul Mayerlink, a missionary among the Tzeltal between 1956 and 1992.

11 Interview in December 1992 with Manual Gomez Hernandez, early convert and current leader of Chamulan Evangelicals.

12 INEGI, "IX Censo generale de poblacion y vivienda," 1990.

13 Even if we exclude marital status and include the never-married, 76 per cent of male converts over the age of twenty were married to an Evangelical. Among all female adults over the age of twenty, 44 per cent had a Catholic spouse.

14 Quoted in Roberts, *Religion in Sociological Perspective*, 111.

15 Snow and Machalek, "The Sociology of Conversion," 175–8.

16 Here the problem of post-conversion reconstruction or exaggeration of a sinful past is most acute. Though I tried to press respondents with demands for specific behavioural indices, the assertion that they had an alcohol problem ultimately rests on the information provided by them. There may be some overstatement, but not by a large margin, as I rejected several claims by younger men that heavy weekend drinking alone constituted at this point a serious problem.

CHAPTER FIVE

1 The official doctrines of Presbyterians and some Baptists do not encompass this notion of certainty, but I am here referring to the perceptions of the laity, who are often unaware of official church teaching. The doctrine of assurance is embraced by the great majority of Pentecostals, though many Mexican denominations and independent churches of a Pentecostal type have very rudimentary formulations of core doctrine.

2 Wilson, *Magic and the Millenium*, 22.

3 Let me reiterate that the total size of the interview sample varies a little from question to question, as I occasionally failed to ask a particular question of a respondent, and some questions were added to the interview schedule over the course of my research. The former situation applies here.

4 Only 3 per cent had not attended in the previous week, whereas this was true of 13 per cent of the congregational sample. To increase the chances of an honest answer to this question, I preceded it by asking how often the respondent typically attended each week. Their average answer was 3.8.

5 Contrary to popular perception, there is no evidence that Pentecostals are any more prone to emotional or mental instability than anyone else. See Maloney and Lovekin, *Glossolalia*, 39–94.

6 Excluded from this calculation are the thirty-five, or 7 per cent of the

total, who admitted to being illiterate or to having a vision problem that prevented them from reading.

7 Maloney and Lovekin, *Glossolalia*, 5.

8 Gran Concilio de la Iglesia Cristiana de las Assambleas de Dios en la Republica de Mexico, *Informe del Superintendente General*, 1984. A later survey by the same denomination revealed that only 32 per cent of 109,199 baptized members spoke in tongues. Gran Concilio de Las Assambleas de Dios en la Republica Mexicana, *Informe del Superintendente General*, 1992.

9 Roughly similar results are to be found in a large survey of Assemblies of God adherents in the U.S. Here, 33 per cent had never spoken in tongues, while 40 per cent regularly did so. Paloma, *The Assemblies of God at the Crossroads*, 12.

10 Assemblies of God pastors and congregations shared similar concerns in the U.S. Ibid., 76.

11 Paloma comes to a similar conclusion when she finds that 34 per cent of her Assemblies of God respondents in the U.S. agreed that divine healing "will always occur if a person's faith is great enough," though this was denied by official church doctrine. Ibid., 62.

12 Modern Catholics (who were perceptually and organizationally separate from the majority practising a syncretistic, folk religion) were the other group most receptive to modern medicine. Harmon, "Medical and Social Changes in a Tzeltal Mayan Community," 32, 153.

13 Converts were obliged to destroy the house cross and house altar on which these magical rituals were centred. Apostates rarely rebuilt these crosses and altars, due to the cost and inconvenience. Thus traditional rites could not be held in their homes, and they continued to attend modern curers. Harmon, "Enclavement, Fusion, and Adaption," 215.

14 Dirksen, "Pentecostal Healing."

15 Finkler, *Spiritualist Healers in Mexico*, 36; Aulie, "The Christian Movement among the Chols of Mexico," 45.

16 Murphy and Stepick, *Social Inequality in Oaxaca*, 52–4.

17 Easthorpe, "Marginal Healers," 63.

18 Ibid., 63–7.

19 For similar conclusions see Wilson, *Religious Sects*, 69; and Allen and Wallis, "Pentecostals as a Medical Minority," 110.

20 Wilson, *Religious Sects*, 100–1. The smaller of the two Adventist denominations I worked with, the Church of God of the Seventh Day, further distanced itself from the mainstream by refusing to celebrate Christmas and Easter, on the grounds that these were really pagan festivals, unconnected to the actual dates of the birth and death of Christ.

21 The total number of women surveyed on this issue is 174.

22 For an overview of some of this literature, see Martin, *Tongues of Fire*, 211–14. Erasmus's work on the Mayo in the 1950s differs from the

other research cited by Martin in that Erasmus found that Pentecostal Mayo "were not saving and not progressing materially more than their neighbours, although many of the men professed that they and their families were living better since they had given up drinking and going to fiestas." Erasmus, *Man Takes Control*, 249–50. O'Connor's later study of the Mayo disagrees. See O'Connor, "Two Kinds of Religious Movement among the Mayo Indians of Sonora Mexico," 260–8.

23 Turner, "Religious Conversion and Community Development," 252–60.

24 Annis, *God and Production in a Guatemalan Town*, 90–8.

25 Ibid., 100–4.

26 The best empirical work in Mexico is the excellent study by Clawson on a Mestizo rural community in the state of Puebla. Clawson concurs with Annis in all important respects, though Clawson's account is of Mormons, who are not part of the Evangelical work, though they might be defined as having evolved from it. They certainly share its ascetic values. Clawson, "Religious Allegiance and Economic Development in Rural Latin America," 499–524.

27 Not one of the fourteen female converts married to a Catholic felt her standard of living had improved after conversion. Another six converts were widows who looked to others for sustenance. There were also nineteen female converts married to second-generation Evangelicals whose economic standing was not shaped by conversion. When these thirty-nine females are excluded from Table 5.7, the proportion of female Evangelical converts claiming to have experienced an improvement in their living standards rises to 46 per cent. The latter is still lower than the rate for males recorded in Table 5.7, but it reduces the gender gap substantially.

28 In all 76 per cent of converts and 81 per cent of the second generation in the labour force were between the ages of twenty and fifty. More of the second generation were clustered in the late teen category, while more of the working converts were over the age of fifty. These exclusions reduce but do not eliminate the effect of general change in the occupational structure. Both converts and the second generation were enumerated in the same time period.

29 The major difference is that Table 5.8 differentiates unskilled from skilled occupations, which are both lumped together in Table 4.1 to facilitate comparison with the census. The discerning reader will note that the percentage in agricultural occupations is lower in Table 5.8. This is because it does not include older men, who are more likely to be engaged in agriculture.

30 The importance of gender differences slowly dawned on me in the course of my investigations. I therefore noted male/female differences in only the second half of my fieldwork.

31 My interview sample of 485, gathered with very different sampling

techniques, was also 64 per cent female, with virtually identical patterns among Pentecostals and others.

32 Davis, *La base economica de la iglesia evangelica en Mexico*, 53.

33 Women could serves as deaconesses along with deacons, but they could not be officially ordained as deacons and hence administer Holy Communion.

34 For those interested in a more precise numerical account, it may be recalled that 73 per cent of female converts were married at conversion. Table 4.10 shows that almost half (47 per cent) of these were married to a Catholic at conversion. Among the fifty-two then married to a Catholic, 64 per cent said that their Catholic husbands were opposed to their conversion. The opposition ranged from beatings, threats of desertion, and prohibitions on attendance to lengthy arguments and ridicule.

35 Brusco, "The Household Basis of Evangelical Religion."

36 Among the fifty-one female converts in the interview sample who were married to a Catholic at the time of their conversion, nineteen, or 37 per cent have subsequently seen their spouses convert. The others are now all either widowed, deserted, or still married to their Catholic spouses.

37 See a variety of articles in Lynn and Dow, *Class, Politics and Popular Religion in Mexico and Central America*; and Ingham, *Folk Catholicism in Central Mexico*.

38 Grayson, *The Church in Contemporary Mexico*, 5; Loaeza-Lajous, "Continuity and Change in the Mexican Catholic Church," 275–6.

CHAPTER SIX

1 This is based on the 495 married women in the congregational sample. In the interview sample, 23 per cent of married women had Catholic spouses, but this smaller sample may be less representative, especially on this issue, because wives with Catholic husbands found it awkward to invite me into their homes, where I normally conducted interviews.

2 Convencion Nacional Bautista de Mexico, *Libro de Informes:* LXXXIII *Reunion Anual* (Morelia, Michoacan, 1992), 128.

3 To be precise, this figure applied to the 347 persons who claimed that they or a member of their family had experienced a serious illness while attending their current congregation.

4 See Dirksen, "Pentecostal Healing," 30; Finkler, *Spiritualist Healers in Mexico*.

5 Bastian, *Los dissidentes*, 70.

6 A time-span of twelve months for current American contributions was set in order to obtain a reasonably accurate and honest reply. If it seems too short a period to the reader, he or she might be advised to see the

data in the next chapter dealing with a variety of indices of past and current forms of American missionary support of Evangelical churches.

7 Higgins, "Martyrs and Virgins," 187–206.

8 Murphy and Stepick, *Social Inequality in Oaxaca*, 149–53.

9 This 9 per cent calculation excludes people with Catholic spouses, who have little choice but to maintain *compadrazgo* links.

10 Excluded here were those who rented or whose Catholic spouse was responsible for construction and repairs.

11 Wilson, *Religious Sects*, 102.

12 Rivera, *Protestantismo Mexicano*, 71–4.

13 *Uno Mas Uno*, 25 Mar. 1990.

14 Penton, "Mexico's Reformation," 262.

15 Pastors were paid directly by the regional association, which received the tithes from all congregations for this purpose. Educational funds were collected separately by the associations, which then provided 50 per cent loans back to the congregations for school buildings or expansions. The association was also able to provide a wealth of practical advice on everything from legal to construction matters.

16 Four (13 per cent) had no formal training whatever; three took correspondence courses, and two attended a Bible institute for a year.

17 Penton, "Mexico's Reformation," 245.

18 Gran Concilio de la Iglesia Cristiana de las Assambleas de Dios en la Republica de Mexico, *Informe del Superintendente General*, 1984.

19 *Noticiero Milamex* 20, no. 242 (April 1991).

20 I was unable to obtain information on the number of regular tithers in two congregations.

21 Their pastors usually received salaries set by the local congregations, rather than the tithe. Their main seminary in Mexico City required completion of junior high school for entry, though completed secondary school was increasingly common. Some were university graduates. However, congregations were free to select pastors regardless of formal training. There were quite a few Baptist congregations without pastors because they could not afford to offer a living wage. For those congregations with resources, there was a surplus of pastors.

22 Since the early 1960s there have been special institutes for the training of Indigenous Presbyterian pastors in Chiapas, where Presbyterianism is especially strong. Though little more than literacy was required, I was told there was marked shortage of pastors because men with sufficient age and maturity to be respected as leaders and pastors were reluctant to take a two-year training course away from home and family.

23 This was not a new problem. In the early 1960s there were 244 Presbyterian congregations in Tabasco served by nine pastors. Bennet, *Tinder in Tabasco*, 149–50.

24 Willems, *Followers of the New Faith*, 104–14; and Lalive D'Epinay, *Haven of the Masses*, 94–5.

25 Gerlach and Hine, "Five Factors Crucial to the Growth and Spread of a Modern Religious Movement," 23–40.

26 Penton, "Mexico's Reformation," 246.

27 Barrett, *World Christian Encyclopedia*, 491.

28 Ibid., 491.

29 I failed to gather this information in one congregation.

30 In six cases a disaffected faction affiliated to an already established congregation or a disaffected congregation terminated its links with its denomination or mother church. Though no new congregations were created in these six cases, I would regard them as schisms since a dissident faction formed and split from an existing body. .

31 Willems, *Followers of the New Faith*, 104–14; and Lalive D'Epinay, *Haven of the Masses*, 174.

32 Wallis, "A Theory of Propensity to Schism," 99–125.

33 Ibid., 173–7. Wallis argues that Pentecostals are most prone to schism because the gifts of the spirit provide them with many bases for asserting their opposition to the established order. Empirically I am doubtful whether schism is more frequent among Pentecostals than Baptists, who do not emphasize the doctrine of the gifts of the spirit. I would therefore reformulate Wallis to say that schism is most likely in conversionist groups that stress the priesthood of all believers.

34 Three of the six Presbyterian congregations suffered a schism, but two were due to disagreements over the Pentecostal practice of tongues. The other, mentioned in the text above, was linked to a wider political conflict.

35 Convencion Nacional Bautista de Mexico, *Libro de Informes de la LXXXIII Reunion Anual* (Morelia, Michoacan, 1992), 129.

36 The neo-Pentecostal church was the mother church of an incipient movement. It gave about 15 per cent of its income to the movement. It also received pastoral services, though not any donations, from American missionaries involved in the movement. The pastors of two other very small churches, with thirty-four and thirty-nine baptized members respectively, said that 20 per cent of offerings to each department were given to the local association, as well as their own tithe. It is doubtful whether these sums amounted to more than 10 per cent of all donations, since no share went to central offices from the substantial giving that was put in the general collection or in special projects. In either case, the amounts received by central offices were very small, since these small and poor congregations were responsible for the upkeep of their church as well as their pastor, his wife, and several children.

37 As a result, Methodists provided much of the leadership. Penton, "Mexico's Reformation," 215–17.

38 Stoll, *Is Latin America Turning Protestant?* 132–4.

39 *Noticiero Milamex* 19, no. 231 (Jan. 1990).

40 Gerlach and Hine, "Five Factors Crucial to the Growth and Spread of a Modern Religious Movement," 26–30.

CHAPTER SEVEN

1 *Uno Mas Uno*, 10 July 1991. See also the claim by the Catholic bishop of Cuernavaca that Evangelicals are like "an epidemic that has invaded Latin America ... We will defend ourselves from these imposters who wish to root out the faith and buy it with dollars." Originally from *El Universal de Morelos*, 10 Dec. 1991, quoted in *Noticiero Milamex* 21, no. 257 (Mar. 1992).

2 From *Tabasco Hoy*, 26 Dec. 1992, quoted in *Noticiero Milamex* 22, no. 267 (Jan. 1993. These notions are also expounded in a full-page newspaper article by William Mendoza, who is a member of the movement "Disciples of the Word," founded by Flaviano Amatulli. See *Noticias: Voz y Imagen de Oaxaca*, 16 Oct. 1992.

3 From the public announcement by the National Presbyterian Church in *Excelsior*, 5 Feb. 1987.

4 Ibid., 8 Mar. 1990.

5 Campbell, "Mexican Presbyterians' Adventure of Faith," 200–9.

6 Patterson, *A Century of Baptist Work in Mexico*, 207–26.

7 Mexico City's size precluded such an effort. Since a host of American churches and missionaries could live on the American side of the northern border with easy access to the Mexican side, it was equally impossible to get a sense of their number and activities. In the oppressive heat of Tabasco, where I spent a summer, there were no missionaries at all. This was due to the active policy of the then-governor of the state, though I was assured that there were no resident missionaries prior to this governor's holding office, when such a policy was not in force.

8 Stoll (*Is Latin America Turning Protestant?* 93) calls them a "mobile version of church camp."

9 Penton "Mexico's Reformation," 220–2.

10 Stoll, *Fishers of Men or Founders of Empire*, 223–32; Stoll, "Con que derecho adoctrinan Ustedes a nuestros indigenas," 9–23.

11 Stoll claims that USAID was the main agency channelling covert CIA support. He says SIL received about 1 per cent of its budget from USAID. Overall, "the $31 million the agency gave eight evangelical PVOs [private voluntary organizations] in 1983–1984 was dwarfed by the $264 million to Catholic Relief Services, 77 percent of the latter's $324 million budget." Stoll, *Is Latin America Turning Protestant?* 271.

12 Stoll (*Fishers of Men or Founders of Empire?* 229) provides a brief account of the breaking of the agreement in 1979, but most of my information comes from interviews with senior SIL people at the time.

13 *Noticiero Milamex* 17, no. 195 (Jan. 1987).

14 *Excelsior*, 26 Feb. 1987.

15 *Noticiero Milamex* 18, no. 220 (Feb. 1989).

16 According to the senior SIL staff I interviewed.

17 According to one of the Reformed missionary couples at the Bible institute from 1961 to 1993, two SIL missionaries worked in the Oxchuc area over roughly the same years. They devoted their time to providing agricultural and craft education, effectively ignoring SIL's tradition of translation or the more general missionary one of church planting. So profound were these differences that they left SIL in the 1970s.

18 Steven, *They Dared to be Different*, 137.

19 Rus and Wasserstrom, "Evangelization and Political Control," 170.

20 No written source assesses the actual degree and nature of missionary contact. My account is derived from interviews with Ken Jacobs, Miguel Gomez's son, Domingo Lopez Angel, and a Chamulan pastor who was part of the 1973 expulsions. I was also helped by Abdias Tovilla, a Presbyterian pastor in Las Casas who headed CEDECH, an Evangelical human-rights association. Chamulan leaders in 1993 spoke of 18,000 refugees. My more conservative figure comes from Vern Sterk, a Reformed Church in America missionary, who had written an as-yet unavailable doctoral thesis on religious persecution in the area for Fuller Theological Seminary. Sterk lived and worked in the neighbouring Tzotzil community of Zinacantan in the late 1960s and 1970s. Thereafter he focused on leadership training for the Tzotzil as a whole and on translation of the Old Testament.

21 Stoll, "Con que derecho adoctrinan Ustedes a nuestros indigenas," 17–18.

22 The other Pentecostal church had been founded by a local who had been converted while working in a Mestizo area. The Methodist mission was formed by another local resident who lived and worked for many years in Oaxaca City, where he was converted in a Methodist church. His mission was established among the initial group of Presbyterians, who predated the missionary.

23 The missionary's account was confirmed by the Mixe Presbyterian pastor I also interviewed. The Mixe convert was a child convert through the influence of a SIL translator who entered the area in 1951. The first house services were not held in the pastor's municipio until 1968. The missionary never made any organized evangelistic efforts, though he did aid and encourage the pastor to attend the Presbyterian seminary in Mexico City for three years. After the young pastor's return in 1971

he initiated an active campaign of evangelism, with the blessings of the missionary but with no material or practical aid from him. In 1993 there were forty-three congregations in the Presbytery, which was founded in 1985. It included some Zapotec and Mixtec churches in addition to the preponderant Mixe base.

24 Beside several interviews with the missionary couple who arrived in 1979, I interviewed another couple who arrived in 1959 and were still resident in Mitla in 1993. From the particular village and church charted below, I interviewed the pastor and ten members of the congregation, including the founder and the principle dissidents. This church is one of the forty-three sample congregations.

25 Hernandez Diaz, *Los Chatinos*, 31.

26 During his absence, the missionary recorded his language helper reading some simple conversionist messages, but he stopped when he found the records were unused, lying around, and being played with by children. He also tried distributing some cheap cassette players, but he also stopped this when he discovered that they were being sold to "non-believers." During the missionary's two-month stay with the former municipal president, who was not a convert, he made only a few brief trips to the village so as not to embarrass his host. There were religious tensions in the village, which his presence exacerbated.

27 During the tenure of the Mestizo leader from Mexico City in the early 1980s it became a mission of this Pentecostal denomination in Mexico City, as did the Mestizo church in the principal town of the municipio. This link was broken in the mid-1980s, with the full concurrence of the Chatino pastor. Though he had been converted in a Pentecostal church, he had never acquired the gift of tongues. The missionary, who was deeply opposed to Pentecostalism, clearly played a part.

28 One couple in another Chatino municipio began working in a village in 1980. Week-long trips throughout the year amounted to about two months of residence in the village a year. In 1993 they had a small congregation of some ten to fifteen families that had not grown for some time. When the other couple arrived in their village in the early 1990s, there was already a small congregation founded by a resident Chatino who had converted through contacts with Mestizo Pentecostals closer to the coast, linked to the same church that initiated the Evangelical presence in the village described in the body of the text.

29 The wife was also a trained medical doctor. Between 1976 and 1986 she and her husband, who initially had not been a convert, lived in a Zapotec village. In 1993 they visited ten days a month. While she ran a medical clinic, he visited the several small Evangelical churches in the area, none of which he or she had founded, though they now offered much advice and encouragement. Both also organized a six-week annual

campaign among migrant crop workers in the northern state of Sinaloa, where they showed films, distributed gospel recordings, and sought converts among the many Indigenous people in the work-camps.

30 Among the two other congregations fully built with foreign money, one was constructed by a Methodist mission in the last century, while the other, on the border, was built by Americans in the process of setting up a small orphanage nearby.

31 I failed to gather data on this issue from one church.

CHAPTER EIGHT

1 This concept, taken from an earlier formulation by David Aberle, is also understood to imply radical, total, or complete change of the individual, as opposed to more partial types of change. Bromley and Shupe, *"Moonies"in America*, 23.

2 Wilson, *Magic and the Millenium*, 22.

3 Alvarez Gutierrez, "Como se sienten los Mexicanos?" 59–81.

4 Excluded from these figures are the 10 per cent of converts who had already broken their family ties before conversion.

5 A coming-of-age party, commonly held for fifteen-year-old girls, involving a special church service and a large party after.

6 There were also several second-generation Presbyterians in a small and struggling rural congregation, with a critical shortage of Evangelical men, who were either apostate or away working. The women admitted they attended the family parties of Catholic relatives. Not a few of the singles confessed to dancing.

7 See Ingham, *Folk Catholicism in Central Mexico*, 90–102; and Chance, "Changes in Twentieth Century Mesoamerican Cargo Systems," 27–42.

8 Based on his review of twenty-three recent ethnographies of Mexican Indian communities, Chance concludes that the former "civil-religious hierarchies are now themselves in the minority." Chance, "Changes in Twentieth Century Mesoamerican Cargo Systems," 30.

9 Hernandez Diaz, *Ensayos sobre la cuestion etnica en Oaxaca*, 33–7.

10 Alvarez Guttierez, "Como se sienten los Mexicanos?" 84–8.

11 It is possible that the Presbyterian army captain was also responsible for sending the army platoon to disperse the crowd around the Pentecostal mission, but I was never able to establish this with any certainty. A similar pattern also occurred in the Methodist church in the Totonac municipio of Ixtepec, which was persecuted for several years, until a Methodist army general was persuaded by Evangelicals to write a letter to the local authorities demanding that they respect the right to religious liberty enshrined in the constitution. The pressure then stopped. See Garma Navarro, *El protestantismo en una comunidad totonaca de Puebla*, 84.

12 Dennis, *Intervillage Conflict in Oaxaca*, 105.

13 In August 1993 474 Evangelicals from twenty communities in Chamula were reported to have been expelled. Abdias Tovilla, a Presbyterian pastor and head of CEDECH, an Evangelical human-rights organization, was said to fear the expulsion of another 1,000 recent converts in Chamula. *Noticeriero Milamex* 23, no. 277 (Oct. 1993).

14 This occurred after a signed agreement had been reached between the state government and CEDECH, the Evangelical human-rights organization. Evangelicals were promised that they would not be forced to buy candles, alcohol, and tobacco associated with religious festivals. In return Evangelicals agreed to respect and not to criticize San Juan, Chamula's patron saint. *Noticiero Milamex* 23, no. 286 (Aug. 1994).

15 *Noticiero Milamex* 24, no. 288 (Oct. 1994).

16 All dates and figures must be treated as approximate. A full and detailed investigation has not yet been done. Apart from press reports of varying degrees of inaccuracy, the scholarly investigators seemed to have had little or no contact with the Chamulan Evangelicals about whom they write. The major written sources are Rus and Wasserstrom, "Evangelization and Political Control," 168–70; Robledo Hernandez, "Dissidencia y religion"; Earle, "Appropriating the Enemy," 115–39; and Lopez Meza, "Sistema religioso-politico y las expulsiones en Chamula, Chiapas, Mexico." My account, which makes no claim to be authoritative, was also guided by interviews with several Chamulan leaders and missionaries, identified in chap. 7, n 20.

17 Robledo Hernandez, "Dissidencia y religion," 48; Lopez Meza, "Sistema religioso-politico y las expulsiones en Chamula, Chiapas, Mexico," 105.

18 Rus and Wasserstrom, "Evangelization and Political Control," 169.

19 Earle, "Appropriating the Enemy," 123.

20 This is because the civil and religious hierarchies had already split in most Indigenous communities. Chance, "Changes in Twentieth Century Mesoamerican Cargo Systems," 30.

21 Gonzales Graf, *Las elecciones de 1988*, 335.

22 Official figures for the same state gave Salinas 142,700 votes and Cardenas 394,534. Gonzalez Graf, *Las elecciones de 1988*, 339.

23 Grayson, *Prospects for Democracy in Mexico*, xxiii.

24 *Uno Mas Uno*, 4 July 1988.

25 Beltran, *Petroleo y desarrollo*, 151–2.

26 Bastian, *Protestantismo y sociedad en Mexico*, 236. I spent the summer of 1989 in the Chontalpa area. Mendez, I was told, was never a Presbyterian, though his wife was, and their children were raised as Presbyterians. Prior to the mid-1970s Mendez was said to have sometimes attended church with his wife, but he was never baptized, let alone ordained. On this were agreed all my many informants, including the

then Presbyterian pastor of the church Mendez's wife attended. Bastian's claim to the contrary is based on an article in *Uno Mas Uno* (18 May 1983), which involved interviews with various PR representatives. This article also contains the rather bizarre assertion, from a reputed member of the PR, that American President Reagan, "who bought our land for us," would help again if compensation was not forthcoming from PEMEX. Such outlandish claims surely call into question all other "facts" cited in the article.

27 The most detailed account of the whole incident and its background is in Beltran, *Petroleo y desarrollo*, 133–5.

28 Beltran, *Petroleo y desarrollo*, 174.

29 Garma Navarro, "Liderazgo protestante en una lucha campesina en Mexico," 126–47. He does say (137) that "members of fundamentalist sects (Baptists and Methodists)" condemned the actions of the former pastor and Pentecostal leader, but he has nothing to say on the response of the three Pentecostal churches in Ixtepec. Garma elsewhere notes that prior to the election, relations between the future Pentecostal leader and the other pastors in Ixtepec were growing progressively "more antagonistic": Garma, *El protestantismo en una comunidad totonaca de Puebla*, 88.

30 See Robledo Hernandez, "Dissidencia y religion," 76–90; Lopez Meza, "Sistema religioso-politico y las expulsiones en Chamula, Chiapas, Mexico," 105–54.

31 Robledo Hernandez, *Dissidencia y Religion*, 84.

32 Lopez Meza, "Sistema religioso-politico y las expulsiones en Chamula, Chiapas, Mexico," 136.

33 I have this from interviews with Ken Jacobs, the SIL missionary, and from a Chamulan pastor in the refugee colonia founded by Miguel Gomez Hernandez,

34 CEDECH was founded in the early 1980s, but it did not become active until the Presbyterians withdrew from CRIACH. My account is partly based on interviews I had with CEDECH's first full-time executive director in July 1992 and May 1993. The other sources are listed in n 16. They include Domingo Angel, the head of CRIACH.

35 *Noticiero Milamex* 18, no. 220 (Feb. 1989).

36 See the beginning of chap. 7.

37 *Noticiero Milamex* 20, no. 247 (May 1991).

38 Evangelical leaders claimed "that the Catholic Church was behind the crackdown." Metz, "Protestantism in Mexico," 72.

39 Bastian, "Editorial," 5–6.

40 *Latin American Evangelist* 70, no. 2 (April–June 1990).

41 *Excelsior*, 8 Mar. 1990. A large poster containing the presentation by the Baptist, Methodist, and Presbyterian churches and the reply of the president was later distributed to the member congregations.

42 *Noticiero Milamex* 21, no. 253 (Nov. 1991); 22, no. 264, (Oct. 1992).

43 *Proceso*, 28 Sept. 1992.

44 *Noticiero Milamex* 21, no. 254 (Dec. 1991).

45 "Ley de Asociaciones Religiosas y Culto Publico," *Diario Oficial de la Federacion de Los Estados Unidos de Mexico*, CDLXVI, no. 11, 1992. See also Blancarte, "Religion and Constitutional Change in Mexico, 1988–1992," 555–69.

46 Blancarte, "Religion and Constitutional Change in Mexico, 1988–1992," 563.

47 *Uno Mas Uno*, 14 Nov. 1992.

CHAPTER NINE

1 The annual baptismal rate of 14.1 per cent in the 1980s recorded in Table 3.4 needs to be balanced by the inevitable losses through death. Applying national mortality rates in the mid-1980s produces an annual growth potential of 13.5 per cent, which yields the 255 per cent increase over the decade.

2 The projected growth of the Mexican population as a whole is based on the census figures indicating a 21.5 per cent increase over the 1980s, which amounts to an annual growth of 1.97 per cent. The Evangelical projection is based on the baptismal rate of 14.1 per cent, adjusted for the national death rate, which yields an annual growth of 13.5 per cent. The projection starts from the census figures of 1980.

3 A recent estimate put the Protestant proportion at 20 per cent. See *New York Times*, 4 July 1993.

4 Martin, *Tongues of Fire*, 290.

5 Stoll, *Is Latin America Turning Protestant?* 310–14.

6 Based on research in the 1960s in Guatemala City, Roberts drew the rather similar conclusion that "joining a Protestant group ... is not an act of withdrawal in the face of difficult urban problems but an active attempt to cope with these problems through an available and suitable form of association." Roberts, "Protestant Groups and Coping with Urban Life in Guatemala," 764.

7 Stark, "How New Religions Succeed," 13–15.

8 Bastian, "The Metamorphosis of Latin American Protestant Groups," 53.

9 Bennett, *Tinder in Tabasco*.

10 Barrett, *World Christian Encyclopedia*, 488; Bailey, "The Church since 1940," 238.

11 Wilson, "An Analysis of Sect Development."

12 Garrard-Burnett, "Protestantism in Latin America," 219.

13 Because of Mexico's proximity to the U.S. and their shared and lengthy land border, I suspect – though I cannot prove – that the *Operation*

World figures cited in Table 9.2 are particularly likely to underestimate the missionary presence in Mexico.

14 Johnstone, *Operation World*, 160.
15 Information on the methodological procedures employed by Evangelical agencies in the 1980s to calculate their percentage of Guatemala's population was obtained from various unpublished reports by Ross Rogde, the senior investigator in the SEPAL project of 1991. Data from the SEPAL study were obtained from the same source and from an interview I had with Ross Rohde in July 1995. In all fairness it must be pointed out that CID, a Guatemalan polling agency affiliated to Gallup, found that 19 per cent of the 1,295 adult Guatemalans it polled in 1991 claimed to be Evangelicals. This is striking confirmation of SEPAL's results, though I remain highly suspicious of SEPAL's assumption that the Guatemalan Evangelical community was 2.3 times larger than its total of Sunday attenders. This assumption does not fit with the minimal requirements of active membership stressed by Mexican Evangelicals and by the Guatemalan Evangelicals I interviewed during a two-month visit during the summer of 1995.
16 A recent projection from the 1980 census and a 1988 survey by the Brazilian Institute of Geography and Statistics together put Evangelicals at about 17 per cent of all Brazilians. Freston, "Popular Protestants in Brazilian Politics," 537, 567.
17 Stoll, *Is Latin America Turning Protestant?* 9; Garrard-Burnet, "Protestantism in Latin America," 219.
18 These findings by Jean Kessler, based on a sample survey of 1,276 adults, are cited in Stoll, "Introduction," 17.
19 Kessler's survey of Costa Rica, cited in the preceding footnote, found that two-thirds of the former Evangelicals now identified themselves as Catholics, while the remainder said they had no religion. Stoll, "Introduction," 17.

Bibliography

Aguilar, Edwin, Jose Sandoval, and Kenneth Coleman. "Protestantism in El Salvador: Conventional Wisdom versus Survey Evidence." *Latin American Research Review* 23, no. 3 (1993): 119–40.

Allen, Gillian, and Roy Wallis. "Pentecostals as a Medical Minority." In Roy Wallis and Peter Morley, eds., *Marginal Medicine*. London: Peter Owen 1976. 110–37.

Alvarez Gutierrez, Alberto. "Como se sienten los Mexicanos?" In Alberto Hernandez Medina and Luis Narro Rodriguez, eds., *Como somos los Mexicanos*. Mexico: CREA 1987. 41–86.

Ammerman, Nancy. "Operationalizing Evangelicalism: An Amendment." *Sociological Analysis* 43, no. 2 (1982): 170–2.

Anderson, Robert M. *Vision of the Disinherited: The Making of American Pentecostalism*. New York: Oxford University Press 1979.

Annis, Sheldon. *God and Production in a Guatemalan Town*. Austin: University of Texas Press 1987.

Aulie, Henry W. "The Christian Movement among the Chols of Mexico, with Special Reference to Problems of Second Generation Christianity." PhD, Fuller Theological Seminary 1979.

Avramow Gutierez, J. "Los partidos contendientes en 1988." In J. Gonzalez Graf, ed., *Las elecciones de 1988 y la crisis del systema politico*. Mexico: Diana 1989. 13–30.

Baez Camargo, Gonzalo, and Kenneth Grubb. *Religion in the Republic of Mexico*. London: World Dominion Press 1935.

Bailey, David C. "The Church since 1940." In W.D. Raat and W. H. Beezley, eds., *Twentieth Century Mexico*. Lincoln and London: University of Nebraska Press 1986. 236–42.

Baldwin, Deborah J. *Protestants and the Mexican Revolution: Missionaries, Ministers, and Social Change*. Chicago: University of Illinois Press 1990.

Banker, Mark T. "Presbyterians and Pueblos: A Protestant Response to the Indian Question, 1872–1892." *Journal of Presbyterian History* 60 (1982): 23–40.

Barranco Villafain, B., and R. Pastor Escobar. *Jerarquia catolica y modernizacion politica en Mexico*. Mexico: Palabra 1989.

Barrett, David. "Statistics, Global." In Stanley Burgess and Gary McGee, eds., *Dictionary of Pentecostal and Charismatic Movements*. Grands Rapids, Mich.: Zondervan 1988. 810–29.

Barrett, David, ed. *World Christian Encyclopedia*. New York: Oxford University Press 1982.

Bastian, Jean P. *Protestantismo y sociedad en Mexico*. Mexico: CUPSA 1983.

– *Breve historia del protestantismo en America Latina*. Mexico: CUPSA 1986.

– "Editorial." *Cristianismo y Sociedad* 27, no. 101 (1989): 5–6.

– *Los Dissidentes: sociedades protestantes y revolucion en Mexico, 1872–1911*. Mexico: Fondo de Cultura Economica & El Colegio de Mexico 1989.

– "El impacto regionale de las sociedades religiosas no catolicas en Mexico." *Cristianismo y Sociedad* 28, no. 105 (1990): 57–74.

– "The Metamorphosis of Latin American Protestant Groups." *Latin American Research Review* 28, no. 3 (1993): 33–61.

Beckford, James A. *Religion and Advanced Industrial Society*. London: Unwin Hyman 1989.

Bellah, Robert. "Religious Evolution." In *Beyond Belief: Essays on Religion in a Post Industrial World*. New York: Harper and Row 1970. 20–50.

Beltran, Jose E. *Petroleo y desarrollo*. 2nd ed. Villahermosa: Instituto de Cultura de Tabasco 1988.

Benjamin Lara, Carlos. "Iglesias evangelicas y conflicto politico en El Salvador." *Cristianismo y Sociedad* 28, no. 103 (1990): 107–21.

Bennett, Charles. *Tinder in Tabasco: A Study in Church Growth*. Grand Rapids: Eerdmans 1968.

Berger, Peter. *The Sacred Canopy*. Garden City: Doubleday 1967.

Bibby, Reg. *Fragmented Gods: The Poverty and Potential of Religion in Canada*. Toronto: Irwin 1987.

Blancarte, Roberto. "Religion and Constitutional Change in Mexico, 1988–1992." *Social Compass* 44, no. 4 (1993): 555–69.

Braden, Charles C. *Man Takes Control*. New York: Bobbs-Merrill 1961.

Bridges, Julian C. *Expansion evangelica en Mexico*. Miama: Mundo Hispanico 1973.

Bromley, David G., and Anson D. Shupe. *"Moonies" in America: Cult, Church, and Crusade*. Beverley Hills, Calif.: Sage 1979.

Bruce, Steve. *A House Divided: Protestantism, Schism, and Secularization*. New York: Routledge 1990.

Brusco, Elizabeth Ellen. "The Household Basis of Evangelical Religion and the Reformation of Machismo in Columbia." PhD, City University of New York 1986.

Butler, John W. "Protestant Christianity in Mexico." *Missionary View of the World* 24 (May 1911): 345–50.

Camp, Roderic A. "The Cross in the Polling Booth: Religion, Politics and the Laity in Mexico." *Latin American Research Review* 29, no. 3 (1994): 69–100.

Campbell, J. Gary. "Mexican Presbyterians' Adventure of Faith: A Case of Moratorium – Two Interviews." *International Review of Missions* 64, no. 1 (1975): 200–9.

Caplow, T. "Contrasting Trends in European and American Religion." *Sociological Analysis* 46, no. 2 (1985): 101–8.

Castaneda, Jorge. "One Party Has Been Well-Engineered in Mexico." *Houston Chronicle*, 15 Aug. 1991.

Catholic Almanac. Huntington, Ind.: Our Sunday Visitor, 1994.

Chance, John K. "Changes in Twentieth Century Mesoamerican Cargo Systems." In Stephen Lynn and James Dow, eds., *Class, Politics, and Popular Religion in Mexico and Central America.* Washington: American Anthropological Association 1990. 27–42.

Clawson, David L. "Religious Allegiance and Economic Development in Rural Latin America." *Journal of Interamerican Studies and World Affairs* 26, no. 4 (1984): 499–524.

Convencion Nacional Bautista de Mexico. *Libro de informes: LXXXIII Reunion Annual.* Morelia, Michoacan, 1992.

Davis, J. Merle. *La base economica de la iglesia evangelica en Mexico.* Londres: Concilio Internacional Misionero 1941.

De la Rosa, Martin. "Iglesia y sociedad en el Mexico de hoy." In Martin de la Rosa and Charles A. Reilly eds., *Religion y politica en Mexico.* Mexico: Siglo Veintiuno 1985. 268–92.

De los Reyes, Alfonso. *Historia de Las Assambleas de Dios en Mexico: Los Pioneros.* Vol. 1. Mexico 1990.

Dennis, P.A. *Inter-Village Conflict in Oaxaca.* New Brunswick, NJ: Rutgers University Press 1987.

Dirksen, Murl O. "Pentecostal Healing: A Facet of the Personalistic Health System in Pakal-Na, a Village in Southern Mexico." PhD, University of Tennessee 1984.

Dominguez, Enrique, and Deborah Huntington. "The Salvation Brokers: Conservative Evangelicals in Central America." *NACLA: Report on the Americas* 18, no. 1 (1984): 2–36.

Dominguez, Roberto. *Pioneros de Pentecosteses.* Vol. 2. El Salvador: Literatura Evangelica 1975.

Earle, Duncan M. "Appropriating the Enemy: Highland Maya Religious Organization and Community Survival." In Stephen Lynn and James Dow, eds., *Class, Politics, and Popular Religion in Mexico and Central America*. Washington: American Anthroplogical Association 1990. 115–139.

Easthorpe, Gary. "Marginal Healers." In R. Kenneth Jones, ed., *Sickness and Sectarianism*. Vermont: Gower 1975. 52–71.

Eckstein, Susan. *The Poverty of Revolution: The State and the Urban Poor in Mexico*. Princeton, NJ: Princeton University Press 1977.

Erasmus, Charles J. *Man Takes Control*. New York: Bobbs-Merrill 1961.

Fagan, Richard, and Wiliiam S. Tuohy. *Politics and Privilege in a Mexican City*. Stanford: University of Stanford Press 1971.

Finkler, Kaja. *Spiritualist Healers in Mexico: Successes and Failures of Alternative Therapeutics*. New York: Praeger 1985.

Freston, Paul. "Popular Protestants in Brazilian Politics: A Novel Turn in Sect-State Relations." *Social Compass*. 41, no. 4 (1994): 537–70.

Garma Navarro, Carlos. "Liderazgo protestante en una Lucha campesina en Mexico." *America Indigena* 44, no. 1 (1984): 126–47.

– *El protestantismo en una comunidad totonaca de Puebla*. Mexico: Instituto Nacional Indigenista 1987.

– "Liderazgo, mensaje religiosso y contexto social." *Cristianismo y Sociedad* 26, no. 95 (1988): 89–100.

– "Los estudios antropologicos sobre el protestantismo en Mexico." *Cristianismo y Sociedad* 27, no. 101 (1989): 89–101.

Garrard-Burnett, Virginia. "Protestantism in Latin America." *Latin American Research Review* 27, no. 1 (1992): 218–30.

– "Conclusion: Is This Latin America's Reformation?" In Virginia Garrard-Burnett and David Stoll, eds., *Rethinking Protestantism in Latin America*, 199–210. Philadelphia: Temple University Press 1993.

Gaxiola, Manuel J. *La serpienta y la paloma*. Pasadena: William Carey Library 1970.

Gentleman, Judith, ed. *Mexican Politics in Transition*. Boulder, Colo.: Westview 1987.

Gerlach, Luther P., and Virginia H. Hine. "Five Factors Crucial to the Growth and Spread of a Modern Religious Movement." *Journal for the Scientific Study of Religion* 7, no. 1 (1968): 23–40.

Glock, Charles, and Rodney Stark. *Religion and Society in Tension*. Chicago: Rand McNally 1965.

Goddard, Jorge Adame. "Iglesia y estadio en el porfiriato." In Jose Francisco Ruiz Massieu, ed., *Relations del estado con las iglesias*. Mexico: Porrua 1992. 1–16.

Gonzalez Casanova, Pablo. *Democracy in Mexico*. New York: Oxford University Press 1970.

Gonzalez Graf, Jaime, ed. *Las elecciones de 1988 y la crisis del systema politico*. Mexico: Diana 1989.

Gonzalez Gary, Oscar. "Poder y presiones de la iglesia." In Pablo Gonzales

Casanova and Hector Aguilar Camin, eds., *Mexico antes la crisis*. Vol. 2. Mexico: Siglo Veintiuno 1985. 238–94.

Gran Concilio de la Iglesia Cristiana de las Assambleas de Dios en la Republica de Mexico. *Informe del Superintendente General*. 1984, 1992.

Grayson, George. *Prospects for Democracy in Mexico*. New Brunswick, NJ: Transaction 1990.

– *The Church in Contemporary Mexico*. Washington: Centre for Strategic and International Studies 1992.

Green, Linda. "Shifting Affiliations: Mayan Widows and 'Evangelicos' in Guatemala." In Virginia Garrard-Burnet and David Stoll, eds., *Rethinking Protestantism in Latin America*. Philadelphia: Temple University Press 1993. 159–79.

Gutierrez Casillas, Jose. *Historia de la iglesia en Mexico*. 2nd ed. Mexico: Editorial Porrua 1984.

Harmon, Robert C. "Medical and Social Changes in a Tzeltal Mayan Community." PhD, University of Arizona 1969.

– "Enclavement, Fusion and Adaptation in a Tzeltal Maya Community." In George Castille and G. Kushnev, eds., *Persistent Peoples*. Tucson: University of Arizona Press 1986. 212–27.

Hellman, Judith A. *Mexico in Crisis*. New York: Holmes and Meier 1978.

Hernandez Diaz, Jorge. *Ensayos sobre la cuestion etnica en Oaxaca*. Oaxaca: Instituto de Investigaciones Sociologicas, UABJO, 1988.

– *Los chatinos: etnicidad y organizacion social*. Oaxaca: Instituto de Investigaciones Sociologicas, UABJO, 1992.

Hernandez Medina, Alberto. "Religion de los mexicanos." In Alberto Hernandez Medina and Luis Narro Rodriguez, eds., *Como somos los mexicanos*. Mexico: CREA 1987. 113–66.

Higgins, Michael J. "Martyrs and Virgins: Popular Religion in Mexico and Nicaragua." In Stephen Lynn and James Dow, eds., *Class, Politics, and Popular Religion in Mexico and Central America*. Washington: American Anthroplogical Association 1990. 187–206.

Hine, Virginia H. "The Deprivation and Disorganization Theories of Social Movements." In Irving Zaretsky and Mark Leone, eds., *Religious Movements in Contemporary America*. Princeton, NJ: Princeton University Press 1974. 646–61.

Hunter, James. "Operationalizing Evangelism: A Review, Critique & Proposal." *Sociological Analysis* 42, no. 4 (1982): 363–73.

Iglesia Cristiana Interdenominational. *50 aniversario: edicion commemorativa*. Mexico, n.d.

Ingham, John M. *Folk Catholicism in Central Mexico: Mary, Michael, and Lucifer*. Austin: University of Texas 1986.

Iturriaga, Jose E. *La estructura social y cultural de Mexico*. Mexico: Cien de Mexico 1987.

Johnstone, Patrick. *Operation World*. 5th ed. Grand Rapids, Mich.: Zondervan 1993.

Jrade, Ramon. "Inquiries into the Cristero Insurrection against the Mexican Revolution." *Latin American Research Review*. 20, no. 2 (1985): 53–69.

Kanter, Rosabeth, 1968. "Commitment and Social Organization: A Study of Commitment Mechanisms in Utopian Communities." *American Sociological Review* 33, no. 4 (1968): 499–517.

Kelley, Dean. "Why Conservative Churches Are Still Growing." *Journal for the Scientific Study of Religion* 17, no. 2 (1978): 165–72.

Kilbourne, Bruce, and James Richardson. "Paradigm Conflict, Types of Conversion, and Conversion Theories." *Sociological Analysis* 50, no. 1 (1988): 1–21.

Lalive D'Epinay, Christian. *Haven of the Masses: A Study of the Pentecostal Movement in Chile*. London: Lutterworth Press 1969.

– "Political Regimes and Millenarianism in a Dependent Society: Reflections on Pentecostalism in Chile." *Concilium*, no. 161 (1983): 42–54.

Loaeza [-Lajous], Soledad. "Notas para el estudio de la iglesia en el Mexico contemporaneo." In Martin de la Rosa and Charles A. Reilly, eds., *Religion y politica en Mexico*. Mexico: Siglo Veintiuno 1985. 42–58.

– "Continuity and Change in the Mexican Catholic Church." In Dermot Keogh, ed., *Church and Politics in Latin America*. New York: St. Martin's Press 1990. 272–98.

Lofland, John, and Norman Skonovd. "Conversion Motifs." *Journal for the Scientific Study of Religion* 20, no. 2 (1981): 862–74.

Lopez Meza, Antonio. "Sistema religioso-politico y las expulsiones en Chamula, Chiapas, Mexico." PhD, Universidad Autonoma de Chiapas 1992.

Lynn, Stephen, and James Dow, eds. *Class, Politics, and Popular Religion in Mexico and Central America*. Washington: American Anthroplogical Association 1990.

McGavran, Donald, Jack Huegel, and Jack Taylor. *Church Growth in Mexico*. Grand Rapids, Mich.: Eerdmans 1963.

Maloney, H.N., and A.A. Lovekin. *Glossolalia: Behavioral Science Perspectives on Speaking in Tongues*. New York: Oxford University Press 1985.

Martin, David. *A General Theory of Secularization*. Oxford: Blackwell 1978.

– *Tongues of Fire: The Explosion of Protantism in Latin America*. Oxford: Basil Blackwell 1990.

Metz, Allan. "Protestantism in Mexico: Contemporary Contextual Developments." *Journal of Church and State* 36, no. 1 (1994): 57–78.

Meyer, Michael, and William Sherman. *The Course of Mexican History*. New York: Oxford University Press 1987.

Moreno, L. "The Linkage between Population and Economic Growth in Mexico." *Latin American Research Review* 26, no. 3 (1991): 159–70.

Moseley, Edward H. "The Religious Impact of the American Occupation of Mexico City, 1847–1848". In Eugene R. Huck and Edward H. Mosley, eds.,

Militarists, Merchants, and Missionaries: United States Expansion in Middle America. Birmingham: University of Alabama Press 1970. 39–52.

Movimiento de la Iglesia Cristiana Independiente Pentecostes. *Bodas de oro: libro historico*. Pachuca, Hidalgo, 1972.

Murphy, Arthur D., and Alex Stepick. *Social Inequality in Oaxaca: A History of Resistance and Change*. Philadelphia: Temple University Press 1991.

Nelson, Lynne, and David Bromley. "Another Look at Conversion and Defection in Conservative Churches." In David Bromley, ed., *Falling from the Faith*. Beverley Hills, Calif.: Sage 1988. 47–61.

Niebuhr, H. Richard. *The Social Sources of Denominationalism*. New York: Holt 1929.

O'Connor, Mary. "Two Kinds of Religious Movement among the Mayo Indians of Sonora Mexico." *Journal for the Scientific Study of Religion* 18, no. 3 (1979): 160–268.

Olivera de Bonfil, Alicia. "La iglesia en Mexico: 1926–1970." In J.W. Wilkie, M.C. Meyer, et al., eds., *Contemporary Mexico: Papers of the IV International Congress of Mexican History*. Berkeley: University of California Press 1976. 295–316.

Paloma, Margaret M. *The Assemblies of God at the Crossroads: Charisma and Institutional Dilemmas*. Knoxville: University of Tennessee Press 1989.

Parnell, Phillip. *Escalating Disputes: Social Participation and Change in the Oaxacan Highlands*. Tucson: University of Arizona Press 1990.

Patterson, F.W. *A Century of Baptist Work in Mexico*. El Paso: Baptist Spanish Publishing House 1979.

Penton, Marvin James. "Mexico's Reformation: A History of Mexican Protestantism from Its Inception to the Present." PhD, State University of Iowa 1965.

– *Apocalypse Delayed: The Story of the Jehovah's Witnesses*. Toronto: University of Toronto Press 1985.

Quirk, R. *The Mexican Revolution and the Catholic Church*. Bloomington: Indiana University Press 1972.

Ramirez, M.D. "The Social and Economic Consequences of the National Austerity Program in Mexico." In H. Handelman and W. Baer, eds., *Paying the Costs of Austerity in Latin America*. Boulder, Colo.: Westview 1989. 143–70.

Read, W., V. Monteroso, and H. Johnson. *Latin American Church Growth*. Grand Rapids, Mich.: Eerdmans 1969.

Riding, Alan. *Distant Neighbours: A Portrait of the Mexicans*. New York: Vintage 1986.

Rivera, Pedro. *Protestantismo mexicano: su desarollo y estado actual*. 3rd ed. Mexico: JUS 1961.

Roberts, Bryan R. "Protestant Groups and Coping with Urban Life in Guatemala." *American Journal of Sociology* 73, no. 4 (1968): 753–67.

Roberts, Keith A. *Religion in Sociological Perspective*. 2nd ed. Belmont, Cali.: Wadsworth 1990

Robledo Hernandez, Gabriela Patricia. "Disidencia y religion: los expulsadores de San Juan Chamula." Diss., Escula Nacional de Antropologica y Historia, Mexico, 1987.

Rolim, Francisco. "El pentecostalismo o a partir del pobre." *Cristianismo y Sociedad* 24, no. 95 (1988): 51–70.

Roof, W.C., and W. McKinney. *American Mainline Religion: Its Changing Shape and Future*. New Brunswick, NJ: Rutgers University Press 1987.

Rus, Jan, and Robert Wasserstrom. "Evangelization and Political control in Mexico: The sil in Mexico." In Peter Aaby and Soren Hvalkof, eds., *Is God an American? An Anthropological Perspective on the Missionary Work of the Summer Institute of Linguistics*. London: Survival International 1981. 163–72.

Sandoval Arriaga, Alfonso. "La poblacion en Mexico." In Alfonso Sandoval Arriaga, Alejandro Rodriguez, et al., eds., *Setenta y cinco anos de Revolution*. Mexico: Fondo de Cultura Economica 1988. 1: 5–110.

Schmitt, Karl M. "American Protestant Missionaries and the Diaz Regime in Mexico." *Journal of Church and State* 25, no. 2 (1983): 253–77.

Simpson, Lesley Bird. *Many Mexicos*. 3rd ed. Berkeley: University of California Press 1959.

Singleton, R., B. Straits, et al. *Approaches to Social Research*. New York: Oxford University Press 1988.

Siverts, Henning. "Social and Cultural Change in a Tzeltal (Mayan) Municipio, Chiapas, Mexico." *Proceedings of the 32nd International Congress of Americanists*. Copenhagen 1956. 175–89.

Slocum, Marianna. "Cultural Change among the Oxchuc Tzeltals." In *Estudios antropologicos en homenaje al Doctor Manuel Camio*. Mexico: Direccion General de Publicacciones 1956. 491–5.

Slocum, Marianna, and Grace Walkins. *The Good Seed*. Orange, Cali.: Promise Publishing 1988.

Snow, David A., and Richard Machalek. "The Sociology of Conversion." *Annual Review of Sociology*, 10 (1988): 167–90

Stark, Rodney. "How New Religions Succeed: A Theoretical Model." In David G. Bromley and Phillip H. Hammond, eds., *The Future of New Religious Movements*. Macon, Ga.: Mercer University Press 1987. 11–29.

Stark, Rodney, and William S. Bainbridge. *The Future of Religion: Secularization, Revival, and Cult Formation*. Berkeley: University of California Press 1985.

Steven, Hugh. *They Dared To Be Different*, Rev. ed. Huntington Beach, Cali.: Wycliffe Bible Translators 1983.

Stoll, David. *Fishers of Men or Founders of Empire? The Wycliffe Bible Translators in Latin America*. London: Zed Press 1982.

– "Con que derecho adoctrinan Ustedes a nuestros indigenas: La polemica en torno al Instituto Lingustico de Verano." *America Indigena* 44, no.1 (1984): 9–23.

– *Is Latin America Turning Protestant? The Politics of Evangelical Growth*. Los Angeles: University of California Press 1990.

– "Introduction: Rethinking Protestantism in Latin America". In Virginia Garrard-Burnett and David Stoll, eds., *Rethinking Protestantism in Latin America*, 1–19. Philadelphia, PA: Temple University Press 1993.

Trudeau, Robert H. *Guatemalan Politics: The Popular Struggle for Democracy*. Boulder: Lynne Rienner 1993.

Turner, Paul R. "Religious Conversion and Community Development." *Journal for the Scientific Study of Religion* 18, no. 3 (1979): 252–60.

Vazquez, Apolonio C. *Los que sembraron con lagrimas*. Mexico: El Faro 1985.

Wallis, Roy. "A Theory of Propensity to Schism." In Roy Wallis, ed., *Salvation and Protest*. New York: St Martin's Press 1976. 174–87.

– "Coping with Institutional Fragility: An Analysis of Christian Science and Scientology." In Roy Wallis, ed., *Salvation and Protest: Studies of Social and Religious Movements*. New York: St Martin's Press 1979. 25–43.

Warner, R. Stephen. "Work in Progress toward a New Paradigm for the Sociological Study of Religion in the United States." *American Journal of Sociology* 98, no. 5 (1993): 1044–93.

Willems, Emilio. *Followers of the New Faith: Cultural Change and the Rise of Protestantism in Brazil and Chile*. Nashville, Tenn.: Vanderbilt University Press 1967.

Wilson, Bryan. "An Analysis of Sect Development." In Louis Schneider, ed., *Religion, Culture, and Society*. New York: John Wiley 1964. 482–97.

– *Religious Sects: A Sociological Study*. New York: McGraw-Hill 1970.

– *Magic and the Millenium: A Sociological Study of Religious Movements of Protest among Tribal and Third-World Peoples*. New York: Harper and Row 1973.

– *Religion in Sociological Perspective*. New York: Oxford University Press 1982.

– *The Social Dimensions of Sectarianism: Sects and New Religious Movements in Contemporary Society*. Oxford: Clarendon 1990.

Wonderly, W.L., and J. Lara-Braud. *Los evangelicos somos asi?* Mexico: CUPSA 1964.

Yinger, J. Milton. *Religion, Society, and the Individual*. New York: Macmillan 1957.

Index

Salinas de Gortari, Carlos, 55, 205, 213–14
Salvation, 76–7, 102–4, 130, 221–2
Samples, 7–11
Sanders, Anna, 42
Schisms, 20, 149–57, 248 nn 33, 34
Sects: conversionist type, 21, 103–4, 157, 227, 232 n 16; defined, 6–7; denominationalization of, 20–1, 74–5, 224–5, 226–7; established type, 21; propaganda on, 21, 164–5
Secularization, 4–5, 15, 19–20
Serrano Elias, Jorge, 4
Slocum, Marianna, 48, 50, 170
Social disorganization theory, 13–14, 82–3, 95, 219
Social service: see Evangelical hospitals, Evangelical schools, Politics
Speaking in tongues: see Glossolalia
Start, Rodney, 5, 7

Stoll, David, 18, 220–1, 229
Summer Institute of Linguistics (SIL), 17, 46–7, 168–78, 224, 249 n 11

Tabasco: Catholic strength in, 35, 57, 59; Evangelicals in, 27– 8, 37, 40, 46, 64, 236 n 62
Tejio, 197
Thomson, James, 24
Tithing, 133–4
Tlacochahuaya, 198–9
Tlatelolco, 54
Toba, 21
Totonacs, 208–9, 252 n 11, 254 n 29
Townsend, Cameron, 47, 172
Tzeltal: see Oxchuc
Tzotzil: see Chamula

United Indian Mission, 175
United States: in Latin America, 4, 17–18; in Mexico, 23, 38, 164–82, 223–4; religion in, 4–5, 13, 15, 18, 41, 42; see also Missionaries,

Summer Institute of Linguistics
Upward mobility: see Economic conditions
Urbanization, 54, 82–3, 95
Uruguay, 3, 228

Velasquez, Gregorio, 32
Venezuela, 32, 228
Villa Aldama, 41
Virgin of Guadalupe, 29, 35, 128–9, 186

Willems, Emilio, 14–15, 18–19, 22
Wilson, Bryan, 7, 17, 21, 103, 226
World Council of Churches, 161
Worship: see Liturgy
Wycliffe Bible Translators (WBT): see Summer Institute of Linguistics

Youth with a Mission (YWAM), 166–7

Zapata, Emiliano, 31, 32
Zapotecs, 25, 177, 251 n 29
Zitacuaro, 28, 36–7